Paylor Str

GU00739305

Best wishes
E Paylor
Up the Boro!

Eric Paylor

Juniper Publishing

First published in Great Britain by
Juniper Publishing, Juniper House,
3, Sandy Lane, Melling, Liverpool L31 1EJ
2000

ISBN 09528622 5 5

Reprographics
P's and Q's Ltd., Unit 10, Gibraltar Row,
King Edward Industrial Estate, Liverpool L3 7HJ

Printed and bound by:
Albion Graphics, Old Connelly Complex,
Kirkby Bank Road, Knowsley Industrial Park North,
Kirkby, Merseyside L33 7SY

Acknowledgments

I WOULD like to thank all the people who are regularly mentioned in this book, particularly Bryan Robson, his coaching staff and the playing squad of Middlesbrough Football Club for their continued support and friendship.

I also want to thank my colleagues at the Evening Gazette and elsewhere in the reporting world, especially Alastair Brownlee and Gordon Cox, and Dave Allan and Louise Wanless from the Boro press office.

Without all their help and amity, this book would not have been possible. A special mention, too, for my good mate John Wilson at Juniper Publishing for his hard work in copy-reading the text and producing this book.

Finally, I am very grateful to Shab at MSV for providing the welcome sponsorship that ensured the original manuscript was turned into the finished product.

Dedication

TO my father Henry and mother Pearl for supporting me in everything I have done.

Contents

Quote Unquote.

Things they might one day say about this book.

Bryan Robson, " Eric Who? "

Alastair Brownlee, " It's in the hands of my solicitor."

Gordon Cox, " My daughter's reading it to me. It's great."

Fabrizio Ravanelli, " Paylor never misquotes anybody."

Bernie Slaven, " Wonderful. Paylor's a living legend."

Roofus the Boro dog, " Only Dawn Thewlis writes better."

Tony Blair, " It's Boro for me in the future."

Bill Clinton, " Splendid. I get the Evening Gazette delivered every night to read Eric Paylor."

The Good, The Bad and The Ugly.

A sideways glance at the 1999/2000 season.

Best Goal: Stephen Carr's own goal at Spurs.

Funniest Game: Boro 0-0 Leeds United.

Unsung hero: Gazza's terrific support for Robbie Mustoe's Testimonial Dinner.

Most caustic comments to a linesman: ME when he allowed Man Utd's fourth goal at the Riverside.

Most passionate interview: Colin Cooper after Villa home defeat.

Best salesman: Gianluca Festa's sales pitch for his new boots.

Best pressbox: Leeds United/Leicester City.

Worst pressbox: Southampton.

Wettest pressbox: Tottenham Hotspur.

Worst socks: Gordon Cox.

Worst overcoat: Nick Wood of the Northern Echo for his impersonation of Dr. Who.

Worst referee: Paul Alcock.

Best food: Leeds United.

Longest scar: Craig Harrison.

Worst beard: Gordon Cox.

Best singer: Neil Maddison.

Fastest talker: Paul Ince.

Coldest match: Coventry v Boro at Highfield Road.

Best away fans: Watford.

Best goalkeeper: Phil Stamp.

Best pies: Leicester City.

Biggest letdown: Boxing Day at Sheffield Wednesday.

Most annoying comment: Press colleague Ken Daley's prophetic, " Dean Saunders has never finished on the losing side against the Boro."

Best refereeing decision ?: Uriah Rennie's booking of Paulo di Canio for diving when he was clearly fouled in the box by Gary Pallister.

Best name for Gianluca Festa's ice cream shop: Giroldo's.

Best potential lynch mob: The 20,000 fans who queued for Frank Worthington Cup tickets blissfully unaware that the club had not received Juninho's international clearance papers.

MSV AND THE BORO

EARLY in 1994, Shab Mehdi had an idea to open an electrical store in Middlesbrough. But he did not want it to be any run-of-the-mill store. Shab wanted to make this one a little bit special.

Since the mid 1970s he had been a devoted fan of Middlesbrough Football Club, regularly travelling the country to see the team in action and supporting them through the bad times as well as the good.

Shab's idea was to somehow combine his plans to become a local businessman along with his love of the Boro. So he set up a meeting with Graham Fordy, the club's commercial manager who was at that time also a director, and the link up was quickly established.

In selecting a name for his business, Shab opted for MSV. No surprise there, MSV and MFC. They sound similar. In fact they go together very well.

At the time, Lennie Lawrence was manager of the Boro and the team was treading water following relegation from the Premier League. Lennie was working hard to stabilise the ship, but the fans were deserting in their droves. So Shab could never be accused of jumping on the bandwagon.

However, unknown to anybody at that time, the wind of change was just around the corner.

The sudden arrival of Bryan Robson lifted Boro very quickly from mid-table obscurity to the heights of the Premier League and later to Wembley. And, as MFC grew, MSV was to grow at a similar rapid pace. Shab said: "Bryan joined Boro almost at the same time as I opened my first store. I was already supplying the club with electrical equipment and when I met Bryan, he could see that I was a big fan.

"I was given permission to use the Middlesbrough FC logo as official suppliers to the club and that was a proud day for me. Since then I have developed a fantastic relationship with the club. It's been a partnership."

He added: "Sometimes I have to pinch myself when I think of everything that has happened. I started watching the Boro in 1975, and players like Stuart Boam, Graeme Souness and John Hickton were my idols. They still are. I look back at that time as being my personal golden era as a supporter.

"But it has not always been great. I had a season ticket in the days when the crowds had fallen to around 3,000. But my attitude was, if you are going to support the club, then you support them through thick and thin.

"My son Waqa was only 11 months old when I first took him to a Boro game. Naturally he didn't know much about it at the time, but now that he is seven he is as keen as I am. Now I've got to take him all over to watch the team."

Shab never missed a match in the season when Boro reached the two cup finals and rarely misses any these days, which is quite remarkable considering that the MSV retail business is bigger than ever - and Saturday afternoons is traditionally the busiest time of the week.

MSV eventually opened a second store in 1997, in the High Street in Redcar, but later closed the Middlesbrough shop at the same time as the £1m+ state-of-the-art superstore in Portrack Lane was opened in July, 1999.

It was only natural of course, that the new superstore would have a strong Boro theme. Not only is there a huge team picture of the Boro on the front wall of the store, facing on to Portrack Lane, but around 40 huge banners portraying individual Boro players are hanging from the ceiling inside. The banners, which are two and a half metres high, cost a total of £8,000 to manufacture. You can't look anywhere without seeing one of the Boro greats like Wilf Mannion or Juninho suspended in front of your eyes.

That's one of the things which gives MSV its individuality. It also makes it a very attractive destination for Boro fans when they are looking for new electrical gear. In fact it takes the pain out of shopping!

It's not just fellow Boro fans who meet up at MSV. You are more than likely to bump into one of the players themselves or a member of the Riverside staff while you are in the store. Maybe even Bryan Robson. Everybody from Boro goes to MSV, bar none. You may even bump into Chubby Brown. Celebrity customers, Shab calls them.

The other attraction, of course, is that Shab makes sure that his prices are competitive. MSV is the only family owned independent electrical business on Teesside, but Shab reckons that he can always do the best deal. The customers must agree. The business has a multi-million pounds turnover.

He insisted: "Our intention is to beat everybody else. And we provide a two year warranty on videos, hi-fis, TVs and DVD players, which you wouldn't get anywhere else without paying for it.

"In addition to that, we also have our own service centre on the premises. If anything needs looking at, then we can give it a full check-out here and so we can return the goods to the customer as quickly as possible.

"I think the people of Teesside appreciate what we are all about. In fact I have 10,000 regular customers who are loyal to MSV. They know that we offer the best deal and the best service, and that is why they keep coming back to us again and again."

INTRODUCTION

IN July 1999 I made the mistake of telling a good friend of mine that I was about to start my 15th season reporting on the ups and downs of Middlesbrough Football Club for the Evening Gazette.

"Hey! That's a milestone. Why don't you write a book about it?" he replied.

It seemed like a good idea at the time. All I had to do was to keep a daily diary.

So here it is. My story of the Boro's 1999-2000 season as it happened to me, day by day.

Little did I know, of course, when I began writing this book, that this particular Boro season would be devoid of many of the major events which make some years so memorable for supporters.

On reflection, maybe that's a good thing. I have had the chance to tell the complete warts-and-all story of the season, without having had the luxury of being sidetracked away from the fact that this job involves a lot more muck, grime, toil, grind, persistence, sweat, slog, struggle and, above all, phone calls, than most supporters would ever imagine. I know that there are lots of fans who would crawl over broken glass to have my job. I can't deny that I thoroughly enjoy it. I do feel privileged to be one of the 50 or so evening newspaper reporters who hold down similar jobs. However it is not as easy as it may look. There are times when I feel I am crawling over broken glass to try to gather my stories.

When I was told that the working title of the book was "Paylor Stripped Bare", I envisaged that I would be revealing lots of exclusive and previously unwritten stories from the inner sanctum of the football club. In fact, when starting out, I fully intended to do so. I can't deny that I hear and see things that I am unable to print in the Evening Gazette. However, despite my original intentions, I gradually began to realise that I could not print the juiciest tales in the book. The funniest stories which come out of football clubs are too irreverent to print anywhere. Then there is the danger of breaching the trust which I have been granted by the football club and which could lead to me being banned from the inner sanctum. This, of course, would prevent me picking up any stories at all and make my job impossible.

However, I have walked the tightrope and printed everything which I feel that I can comfortably get away with. This book has to give a true representation of what my job entails, and hopefully I have achieved this aim.

Basically Paylor Stripped Bare will give an insight into what it is like for a local sports writer to report on the day-to-day fortunes of a local football club.

What the book has told me, is that my job has changed dramatically since the summer of 1985 when I first picked up my pen and notebook and set off for Ayresome Park.

Naturally typewriters have given way to computers and hired phones have been superseded by mobiles. Some pens and notebooks have also been replaced by mini-cassette recorder dictaphones, though not in my case. I like to think that my shorthand note rarely lets me down.

The biggest change in my job has come about with regard to how I gather my information. When I was first appointed chief sports writer of the Evening Gazette, I enjoyed the luxury of travelling to away games on the Boro team coach. Away day Friday nights were spent eating an exotic meal at a swish hotel, followed by liquid refreshment while in deep conversation with the manager and coaches. Now I hit the road early on a Saturday morning, just like the fans, and travel to away games and back on the same day.

In 1985, if you wanted to find out about the Boro, you picked up the Evening Gazette or the Northern Echo. I had my 9.45am briefing with the manager and Ray Robertson from the Echo followed suit at 1pm. Any other media organisation which ever mentioned the Boro in its pages or on the air, merely scratched the surface.

Now, it seems, everybody wants to know what it going on at the Riverside. You can't pick up a newspaper, switch on the radio or watch TV without some modern-day 'expert' giving you 'revelations' about the club.

The Evening Gazette's daily press briefing has now been replaced by an occasional cavalry charge, which often sees myself, Alastair Brownlee from Boro TV and Century Radio, Gordon Cox from the Boro Web-site and PR officer Louise Wanless from Boro Clubcall all crowding into Bryan Robson's office at 9am on a morning.

There are times, too, when I pick up an interview with a Boro player without asking more than two or three questions. Often I have to approach a player in unison with Alastair and Gordon who, because they are using microphones and modern tape machines, have first crack of the whip in asking questions. This is to prevent the player from having to undertake two full interviews. Once Alastair and Gordon have finished, I have the opportunity to put my own questions afterwards, though usually most of the obvious ones have already been asked.

In this respect, it is harder than ever to get the stories first, but I like to think that the Evening Gazette does pretty well in such a competitive marketplace. In fact we use the word 'exclusive' a little too sparingly. There are many occasions when we could easily pat ourselves on the back over some of our individually-researched Boro stories.

This is what makes reporting on the fortunes of Middlesbrough Football Club in the New Millennium such an ongoing challenge, and so rewarding. The ability to build up the personal contacts, make the discreet phonecalls and ask the correct questions all make this job a bit special.

I've enjoyed virtually every minute of this season, despite the lack of drama. And, as a workaholic, I've thoroughly enjoyed writing this book. I hope you readers will be a little wiser and more fulfilled at the end of it.

Eric Paylor

Chapter One

AUGUST

Monday, August 2

BRYAN Robson is always amenable. Today he was in a particularly buoyant mood. After months of hard work and patience, with the fans starting to become a little worried, the Boro boss had finally completed his first two signings of the summer.

It was in the nick of time. The new season was just five days away. But both new boys, Paul Ince and Christian Ziege, were today training with the squad at Rockliffe Park.

The German Ziege, a £4m signing from AC Milan, was a cultured wing-back with a top class pedigree. Ince, signed for just £1m from Liverpool, was at the peak of his career. Both players were seasoned internationals. They could only add even more strength to Boro's experienced dressing room.

When I arrived at Rockliffe Park, Ziege was already sitting in the restaurant. He looked lean and tall, and a natural athlete.

Robbo enthused about both new boys. "I still have to pinch myself to think that I've signed a player of Ince's calibre for £1m," he declared.

Talk then drifted on to the opening game of the new season. Boro were entertaining Premier League new boys Bradford City on the Saturday. Bradford, who were expected to find the going tough in their first ever season in the Premier League, were already struggling. They had lost their last three friendly games, including one against Third Division Halifax Town.

Robson said: "We've watched Bradford a few times and they've always looked very poor. But we won't under-estimate them. They'll still give us a hard game because it's their very first match in the Premier League. I just wish we were playing Bradford eight games into the season, when they were beginning to feel it."

Afterwards, I spoke to Ziege on the restaurant veranda, along with Alastair Brownlee from Boro TV and Gordon Cox from Boro's official website.

Ziege matched his impressive physical stature with a clear commitment to the club. He left no doubts that he was delighted to be at Hurworth.

"Look at this," he said, in excellent English, looking out over the sunswept training pitches towards the tree lined River Tees beyond. "This is marvellous. I love it. I want to build a house over there, in the corner, with a big garden."

When we walked into the restaurant, Ziege had been chatting to Gianluca Festa in Italian. The German was a welcome new colleague for the popular Italian defender. Ironically, Ince speaks Italian as well. Both Festa and Ince had played together at Inter Milan, while Ziege was with AC Milan.

Gordon Cox and I decided to grab another quick interview and quizzed Festa about the two new boys. He stressed that he was happy to have both of them aboard.

Soon we had another interview in the bag. This time Andy Campbell was collared outside in the sunshine. The 20-year-old Middlesbrough born striker had scored a hat trick in Saturday's final friendly at Huddersfield Town, which Boro won 5-2.

Andy's pre-season tally was six goals and he could hardly have done any more to stake his claim for a place in the starting line-up against Bradford. He had outshone the better known strikers at the club with his pace and clinical finishing, though to be fair, Brian Deane had also played well at Huddersfield.

I phoned in the Ziege story to the Evening Gazette for today's back page, and drove back to the office in Middlesbrough to get through some more work.

Boro's pre-season photo session at Hurworth was timed for 1.30pm, but I decided to give it a miss in order to catch up on a bit of writing. However, soon I was back in the car to return to the training headquarters for 3pm. I wanted to monitor the press conference announcing the double signing. This press conference gave the TV, radio lads and national press the chance to pick up the story.

Robson was flanked by both players in the press room at Rockliffe Park. Most of the questions were directed at Ince. However the unfortunate Ziege was handed a naughty question. "If the Italian League is so good, why did you come here?" he was asked. The German showed quickness of mind in providing a diplomatic answer, insisting that the move to Teesside could revive his own career and help his international prospects.

Before leaving Rockliffe Park, I bumped into the Academy director Dave Parnaby and interviewed him. I wanted to pick up the latest news from the club's youth scene. Dave was full of new ideas and was running the youth set-up with great passion. He was also keen to publicise the lads' activities and achievements, which suited me fine.

I was happy to help the club's Academy players achieve a higher profile.

Tuesday, August 3

BORO'S coaching staff were excited about a 17-year-old wonderkid who had played for Boca Juniors against Boro's reserve side at Hurworth the previous week.

The player, Carlos Marinelli, had apparently produced a blistering performance, the likes of which most observers had never seen before.

Bryan Robson insisted: "Everybody feels that he is the best 17-year-old they have ever seen."

Praise indeed. Naturally Boro were keen to sign the lad. They had wanted to organise a two-weeks trial at Rockliffe Park for Marinelli, but were told: "Carlos doesn't go on trial. If he plays for another club, he moves for money."

Undeterred, Boro had already put the wheels into motion to try to hammer out a price with Boca Juniors. If the fee was reasonable, then it looked as though Robbo would push for a permanent deal.

Boro had been successful in hanging on to one of the Boca Juniors lads on trial. Facundo Bonvin, a striker, was spending two weeks with the club on trial. Bonvin, 18, looked strong and powerful for his age. A third player from the Boca team had also been offered a trial, but his father had taken ill in the Argentine and he was forced to return home.

Robson added: "We hope to get him back over here for a trial once his father is OK."

Unfortunately I was not given permission by Robson to use the Marinelli story.

Robbo added: "We can't take the risk that other clubs will read the story and move in as well. The lad has indicated that he is keen to come here. So it's important that we stay ahead of the field. You'll get the story first if we can sort something out."

Boro were staging a full scale practice match at Hurworth, to which I was not invited. In any case I had already accepted a lunch invitation from Dave Allan, Boro's head of PR, at the BT Cellnet Riverside Stadium.

I was accompanied by the Evening Gazette sports supremo, Allan Boughey, while Mark Hooper, a PR officer at the club, joined us.

The object of the lunch was to discuss the Gazette's working arrangements with the club for the new season. We made a lot of progress. In particular we talked about ways and means of improving the coverage in the Gazette of the junior teams at the club. Dave also informed us of Boro's plans to develop their home reserve games into family nights, especially with a view to attracting those fans who could not afford to take their families to watch Premier League football. It was a productive meeting, and an excellent meal.

Wednesday, August 4

THE Marco Branca saga reared its head again. The Premier League issued a statement announcing that they had rejected an appeal by the Italian striker, who was still angry that his contract with Boro had been cancelled.

Boro chief executive Keith Lamb then gave me an official statement from the club, which welcomed the Premier League's decision but also wished Marco well for the future.

The whole situation was very unfortunate and should not have degenerated in the way that it had. I could see all sides of the argument. Boro did not want to lose Marco. He was a clinical finisher. Similarly Marco did not want his career to end.

However, the official medical evidence which was given to Boro was overwhelming. Three orthopaedic surgeons' reports stressed that Marco's knee was no longer strong enough to stand up to the rigours of Premier League football. Under the circumstances, I felt that the club's hands were tied behind their back when it came to making the difficult decision.

Friday, August 6

PHIL Stamp was in a positive mood today. The Middlesbrough-born player was looking forward to starting the new season in the team against Bradford City tomorrow.

But the 23-year-old told me that he was under no doubts that he needed to produce the goods this season.

"This is the most important season of my career," he admitted. "Hopefully I can steer clear of injuries and show people what I can do."

Phil can claim to have been the unluckiest player in the squad over the past couple of seasons. Every time he forced his way into the team, he picked up a new injury.

Surely the tide must start to turn in his favour.

I chatted to Phil following the usual pre-match conference with Bryan Robson. The manager was in one of those moods where he was determined to give nothing away about his starting line-up, so as not to give Bradford a head's start. I hoped that Robbo's reticence was unfounded.

Saturday, August 7

DISASTER! Boro lost their opening Premier League game against newly promoted Bradford City, after conceding a last minute goal to Dean Saunders.

I could not believe it at the final whistle, and nor could anybody else in the ground - except those who were supporting Bradford.

Boro had been dire in the second half, and it was all very worrying. No work-rate, no closing down, no commitment. The feeling of abject and complete deflation was evident everywhere.

Bryan Robson did his best to talk positively to the press afterwards, but the players were dazed and confused. I spoke to acting captain Robbie Mustoe and then Christian Ziege. They were completely shattered.

"It's incredible that we lost," admitted Ziege, whose cultured performance was the only bright spot in the match.

What worried me most was that the players might find it hard to lift themselves quickly after such a nightmare experience. Yet, with away games to come at Wimbledon and Derby County, they could not afford to go three games without a win at the start of their fixtures. Otherwise they would always be playing catch-up and the season would be wasted. All this after one game!

It was no consolation to be informed by my press colleague Ken Daley on leaving the ground that Saunders had never finished on the losing side against Boro. I just wanted to go away somewhere and hibernate.

Monday, August 9

BRYAN Robson was not due in until later, so Viv Anderson handled the press briefing for the local media. Alastair Brownlee was there, along with Gordon Cox. I was taken aback to see that Gordon was growing a beard. Must be shock, following Saturday's defeat by Bradford.

Viv is a great talker, and always provides plenty of words in an interview. However he rarely discusses transfer targets and usually gives less away than Robbo.

Viv had spent the weekend watching the nightmare video of the Bradford game, and was assessing it again this morning.

"We put 24 or 25 crosses into the Bradford box in the first half and got on the end of only one of them," Viv groaned.

"The video has told us plenty of things about where we went wrong. We have to work on putting them right immediately."

The air of despondency felt by the fans was not shared by Viv, though the general mood at Rockliffe Park was different to what I would have witnessed if Boro had won on Saturday.

Steve Vickers appeared sporting five stitches in his forehead following a clash of heads against Bradford, but promised that he would be fine to play at Wimbledon the following night. It was a relief, because Boro were decidedly short of experienced, fit centre-backs.

Two young Italian-speaking lads turned up in the company of Argentine trialist Facundo Bonvin. One was carrying a Juventus holdall, while the other one had a Roma bag.

I went to see Academy director Dave Parnaby. "Don't put anything in the paper," he requested. "They've been recommended to us, but we're not sure about them. All we are doing is agreeing to have a look at them. But I wouldn't want to raise people's hopes."

Tuesday, August 10

BORO turned their season around by winning 3-2 at Wimbledon tonight. Thank heaven!

As they did so, I realised that I was completely to blame for Saturday's defeat by Bradford City. Instead of wearing the lucky tie which I had worn throughout last season, I threw caution to the wind against Bradford and deliberately put on a completely different tie because I thought Boro could not lose. How wrong I had been. I would like to apologise publicly to the Boro players for being solely responsible for the Bradford defeat.

I wore my lucky tie all the way to Wimbledon and during the match. It paid dividends. Hamilton Ricard scored twice, including one from the penalty spot, while Christian Ziege grabbed his first goal for the club.

However the best individual performances came from Paul Ince and Paul Gascoigne, who were superb together. This was Ince's debut for Boro and his contribution indicated that he could turn out to be the British bargain buy of the summer.

Before setting off from Middlesbrough to catch the train to London, I received a solid tip-off that Boro chief executive Keith Lamb was flying out for talks with Atletico Madrid. Apparently Atletico Madrid were now willing to do a cut-price deal on Juninho. The more that Juninho's price dropped, the more likely that Boro might show interest.

Selhurst Park is OK as a stadium, but finding the place can be a nightmare. It's in the middle of nowhere. It takes ages to reach the stadium, by car or by train, even after you have arrived in London. It's one of those fixtures you always look for first on the new fixture list, and one you always like to put behind you. However, evening kick offs at Selhurst are not too bad, because they necessitate an overnight stay and you can spread the travelling over two days.

I normally stay in a hotel within walking distance of Selhurst Park, but it was fully booked up. The nearest I could get on this occasion was a hotel at Bromley, which turned out to be eight and a half miles away from the stadium. I was grateful that the Evening Gazette was footing the taxi fares.

My taxi driver on the outward journey from the Bromley Court Hotel turned out to be a Brentford fan, and a lovely fella. He never stopped talking and gave me the full run-down on how Ron Noades had turned the Bees around.

I arrived at Selhurst Park early, before the press turnstile was open. But I bumped into Bernie Slaven, the Living Legend, and he used his Irish, or is it Scottish, charm to wangle us in through another gate. Two hours to kill gave me plenty of time to chat. I had several long conversations with Clive Hetherington from the Northern Echo, Tim Rich from the Newcastle Journal, and Shaun Custis from the Daily Express. Shaun had just flown in from Zurich where he had been reporting on England's opening bid to win the right to stage the 2006 World Cup.

I also met Chris Harte from the London Sports Reporting Agency. He's a friendly, warm chap, who has written three books similar to this one about his own experiences as a journalist. In fact Chris's books were one of the inspirations for me sitting down to compile this marathon effort.

I spent half-time talking to Gordon Cox. Still unshaven. He was giving designer stubble a bad name.

After the final whistle, Bryan Robson was brought up to the press room for the post-match interview, and was pounded with questions about Paul Gascoigne and Paul Ince by the London-based press.

"Paul Ince doesn't have to prove anything to anybody," said Robson. "He's a top class player. He may have said that he wants to see Gerard Houllier and Phil Thompson get the sack but I don't see what is the big deal about that."

I left the press conference and managed to pull Gianluca Festa to one side as he was about to join the coach. Festa had enjoyed a much better performance than he produced against Bradford and he knew it, though he admitted he was still feeling a hamstring niggle. The interview gave me a nice story for the Sports Gazette which I could write up when I arrived back at the office early tomorrow afternoon.

I had arranged for the Bromley taxi company to pick me up at 10.30pm, but when I reached the meeting point outside the Crystal Palace club shop, the car was there ten minutes early. It was a bonus, and the journey was again enjoyable. This time the driver was a Millwall fan. He was the salt of the earth. He was now a fully respectable guy, but he delighted in telling me about all the fights he had got into during his teenage years supporting the club.

He also told me a wonderful story about a good friend of his who had been thrown out of the Communist Party for being too left wing. It was a pity that the journey had to eventually come to an end.

I was back in the hotel for 10.45pm and it took an hour to write up the two reports, and the match statistics, ready to phone them over to the Evening Gazette in the morning. Into bed at 11.45pm. It had been a pretty good day. But then it always is when the Boro win.

Wednesday, August 11

THERE was a full eclipse today. So they tell me. I slept through it on the train on the way back from last night's match at Wimbledon. I must make sure that I'm awake for the next one in 90 years' time. When I returned to the office I discovered that I had not missed the 'wonderful experience' which TV and the tabloids had promised me.

Before sitting down to hammer out a few Boro features, I glanced through the morning papers. I was correct in believing that Paul Gascoigne had impressed the London press. The clamour for his England recall was increasing.

Friday, August 13

I HAD a chat with Keith O'Neill outside the training headquarters at Rockliffe Park and picked up a few decent quotes for a story. The Irish lad had been a revelation since he moved north from Norwich City for a bargain £700,000.

The great thing about Keith is that he can play anywhere. He has all the attributes. He can tackle and defend, is superb in the air, has pace, runs strongly with the ball and is a good passer. If he had Hamilton Ricard's goalscoring ability then he would be the complete player.

Like most of the Boro squad at the moment, Keith was delighted just to be involved. The players' confidence had fully returned following the Wimbledon win and now they could hardly wait for tomorrow's game at Derby to come along.

Bryan Robson was also upbeat. Apparently he had not been in the same frame of mind yesterday, when I was on my day off. Robbo had been spitting blood after reading an article in the Daily Mail which claimed that Paul Gascoigne had been drunk at a celebrity party which followed the premiere of Hugh Grant's new film Mickey Blue Eyes at the Waldorf Hotel in London's West End.

I believed Robson when he said that Gazza could not have spent more than 90 minutes at the event and, while it was physically possible to become drunk in this period of time, the allegations were rather dubious. And that's not denying the fact that Gazza probably did have a drink or two. What player wouldn't, after a 3-2 win at Wimbledon that night? However, the facts indicated that Gazza had been set up. The "exclusive" photo which showed him blinking, and alleged that he was drunk, was a little unfair. The Daily Mail is regarded as a fair-minded newspaper, but you couldn't help thinking they had been taken advantage of in this instance.

Anybody following Gazza's progress during the summer, as I had done, knew that he had been totally dedicated towards reaching full fitness, especially with the carrot of a potential England recall.

One of the problems that I, and the other members of the local press, had encountered since Gazza arrived on Teesside was getting interviews from him. The reason was obvious. Gazza was always wary of being stitched up. Even if he believed that I would present his quotes fairly, he knew that somebody else might lift them from the Evening Gazette and use them out of context to knock him.

While the newspaper report in the Daily Mail was a blow for Gazza, he suffered a real Friday the Thirteenth setback when his good pal Jimmy Gardner was sent down for six months for a firearms offence.

The two are inseparable at times, and the loss of his best mate for some time would certainly be hard for Gazza to come to terms with.

On the plus side, I was relieved to see that Gordon Cox had had a shave. His face now looked like a baby's bum.

Back at the office, I answered a couple of calls from fans who were angry over some of the developments at the Boro. Despite the fact that Boro finished in their highest position for 20 years last season, I'd had more calls from frustrated fans than I normally received at the start of a season. I try to listen to all fans who contact me. When they ring, I know that it is usually through sheer frustration, because they have nowhere else to turn in an effort to voice their concerns. Usually they are annoyed about developments at the club, or perhaps a lack of them. In this instance, the fans who were ringing me revealed grouses which completely lacked substance. In fact I found their concerns a little worrying.

Bradford apart, I had been delighted with the way things were going at the Boro. I came to the conclusion that there were a few fans who had renewed their season tickets this year who should never have done so. They had already made their minds up that they would not get value for money, whatever happened on the pitch. It all seemed so pointless to me. Surely there's no point forking out for expensive season tickets unless you genuinely want to watch the football fare being provided. It was just wasted money.

One fan who rang today accused me of concealing the "truth" about Alun Armstrong, who was not in the team at the moment. He said that the club was pulling the wool over my eyes with regard to the Armstrong situation.

Not so. I had asked several questions already about Armstrong directly to Robson this season and printed the facts in the Evening Gazette. The manager said that Armstrong's Achilles tendon problem was now fully healed, but he had a niggle in his back. At the same time Alun apparently needed games to restore his form and confidence. At the moment Alun was fourth choice striker, so these games were not going to come in the first team.

Saturday, August 14

THINGS were getting better! Boro won again, by 3-1 at Derby County, to cruise into fourth position in the Premier League.

It was another great day out, especially for the travelling fans, who gave Boro fantastic support throughout the 90 minutes.

Pride Park, of course, is built to the same specifications as the BT Cellnet Riverside Stadium. But it doesn't have the same warmth, maybe because it is painted black and white. There's something about those colours. The lay-out behind the scenes at Pride Park is different to the Riverside, and the press facilities are better. There is a large airy press room, while the press box is much nearer to the pitch. You can actually make out the numbers on the shirts.

Boro were 2-0 up in 20 minutes thanks to goals from Brian Deane and Christian Ziege, and the fans reacted by chanting one of the songs which they had learned from Arsenal at the end of last season.

"Shall we sing a song for you?" they asked of the dismally silent home fans. "Derby, Derby, Derby," came the chant from the Boro end. It was the ultimate mickey-take, but then the fans had every right to thoroughly enjoy themselves because Boro were absolutely rampant on the pitch. Derby did pull a goal back shortly before half-time, but Boro won at a canter once Hamilton Ricard had slotted home a second half penalty. My lucky tie had paid massive dividends again.

The press conference afterwards should have been a celebration, but it became a bit tense when the national press showered Bryan Robson with fresh questions about Paul Gascoigne.

Robson revealed that Gazza had been rested, though he was also suffering from a mild bout of sciatica. "I always intended giving my midfielders two games each in the first week of the season and that's what I've done," Robson stressed.

But the press were not convinced and the questions continued. I could understand their need to piece together the complete picture, because Gazza was higher profile than ever, especially with a potential England recall in the offing. Maybe the high media attention would die down once England's Euro 2000 qualifiers against Luxemburg and Poland were over.

Gazza had attended the game at Pride Park, and watched from the dug-out.

There were a few old friends in the press room, including Mike Walters from the Daily Mirror. Our friendship goes back many years, to the time when he was a junior reporter on the Evening Gazette.

Mike is a rampant Watford fan, and was in great heart following the Hornets' 1-0 win at Liverpool that afternoon. The winning goal had been scored by Tommy Mooney, who hailed from Billingham.

Mike was completely made up when I told him that Tommy used to play five-a-side with us occasionally when he was a 14-year-old. "I've played with Tommy Mooney, I can't believe it," he kept insisting.

No players were brought anywhere near the press room for interviews after the game, so I spent some time talking to one of the stewards instead. A friendly chap, he revealed that he made a 45-minute bike ride in for matches. True devotion indeed.

The post-match period is often the least glamorous side of football reporting, especially when you start nibbling at the now soggy few remaining sandwiches. It was two minutes before seven when Gordon Cox and I finally left Pride Park. Maybe some Boro fans had already arrived home by that time. After leaving the stadium, we drove into Derby to rendezvous with our regular travelling companions Len Shepherd, his son Andrew, and Nigel Gibb, at a local hostelry.

Len and Co had spent a couple of hours in the pub exchanging views with a quartet of Derby fans, who clearly had been drinking solidly since the final whistle. Maybe they had been drowning their sorrows. These Derby fans insisted that they were planning a long session that night, though I wondered if they would last the pace.

However, they were very friendly and chatty, and philosophical about the defeat. They were not particularly supportive of former Boro striker Mikkel Beck, now with Derby, who had been substituted by manager Jim Smith at the interval. As we were leaving, they insisted that I sent them a copy of my match report.

We finally hit the road at twenty past seven. I arrived home at five to ten, and settled down to enjoy Match of the Day.

Monday, August 16

THE tabloids had been full of new 'Juninho for Boro' stories, following revelations by Yorkshire based journalists that Atletico Madrid would pay the down payment of £6m to Leeds United for Jimmy Floyd Hasselbaink once they had sold Juninho to Boro.

So I had to broach the subject with Bryan Robson.

I knew that chief executive Keith Lamb had flown out to Madrid last week, and I had revealed the story of the new negotiations in the Evening Gazette.

But Robbo made it clear for once and for all that Boro had no intentions of paying cash on the nose to bring back Juninho. He stressed that he felt that the Brazilian was still very talented, but had not looked as effective in Spanish football as he was before his broken leg.

However, Robbo did reveal that Boro had been trying to negotiate a 12-months loan deal with Atletico to bring Juninho back to Teesside. So far they had not been successful.

The inference was that Boro were not prepared to take any financial risks. They knew that Juninho would regain his self belief if he returned to Teesside, but they did not know if he would ever become quite the same player again.

Unfortunately I was not given permission to use the story about the attempted loan deal in the Evening Gazette. It was disappointing, because the loan bid was a completely new slant on the story, and an exclusive. But I had to play ball. The trust between a local reporter and a manager is vital. The price you pay for having 'the ear of the club' is a small price considering all the other stories you are given.

At the end of our interview, Bryan declared: "I can't believe that you haven't asked me a question about Gazza."

The fact that Robson was being bombarded with Gazza questions from all areas was clearly touching a raw nerve. But there had been no need to delve into the Gazza situation any further. Robson told me at Derby on Saturday that he had rested the midfielder. End of story.

However, Gazza must have received a massive boost with the news that his best pal Jimmy Gardner was to be released from prison after only three days inside, pending an appeal.

Before leaving Hurworth, Louise Wanless came walking past me with a huge wad of letters, most of which had arrived for the players.

Louise is the PR officer at Rockliffe Park. There's nothing goes on at the training headquarters which Louise doesn't know about. She's dedicated to her job, and looks after the players as well as the press. Weighed down on this occasion with letters, she revealed: "Most of these are for Christian Ziege. Already, he gets more letters than any of the other players."

The German wing-back had made a big impact in more ways than one. After lunch I phoned David Parnaby to pick up the latest information from the youth scene in order to kick off the new Academy column in the Sports Gazette.

Towards the end of the afternoon I contacted Boro chairman Steve Gibson for a chat. He is always so enthusiastic about the club. Naturally Steve was delighted to see the team win its two away games and wipe away the bad memories of the Bradford defeat.

"Phew," he said. "What a difference a week makes."

Too true.

I probed with a couple of Juninho questions. Steve has always been Juninho's biggest supporter and I needed to know how keen he was to see the return of the Brazilian. But the chairman was not prepared to give anything away.

I was on Boro duty again in late evening when Boro TV asked me to be a telephone guest on Alastair and Bernie's chat programme.

I was delighted, and enjoyed ten minutes or so exchanging 'barbed' comments. I get on very well with both guys and thoroughly enjoy their company.

Bernie's first question was: "Why do you keep writing about Juninho?" I stressed that my own personal opinion was I was unsure whether it would be a good decision to bring back Juninho. I wanted the club to look forward rather than back. But I knew that many Boro fans felt that Boro should try to re-sign Juninho, and I had to represent their interests as Evening Gazette readers by reporting the facts as best as I could. In any case, I felt there was a need to bring in an exciting attacking player of some description.

Tuesday, August 17

BRYAN Robson announced the anticipated news that Dean Gordon had suffered a cruciate knee ligament injury at Derby County on Saturday. Deano, who never missed a game last season, would probably miss most of the rest of this one.

Afterwards, Gordon Cox and I arranged an interview with Keith O'Neill, who had been promoted from Republic of Ireland stand-by duty to the full squad for the forthcoming Euro 2000 qualifiers. It was a case of justice being done in the end. Nobody had been able to understand why Keith was merely on the stand-by list when the squad was originally announced. Keith, very wisely, was diplomatic about the whole thing, though I guessed he had been hurt when his name was originally omitted.

Coxy and I had hoped to chat to Curtis Fleming as well. The Irish defender was thankfully back in full training again following his knee operation and was pencilled in to play in a friendly reserve match against Derby County next week.

However, Curtis politely declined the request for an interview. "If I talk to you lads, I'll probably be unlucky and have a setback or something. Just give me another week or so will you?"

We were happy to oblige. Curtis was one of the nicest guys in the Boro squad and deserved a change of luck this season.

Gordon and I then retired to our cars to phone in our stories about Dean Gordon. But as we were sitting there with our mobiles at our ears, Dean walked past us unexpectedly and went into the dressing room area at the training headquarters. He was limping, but not as badly as you would expect from a player with a cruciate ligament problem.

Coxy and I looked at each other. I could see he was feeling the same doubts which were crossing my mind. I had already phoned in most of today's back page lead, but I decided to totally rejig my story and water it down, just in case. Fortunately I had an understanding copy-taker in Carole on the other end of the line. In the event I managed to file my copy just in time for first edition.

I raced back to the Evening Gazette to write up my Paylor on Wednesday column for tomorrow's paper. On the afternoon I stayed busy by putting together a Paul Gascoigne-Paul Ince feature.

After tea I phoned Steve Vickers for an interview for the Sports Gazette. Steve was out when I first called. He was apparently surveying the progress being made on his new house. It was being built on the very next plot to where he lived at the moment. Should save on removal expenses.

Steve had made a good start to the Premier League season, which was crucial considering the team's centre-back problems. He was happy to talk at length about the club's fortunes. The whole squad was on cloud nine following the two away wins.

Wednesday, August 18

THE Juninho stories and rumours were coming thick and fast. It seemed inevitable that the Brazilian would end up back on Teesside, whether it took weeks, months or years. It was the will of the fans.

However, I had my doubts when yet another fax from Spain arrived on my desk, insisting that Boro had reached an agreement to buy back Juninho for £7.2m. According to the press release the deal was to be completed tomorrow. I knew it was not going to happen that quickly.

I did not know who was trying to sell the Brazilian midfielder the hardest - Atletico Madrid or the English-speaking news agency in Madrid which continued to send these press releases to all and sundry in the North-east.

Friday, August 20

PAUL Ince had been gagged by Bryan Robson this week from talking about tomorrow's game against Liverpool.

So it was up to Robbo to talk about Ince's big game against his former club. The manager, wary about saying anything which might give the tabloids a "Time Bomb Ince" story, came out with a few diplomatic quotes.

The second biggest disappointment of the week, after it was officially confirmed that Dean Gordon was definitely out for most of the season, was the news that Robbie Keane had signed for Coventry for £5.75m. Bryan had been hell bent on signing the Irish teenager. His £6m offer for Keane had been accepted by Wolves weeks ago.

But Boro were unwilling to meet the apparent inflated wage demands of Robbie's agent, Tony Stephens, and the negotiations eventually broke down. Coventry, without a win in their first three games, were struggling - so they agreed to fork out the cash for the young striker.

It's a sad state of affairs where money is now more important than ambition in the game, but Robson's general feeling was "good luck to both of them". The Sky Blues would clearly struggle to stay up again this season, though I suspected that Keane's goals would now ensure their survival.

I had been asked by my editor, Ranald Allan, to ask Bryan and Paul Gascoigne to provide a few words for the special newspaper which the Evening Gazette was producing to support Middlesbrough's bid to become a city. Robson was happy to provide some quotes, but Gazza seemed a bit suspicious and asked me to see him later about it.

After leaving Robbo's office, Alastair Brownlee, Gordon Cox and I grabbed Alun Armstrong for an interview. The Geordie striker had completed his first 90 minutes of the summer for the reserves in midweek, and was at last beginning the build-up for full match fitness.

He needed more games in order to reach his peak, and deserved a bit of luck in the process.

Saturday, August 21

BRIAN Deane's second goal of the season was enough to earn Boro all three points in a hotly contested clash at home to Liverpool. Lucky tie comes good again.

The win took Boro into second place in the Premier League, trailing Spurs only on goals scored. However, nobody was getting carried away. "There's a long way to go," insisted Bryan Robson.

The game brought a major bodyblow for Paul Gascoigne, who limped off after 18 minutes with a bruised calf. To make matters worse, England boss Kevin Keegan was watching from the directors' box. It was obvious that Keegan could not possibly bring Gazza back to the international arena now.

However, Keegan must have been impressed with Paul Ince, who did well against his former club. Fortunately Paul did not get embroiled in any of the rough stuff which had been forecast by the media, following his outspoken comments when leaving Anfield.

Many big name reporters from London and Manchester were there, purely to monitor Gazza's performance, so they must have been mortified when he limped off.

However, it was a good afternoon for Christian Ziege, who had attracted a number of German journalists to the game. The German assistant manager Uli Stielike was also watching from the directors' box.

Before the game I bumped into Charles Porter, who is a member of Robbie Mustoe's testimonial committee. He confirmed that Glasgow Rangers had agreed to play in Robbie's big game. It was quite a coup and I was delighted for Robbie. I agreed with Charles that the story would be embargoed until the following Thursday.

I was accompanied to the game by Evening Gazette sports writer Emma Chesworth, who was brought up in St Helens and still retained a soft spot for Liverpool.

But the only Scouse comments in the press box came from behind me, from three Liverpool fans who were surprisingly plonked in media seats.

At one time I thought that one of them was trying to put his hand in my pocket, until I realised that he was occasionally kicking me, no doubt accidentally.

All three generally behaved themselves quite well, though Liverpool's lack of punch gave them little to shout about.

After the match I had good reason to feel sympathetic for their situation. The three Scousers revealed that they had bought tickets for the game, only to find that their seat numbers coincided with those of three

Boro season ticket holders. When stewards moved them to other seats elsewhere in the West Stand, the same thing happened.

Eventually, after missing much of the first half hour of the game, the trio were directed to the press box. I could understand Boro's problems. The crowd of 34,783 was a stadium record and seats were at a premium everywhere.

Monday, August 23

I received a call from German journalist Ronnie Reng at lunchtime to tell me that Christian Ziege had been recalled to his country's international squad for the first time since the World Cup Finals in France.

It was great news, though not so good to hear that German assistant manager Uli Stielike had told the German press that Christian had played OK against Liverpool on Saturday, but added that Ziege was playing for a poor team. It was a bit of an insult considering that Boro were in third place in the Premier League. I could not imagine that all German sides were as good as Bayern Munich.

There was little chance of picking a quick comment from the club about Ziege's call-up, as I had only enough time to squeeze the story into the main edition of the Evening Gazette.

Earlier in the day, Alastair Brownlee, Gordon Cox and I interviewed a few players to build up a collection of stories for use during the early part of the week.

The best interview was with Paul Ince. It was the first time I had spoken to him face to face. He was confident and articulate, but spoke very quickly. However, Incey provided some excellent quotes, stressing how disappointed he was that Paul Gascoigne's injury prevented him from returning to the England squad.

We also chatted to Steve Vickers and Brian Deane. Brian is relatively shy for a big man, and it's easy to tell that he does not enjoy being interviewed. However, he was very pleasant and answered every question.

Alastair and Gordon then did a disappearing act when Mark Schwarzer appeared on the scene. The pair owed Mark yet more money after losing out on bets made on the result of the final cricket Test between England and New Zealand. Will they never learn? At one time Gordon was on his hands and knees trying to hide behind a plant pot. However, Schwarzer was eagled eyed, and Coxy was forced to pay up.

Bryan Robson revealed earlier that the FA had dropped plans to carpet Paul Ince following the comments he had made about the Liverpool management team. However, Graham Bean, the FA compliance officer, paid a visit to Rockliffe Park to air the FA's strong views on the matter.

Everybody was disappointed for Gazza, and Robbo was annoyed that Kevin Keegan had planned to watch him in only one game before selecting his England squad for the Euro 2000 qualifiers. He said: "I feel that it's a little unfair on Gazza that Kevin watched him only the once. He should have been judged over a period of games."

Robbo was also annoyed that Andy Townsend had been booked for nothing after half an hour of the Liverpool game, though relieved that Gianluca Festa's punch thrown at Robbie Fowler had been missed by the match officials.

Wednesday, August 24

THE spectre of Leicester City returned to haunt Boro yet again. On a night of total misery for players and fans alike, Leicester won at a canter by 3-0 at the Riverside.

It was a dreadful game. The harder that Boro tried, the worse they got. And their defending was woeful. It was a complete disaster all-round. So much for my lucky tie. I've made up my mind to take a week's holiday to coincide with the home game against Leicester next season.

Middlesbrough-born Leeds United and England star Jonathan Woodgate was in the press room before the game, and reappeared again at half-time. When I first saw him, I could not quite place him, mainly because you don't expect to see England players in the Riverside press room. By the time I realised who he was, it was too late to have a chat. Maybe I'll have the chance next time.

One person I did meet up with was Paul Kerr. He was attending the game as a guest of Radio Cleveland. It was great to see Nookie again. He was always very friendly, and ready to give interviews when he was a player.

After the game, it was not surprising to see Martin O'Neill enter the press room in a state of triumph. However, he was shot down a little when one reporter, asking the first question, called him Brian! Mr O'Neill was none too pleased.

I had been informed that the air in the Boro dressing room was blue, both at half-time and after the final whistle, as would be expected. However, Bryan Robson had clearly calmed down by the time he arrived in the press room.

Robbo blamed the team's defending for the defeat, which was fine, but I felt he should have taken some of the blame himself because Boro were clearly out-thought on the night. Boro's game plan had been totally inadequate.

The players were devastated by the debacle, so I was grateful to Robbie Mustoe for agreeing to give me an interview. We talked about about his forthcoming testimonial match against Rangers, and then Robbie gave me his reasons why the game had not gone Boro's way. It was an in-depth interview and would give me a nice piece for the Sports Gazette on Saturday night.

Wednesday, August 25

A good mate, Simon Clifford, rang to inform me that there was a new story brewing about Juninho. The news that Boro had tried to sign the Brazilian on loan a couple of weeks ago was now out of the bag, and there were indications that the tabloids were preparing to carry stories insisting that he was about to sign for the Boro.

Simon, a personal friend of the Giroldos, said that he would contact Juninho's father Osvaldo in Madrid to try to ascertain any latest developments.

Simon rang back later to say that Osvaldo was not aware of any real change in the situation, which was what I had expected.

Thursday, August 26

I WAS surprised that Bryan Robson came out with some on-the-record quotes about Juninho today, following the stories in the tabloids.

Robbo confirmed officially that negotiations had taken place with Atletico Madrid, though he inferred that an agreement was nowhere near.

I suspected that Boro still wanted to take Juninho on loan for the rest of the season, possibly with a view to completing a permanent signing next summer if the Brazilian produced the goods. However, Atletico Madrid were still trying to negotiate along a different route. They wanted money and were looking for a pay-per-play deal.

Robson said that Atletico had changed their stance on some aspects of the negotiations. However, he made it clear that Boro were intransigent on the matter, and it was up to Atletico to make the next move.

There were plenty of stories today. Keith O'Neill had pulled out of the Republic of Ireland squad with a groin strain, Neil Maddison had been back to hospital for a scan following a clash of heads during the Leicester game, while Paul Gascoigne was progressing well and had a chance of being fit for Saturday's trip to Aston Villa.

Alastair Brownlee and I also had a chat with Robbie Mustoe, who officially revealed today that Glasgow Rangers had agreed to travel to Teesside to play in his testimonial game. The date was yet to be fixed, but the match would take place towards the end of the season. I was pleased for Robbie, because it should guarantee him a big night.

The reception lounge at Rockliffe Park had been packed when I arrived. A party of officials from Boca Juniors had arrived to open negotiations over the transfer of Carlos Marinelli to the Boro. The Argentine club had sent a huge entourage, which no doubt would test chief executive Keith Lamb's negotiating skills to the full if they all tried to speak at once.

Saturday, August 28

ANOTHER defeat. Boro were uninspiring on a strength-sapping afternoon in the hot sun at Villa Park.

They conceded a bad goal after only five minutes when Dion Dublin scored, and never looked like pulling it back.

Christian Ziege and Keith O'Neill were both missing through injury, as Bryan Robson rightly pointed out afterwards, but Boro still could have done better.

The press, it seems, are no longer impressed by Boro.

"You've got a very old team," Janine Self from The Sun told me before the kick-off. Maybe, but not that old, I thought, considering that teenagers Jason Gavin and Robbie Stockdale were lining up in the defence. Gavin, in only his third game, was a clear-cut man of the match. He never made a mistake throughout the whole game.

The interview procedure is a bit weird at Villa Park, so I missed the opportunity to grab Gavin for a chat afterwards.

Villa hand out six special slips to the press, and only the holders of these slips are allowed near the players before the two managers have completed their interviews. When I finally entered the area outside the players' lounge, Gavin was already sitting on the coach. The Aston Villa directors' cars were parked here. One bore the numberplate AV1, and another S4OTS.

I needed an interview, and fortunately Gary Pallister stopped to answer a few questions. I spoke to him in tandem with Gordon Cox from the Boro web-site.

Pally blamed the injuries for upsetting Boro's rhythm in the early stages of the match, but was full of praise for Gavin's performance. "These games don't come any harder than Dublin and Joachim," he insisted.

Tony McAndrew also came over for a chat. He is on the coaching staff at Villa Park. It was good to see him again. He always has a friendly handshake and a few words , and follows the Boro's progress with interest. Boro had been paired with Chesterfield in the second round of the Worthington Cup, which was drawn today. It was a pairing which would bring back memories of the FA Cup semi-final clashes for most Boro fans.

But not Pally. He instantly recalled a Freight Rover Trophy tie at Saltergate from about ten years ago, when he scored an own goal with a long range lob from well outside his own box and then later conceded a penalty.

"I remember it well," he admitted. "I got a bollocking from Bruce Rioch afterwards. I'll have to make sure that I do better this time."

Tuesday, August 31

I NEEDED to discover whether Christian Ziege's calf strain had prevented him from training with the German international squad today. I knew that Christian would have been mortified if he had been forced to drop out of the squad because of injury, after waiting 15 months for a recall. I phoned my German friend Ronnie Reng, who offered to put a phonecall into the German training camp near Frankfurt.

I like to keep in touch with all of the foreign journalists I meet during the course of my job, because they often prove to be invaluable contacts. The game is now global, and you need journalistic friends in other countries with whom you can swap information. Ronnie is one of my latest such friends, having contacted me initially when Boro signed Christian Ziege. Ronnie is currently based in the London office of his German newspaper, and speaks excellent English, as do most of the foreign journalists with whom I keep in touch.

Ronnie phoned back within half an hour to say that Christian was fine and due to train that day, while he also gave me a couple of quotes about Ziege from the German manager Erich Ribbeck which were most useful.

I needed to finish off my Paylor on Wednesday column for tomorrow, so I gave Bernie Slaven a call. The Living Legend revealed that he and Boro Under-17s coach Mark Proctor were in full training for the London Marathon next year.

Pretty good for a guy who told me "Never Again" after completing the Redcar Half Marathon!

Bernie revealed that Paul Kerr and Gary Gill would also be running in the London event. Gilly, who is Radio Cleveland's matchday Boro reporter, was the official representative of the Boro in the marathon. All four would be running on behalf of different charities.

Bernie loves a laugh, but began to get a bit too deep for me when he described how you closed your mind off when you were running and thought about things which you normally did not have time to contemplate. However, he deserved to complete the marathon because he was so committed with his training.

Later in the day, Simon Clifford tipped me off that the Juninho deal was back on in a big way. With a little bit of research I discovered that Bryan Robson and Keith Lamb had flown back out to Madrid today.

Simon was calling Osvaldo tonight to get the story from the horse's mouth. I phoned Simon at ten o'clock at his home in Leeds hoping to get the full facts. But there was no answer. Damn!

Chapter Two

SEPTEMBER

Wednesday, September 1

START the month with a bang! I received a couple of calls that Juninho was definitely coming back, after all. The rumour-mongers were also in top gear. "He'll be at the training headquarters at nine o'clock today," said one caller.

There was little chance of Juninho being at Hurworth. He hadn't even agreed personal terms. But we have to take all tip-offs seriously. So chief photographer Dave Jamieson suggested that photographer Steve Elliott accompanied me to the training headquarters, just in case.

I drove up to Rockliffe Park, certain that the story of Juninho's signing would be confirmed, and it was great to be given some exclusive quotes from Viv Anderson admitting that a deal with Atletico Madrid was near.

However, I wondered how Juninho would receive a work permit, having failed to win a Brazilian cap for two years. "We've got something up our sleeves," Viv said.

I had also been tipped off on the grapevine that Boro were very close to signing Frenchman Ibrahim Ba on loan from AC Milan. I put this to Viv, and he declined to comment. It was the kind of 'no comment' which made me believe that the story was true, so I decided to use it as well. Naturally there was no picture opportunity for photographer Steve, because Juninho was still in Madrid. I phoned the office to give them the facts about Juninho's signing and they advised me to come straight back. The office car was a little red Corsa. I had never realised that it would go so fast.

When I walked into the Evening Gazette, I was disappointed to discover that the Juninho story was not to be the front page lead. I felt it was strong enough. However, I had to settle for a large chunk of the back page, plus a banner story across the top of the front page - which meant extra work. Both stories were written up just in time to beat the first edition deadline.

During the day we received the usual calls from fans wondering whether it was true that Juninho was returning. Yes it was. They were beside themselves with glee.

The rumours continued. "Juninho is arriving on a charter flight at Teesside Airport at four o'clock." said one well-meaning caller. We didn't even bother checking that one. Why Juninho would even consider spending a lavish £20,000 to charter a plane when he could take a routine flight for less than one per cent of the cost beats me.

Friday, September 3

BACK at work after a relaxing day off on one of the hottest days of the year. I drove up to Rockliffe Park to check out the latest situation regarding new signings Juninho and Ibrahim Ba. My colleague, Andrew Wilkinson, had received confirmation of the Ba loan signing yesterday.

Viv Anderson was in a buoyant mood, as usual, as well he might be. Two signings virtually completed in two days, while Bryan Robson and chief executive Keith Lamb were currently in Argentina trying to complete a double swoop for teenagers Carlos Marinelli and Facundo Bonvin from Boca Juniors.

Viv made it clear that Boro had been unable to sign Juninho on loan, as had been previously announced, because loan signings from non-EU countries did not qualify for work permits. So Boro had arranged a short term contract with Atletico Madrid and had forked out £1.4m for the privilege.

Boro's application for a work permit from the Department for Education and Employment for Juninho was immediately turned down. However there was an appeals procedure and Viv was confident that Boro would eventually be successful. Unfortunately the whole thing could take up to a month.

There were no apparent problems regarding Ba, and Viv revealed that the Frenchman was due to fly in from Milan on Sunday evening. The speedy winger would have medicals at Rockliffe Park on Monday and then hopefully start training with his new teammates immediately.

Viv revealed that Christian Ziege, a former teammate of Ba at AC Milan, had played a big part in recommending Boro as a good club to join. In fact Viv rubbished one naughty report in a tabloid which had suggested that Ba was flying in next Wednesday to have a look around the area, before deciding whether to accept Boro's offer. In any case, one look around Rockliffe Park on Monday, and the Frenchman would know that he had made the correct decision.

Viv also told me that he was flying out to Helsinki tomorrow to watch the Euro 2000 qualifier between Finland and Germany. Christian Ziege was hopefully playing for Germany. However I suspected that Ziege was not the subject of Viv's trip. Maybe Christian had recommended one or two of his teammates as potential Boro signings. I decided to keep my nose close to the ground on this one.

After phoning over my story to the Evening Gazette, I spotted Dean Gordon arriving at the training headquarters. The wing-back was hobbling on crutches following his cruciate ligament operation on his knee.

As ever, Dean was amiable and upbeat when I walked over for a chat. He said: "The surgeon who performed the operation did the same for Niall Quinn at Sunderland and got him back in four months."

That was great news, and it gave Deano something to aim for as he started his rehabilitation. Hopefully the initial suggestions that Dean could be out for the whole season would be well wide of the mark.

After a busy afternoon helping to finalise the advance pages for the Sports Gazette, I stopped off for petrol on the way home.

Who should I bump into but none other than Jamie Pollock, formerly of Boro and now with Manchester City. It was good to see him again. It was the first time I had seen Jamie for a couple of years, though we had spoken on the phone.

I wanted to know why Jamie was not in the City team this season. It transpired that he'd had a little difference of opinion with manager Joe Royle, and was at this moment considering the chance of a move. To which club, I asked. "I can't say," said Jamie, "But it's a big club. In any case it's decision time. Either I move on, or I stay and the gaffer brings me back in and I get on with it."

I suspected that, deep down, Jamie would prefer to stay, and that he would knuckle down and get on with it.

Saturday, September 4

SATURDAY afternoon, and no game. All Premier League football was cancelled because it was an international weekend. I was consigned to the office all day to help bring out the Sports Gazette. I wrote up a lead story on Ibrahim Ba, thanks to some useful quotes I had saved from the Viv Anderson interview yesterday.

However it is so frustrating being stuck inside on a Saturday. I spent a bomb on sandwiches and sweets trying to console myself. I love international football as much as I love Newcastle United.

Monday, September 6

WHAT a morning! It was all rather hectic. No sooner had Bryan Robson talked glowingly about new signings Carlos Marinelli and Ibrahim Ba, than it was revealed on Ceefax that Ba had reneged on his agreement to join Boro.

Ba had been due to fly into Teesside today, and I had announced that fact in my story to the Evening Gazette. The latest revelations caused me a bit of a panic,. I had to organise a Ba rewrite and get all today's news into the first edition. Fortunately I made it, with a little help from my friends.

When I walked into Robbo's office, he looked tired, but relaxed following his week away. He had travelled throughout Europe in the early part of last week, signing Juninho and Ba. Then he jetted off to South America to sign Marinelli, but missed out on his Boca Juniors colleague Facundo Bonvin.

"All part of the job," he insisted, as he prepared to take training.

Bryan had met Marinelli and his father, and the 17-year-old starlet had agreed a five-year contract. But Bonvin's family were not too happy that Boro initially only wanted their 18-year-old son on loan. So they said "No".

"Ideally I would have liked to bring them both back together," said Robbo, "But Carlos will have no problems settling in."

Robson also came out with some positive quotes about Ba's qualities and gave the low-down on several other stories. There were no hints at that time that Bryan was aware of any problems with the Ba deal.

Outside the main building, I joined Boro TV presenter Alastair Brownlee in talking to Andy Townsend, and then Gordon Cox from the Boro website joined us for an interview with Mark Schwarzer. The Boro goalkeeper had been asked by new Australian national coach Frank Farina to end his self-styled exile from the international scene. The two were due to meet up in Teesside later in the month.

After phoning in my back page story, I popped back inside the training headquarters to link up with Dave Parnaby for our weekly get-together for the Boro youth scene report.

It was on my way to chat to Dave that I discovered that Ba had decided against joining Boro after all. He had revealed his change of mind in an Italian newspaper. Ba's quotes had just appeared on Ceefax.

It was a complete sickener. What a lousy way to announce a decision, and what a complete lack of ambition shown by the player. I phoned the office immediately to warn them, and then sat down with Dave to jot down the juniors' details.

The interview complete, I phoned the office again and, with the help of my colleague Emma Chesworth, while the rest of the staff desperately checked out Ba's quotes, we put the new back page lead together.

When I drove back to the Evening Gazette, everybody was asking me why Ba had changed his mind. I knew no more than they did. But I had long suspected that Boro's name was mud among a section of the Italian footballers because of the Marco Branca incident. It was possible that Ba's head had been turned by some of his Italian colleagues. Certainly nothing had happened at the Teesside end to change his views.

Ironically, I arrived back at the sports desk just as Anthony Vickers became embroiled in an argument with a guy on the phone. The caller was insisting that we should criticise Boro heavily in the Evening Gazette for having annulled Branca's contract 12 months early because of injury. This followed an alleged announcement by FIFA that Boro had been wrong to take this decision.

Vic's heated phone argument was one that I was happy to miss at that time. In any case I knew that FIFA had no right to make such a statement - if they did - when Boro had not been invited to attend an official hearing, or take part in any discussions. There was something very fishy about this FIFA announcement. It lacked substance. But I had spoken to this particular caller on previous occasions on the phone, and I knew that he fervently supported Branca's stance against the club. I did not agree with his views, but I respected his right to hold them.

While Vic battled on, I toned up the Marinelli-Ba story for the main edition. I decided I would give Robbo a chance to recover from the shock news before asking him for his reaction tomorrow.

Tuesday, September 7

I HEARD a harrowing story today from Craig Harrison, who finally returned to the club's training headquarters after being taken severely ill during the summer. The 21-year-old left back had suffered an appendix problem at the end of last season which eventually led to peritonitis, and two serious operations.

When Craig revealed that he almost died, I was shocked. Bryan Robson had told me on several occasions that Craig had been very ill, and that he did not want anything to appear in the paper at the time. But when I discovered the full extent of Craig's close shave with death, it was quite alarming.

Craig had recovered only thanks to a committed medical staff, and the support of his family and girlfriend Corrina.

"I owe a great deal to everybody who supported me," he said. "Without them I don't know if I would have pulled through."

Craig's weight had dipped from 12st 7lb to less than ten stones as a result of his illness, though fortunately he had now put most of it back on.

"I've been eating a lot of burgers," he admitted, with a wry smile.

Craig then showed me the ten inch long scar on his stomach which would remain with him for the rest of his life. It was a nice example of needlecraft. But I wouldn't particularly want it on my stomach.

Remarkably, even now, almost five months after the second operation, Craig was still unable to do anything more physical than walking. He could not begin running until he was given permission by his surgeon.

Earlier, I had gone in to see Robson along with Alastair Brownlee and PR officer Louise Wanless. Bryan was not a happy man today. It was only to be expected. Huge headlines, claiming that Ibrahim Ba had decided against joining Boro, had been blasted across the newspapers over the past 24 hours.

Bryan was angry because the journalists had lifted a series of quotes from Ceefax which were claimed to have been made by Ba. The Boro boss suggested that nobody had bothered to check these quotes before using them, and he had a valid point.

As a result, Bryan was reluctant to discuss the Ba situation with me. It was clear that he did not believe that the deal was completely dead, though I suspected that deep down he knew that the writing was on the wall.

Robson had recently spoken with Ba's agent, while Christian Ziege had also spoken with the player. It emerged that Ba had a problem with his club, AC Milan, presumably over cash, which he wanted to sort out before leaving the club.

Even so, I could not believe that Ba had any intentions of linking up with Boro. He had not arrived as planned, and he did not warn Boro that he was not coming. Not the actions of a man who had honourable intentions, I thought. Boro had been along this road many times before and the best way out was the quickest one.

I did not have enough fresh information to lead off the Evening Gazette back page on Ba, so I phoned in a story on Christian Ziege. The wingback was expected to shake off a shoulder injury to play for Germany against Northern Ireland tomorrow. It was another honour for Boro, especially as Ziege was the club's only player to make an international appearance so far this season.

On the afternoon I exchanged a bit of gossip on the telephone with my old friend Graham Hiley, who is the Eric Paylor of the Southampton evening newspaper. Boro were playing the Saints on Saturday.

The only problem when swapping such information, is that you must learn to keep some of it back. I don't like to hand over too much info to other journalists, in the belief that the opposition manager might have a chance of working out Boro's possible team if he sees detailed team news about his rivals in his local paper.

I don't doubt that Graham, and all the other local paper hacks, do exactly the same.

Wednesday, September 8

SIMON Clifford rang me today on his mobile. We tried to pick each other's brains to work out whether Juninho would be awarded a work permit on Friday.

"I've been speaking to Juninho's father," said Simon, "And all they want to do is to get it over with."

I felt the same way. But I was desperately keeping my fingers crossed that the outcome was positive, because the Boro fans desperately needed a lift. The team's last two performances had been a big let-down. The make-up of Friday's appeal panel did not fill me with particular glee, especially as it included the PFA and one or two others who might not be supportive of foreign players coming into this country. However I believed that the honest and fair decision would be to grant the permit.

Earlier, I did not make the trip up to Hurworth because I suspected it was a very quiet day at the training headquarters. Bryan Robson was at his desk, but the players were on a day off. So I rang Bryan to find out if anything was afoot. He was happy to answer my questions, but clearly there was nothing happening. It gave me the opportunity to write up my story about Dean Gordon, which had been burning a hole in my notebook since I interviewed him on Friday.

Friday, September 10

CHRISTIAN Ziege reported back at Rockliffe Park following his superb hat trick for Germany against Northern Ireland on Wednesday.

One of many congratulations came from Bryan Robson.

"Hey, you have to save your hat tricks for when you are playing for us," Bryan insisted, as they shook hands.

I had a brief chat with Christian before he disappeared into the treatment rooms for a massage. I could tell that he was tired following his two games with Germany, and it was no surprise to hear that he had been excused training for the day to give him the chance to recover fully.

"No doubt you'll be busting a gut to get a goal or three against Southampton tomorrow," I asked him.

But Christian was already well schooled in the Art of English Football Diplomacy. "It's not important who scores the goals as long as we win," he told me.

It's remarkable how Christian's world has changed since joining Boro. Just a short while ago he was going nowhere, outside of the AC Milan first team picture and without any international prospects; now he was Boro's new superstar and a hero in his home country again.

The change of fortune had delighted Christian, especially the reaction he received in Germany. "It was important for me to have the German supporters on my side because it has not always been that way. But they were all behind me this week," he revealed.

Robbo had arrived at Rockliffe Park in suit and tie. He was not supervising training because he was racing off to Manchester for the appeal hearing over the Juninho work permit application.

How confident was he? "We are hopeful. We believe that we have put together a strong case, but all we can do is put it forward and then wait and see."

Emma Chesworth, my colleague on the Evening Gazette sports desk, phoned the Department of Education and Employment for me to find out if there was any chance of a decision on the work permit this afternoon. "No chance," they said. "It will be Monday at the earliest."

But the supporters could not wait. The phone was ringing from mid-afternoon onwards with eager fans wanting to know if the crucial decision had been announced.

Another call which came in was from Bernie O'Hagan, the chairman of the Derbyshire Reds, which is the Midlands-based 'branch' of the supporters organisation.

Bernie told me that the Derbyshire Reds were planning to play Lincoln City Supporters Club in a game to commemorate 100 years of Boro league football. The very first game played by Boro in the Football League in 1899 was against Lincoln.

The Derbyshire Reds, who play under the name of the Boro Fishbar XI, were planning to wear Boro's original strip of white shirts and baggy blue shorts, but without the customary hobnail boots.

"However, we'll still be slicking back our hair," Bernie insisted.

If the Fishbar XI were to beat Lincoln, it would be their first ever win. Good luck!

Saturday, September 11

I DONNED T-shirt and jeans today to enter the vaults of the Evening Gazette and begin researching my next book, which is to be a detailed biographical study of Teesside's top sportsmen and women through the ages.

One hundred and thirty years of treasure is locked in the Gazette vaults. That's how long the newspaper has been in existence. It's a stuffy, but quite magical place, for history lovers like myself.

First I had to unlock the outer protective layer of the vaults, which was a heavy steel door built into the wall in the basement of the Gazette building. Then a second key is needed for the inner sanctum of the vaults, where most of the prized files are kept on rows of sturdy wooden shelves.

Unfortunately time has taken its toll on some of the yellowing files. Paper does become brittle on prolonged exposure to air. In addition there is dust everywhere. But a little bit of muck and grime is a small price to pay for handling and reading these irreplaceable chronicles.

I had no luck researching the history of Middlesbrough-born boxer Johnny Summers before and after the First World War, but some of the news stories in those ancient papers made enthralling reading. One wretched woman, from Hutton Henry, had murdered her own four children and tried to commit suicide. But she failed in her attempts to take her own life, and was arrested. The outcome of her court case was pretty straight forward. Naturally, in those days, she would hang.

I moved nearer to modern times and checked out the obituary of Harry Makepeace, following his death in December, 1952. Success! There were plenty of details. Makepeace was a Middlesbrough-born double international at both football and cricket, though unfortunately played his sport for Everton and Lancashire respectively.

However, the full details of his sporting exploits listed in the Evening Gazette were excellent.

Funny how you get sidetracked though. The same files recorded the infamous Derek Bentley court case. Bentley was the 18-year-old who was sentenced to hang for allegedly telling his 16-year-old pal to "Let him have it" when facing a policeman on a roof during a botched attempted burglary. The 16-year-old was holding a gun and the copper was shot dead. The other lad pressed the trigger, but Bentley was sentenced to hang. The other lad was too young to go to the gallows. Bentley, of course, has been reprieved in the last two or three years. A very sad case, and it helps to put the Boro's ups and downs into context. There were plenty of ups and downs at the Riverside on the afternoon.

Boro twice trailed to Southampton but eventually won 3-2 thanks to a late winner from Brian Deane. It was a crucial win. The other goals came from Gary Pallister and Paul Gascoigne.

It was a hot, sultry day, despite the lack of sun. I don't think I can remember a hotter day in September. The press room was unbearably hot, a fact which was noted by Bryan Robson when he appeared for the post-match press conference.

Afterwards I had a brief chat with Brian Deane, along with Gordon Cox, and we moved on to talk with Colin Cooper, who had been grabbed by Gary Gill.

While we were talking, I shook hands with Stuart Ripley, who was enjoying a resurgence of form with the Saints. Not today though. He was crocked in the first half by a tackle by Coops.

"I'm really sorry for Stuart and I've already apologised profusely," said Coops, who had been playing his first game of the season after recovering from a medial knee ligament injury.

Monday, September 13

I RECEIVED rather a surprise when Juninho suddenly walked into Rockliffe Park today. The Brazilian's work permit application was still under review and I had not been aware that he was allowed in the country.

However, while it was a coup on my part, it was not something which I could publicise in the Evening Gazette. I have to accept that when I am standing in the reception area at the club's training headquarters, I am in a privileged position. There is sometimes a small price to pay for this licensed freedom, because I cannot report anything out of the ordinary without first asking permission.

There was no point even trying to get clearance from the club to print this story.

Juninho arrived at around 10.20pm with his father Osvaldo, and Boro chief executive Keith Lamb. I felt a little bit awkward, because I knew that I was not supposed to witness Juninho's arrival. But Osvaldo put me at ease by walking across and firmly shaking my hand.

Osvaldo remembered me well from Juninho's last term on Teesside and, although Osvaldo did not speak the best of English, he gave me a warm "Hello" and a broad smile.

I was the only journalist in the building, and therefore the first one to see Juninho make his return to the Boro. It was an unreal situation, because it was completely unexpected. But it was still a coup.

The problem was, that when I eventually returned to the Evening

Gazette, I could not tell anybody on the sports desk what I had seen. I would have been expected to report the story in the paper; yet I knew I could not. A national newspaper reporter would have been straight on his mobile to his news editor as soon as he saw Juninho. A local sports reporter would not. He has too much to lose.

However, I had already written a very positive report for the back page informing the fans that Juninho's work permit would be awarded on Wednesday when the employment minister Margaret Hodge returned from her trip to the United States,

My story was virtually confirmed when I returned to the office, because Middlesbrough MP Stuart Bell contacted me to say that he was 99 per cent hopeful that Ms Hodge would look favourably upon the work permit. I was also tipped off that the voting at Boro's tribunal hearing on Friday had been unanimous in Juninho's favour.

Earlier I had climbed the stairs at Rockliffe Park, along with Alastair Brownlee, Gordon Cox and Boro PR officer Louise Wanless, to see Bryan Robson.

One of the subjects under discussion was a huge 'exclusive' story in the Daily Star, in which a waitress claimed that she had slept with both Ruud Gullit and Paul Gascoigne.

Nothing disgusts Robbo more than the constant flow of Gazza-knocking stories in the tabloids, most of which never give the Boro midfielder the right of reply.

However on this occasion Bryan was able to see the positive side, especially as the waitress insisted that Gazza was a better lover than Gullit.

The fact that this was seen as a 'positive' story at Rockliffe Park was borne out by the raucous reception Gazza received from his teammates when he arrived. They were certainly impressed. This was one of the few Gazza knocking stories which did a great deal to inflate his ego, rather than try to grind him down.

Robson had revealed that Irish defender Curtis Fleming, who had been sidelined through injury since early in the year, would definitely make his return to first team action in tomorrow's Frank Worthington Cup second round first leg tie at Chesterfield.

It was great news, especially for Curtis, after eight long months fighting for full fitness.

Afterwards, Alastair, Gordon and I interviewed Curtis in the warm sunshine outside the training headquarters.

Curtis has a wonderfully special Irish way of saying "I'm thrilled" but this time he merely stuck to "I'm delighted". I'm sure that he was mightily relieved as well. I sincerely hoped that everything would go well for him.

While Alastair and Gordon zoomed off, I stayed behind to interview Dave Parnaby for the latest Academy details. It was then that I was confronted with the sight of Juninho. If nothing else, it confirmed that my positive back page story was correct.

Tuesday, September 14

I MET up with one of Hartlepool's football legends tonight - in Chesterfield.

After the game, I bumped into Bob Newton, a folk hero in the Pool. As a Seventies centre-forward he was strong, ruthless and utterly fearless and he led the Pool attack with great power for a few years.

He was also pretty popular in Chesterfield, which was his home town, and that's why he had since become a football pundit for local radio.

"I absolutely loved it at Hartlepool," Bob admitted. "I had some great times there. And my son is a monkey hanger. He was born at Cameron Hospital."

We discussed the current de-merits of Pool, who were second bottom of the Third Division. "They need a guy like me in the dressing room," he insisted. "There would be no messing with me. The problem is that I've got a good job outside of football. But maybe the time is right for me to give football management a shot."

If Bob did return, you could be certain that none of his players would ever try to take any liberties.

I chatted to Bob after Boro's goalless draw against Chesterfield in the Frank Worthington Cup second round first leg. It was good to go back at Saltergate. A lovely little ground. I vividly remember Gary Pallister scoring his incredible own goal from about 35 yards in a Freight Rover Trophy match at Saltergate about 13 years ago. Tonight Pally was man of the match.

I journeyed down to the North Midlands with travelling colleagues Len Shepherd, his son Andrew, and Nigel Gibb. They were meeting up before the game with two Nottingham Forest fans, Mike and Mark, with whom they had been good friends for several years.

It gave me plenty of time to kill before the kick off. I spent much of it chatting to Nigel Gardiner from Raymonds news agency. The press box was very small, but I grabbed a seat next to Nigel on the back row. Tim Rich from The Journal was not so fortunate. He had been refused a seat in the press box because there was no room. Instead he was allotted a seat in the main stand, in the middle of the Chesterfield fans. And The Journal had to fork out £10 for the seat, because otherwise the club could have sold it to a home fan.

I knew how Tim felt. Two seasons ago I was handed a seat among the West Brom fans when Paul Gascoigne made his Boro debut at The Hawthorns. I had my notepad on my knee, my stopwatch in one hand, my mobile phone in the other and my pen in my mouth. The West Brom fans were wonderful, but they did not make my job any easier. Every time that the crowd jumped up I missed the action because I could not move.

There were no such problems for me at Chesterfield. The match was OK, but incident free. The first person I spoke to afterwards was Curtis Fleming, following the team's warm down. We chatted in the dressing room tunnel. It was Curtis's first senior game since January and he was delighted to have come through it with flying colours. Our chat gave me plenty of quotes and a good exclusive feature for the Sports Gazette.

Then Bryan Robson came out of the dressing room for his press interviews. He revealed that talks had been going on with West Brom over the likely transfer of Andy Townsend, who had been withdrawn from Boro's team for the Chesterfield game at the last minute. In some ways I was pleased for Andy, because there was a three-year contract on offer at The Hawthorns. Not bad for a 36-year-old. But I would still be disappointed to see him leave Teesside because he was a committed clubman.

It was eleven o'clock before we left Chesterfield and 1.20am when I climbed into bed, looking forward immensely to my five hours and ten minutes of sleep.

Wednesday, September 15

STUART Bell, Middlesbrough's MP, phoned me this morning to reveal that Juninho had been awarded a work permit to return to the Boro.

I was the first journalist to hear the news, and immediately began writing the 'splash' story for the front page of the Evening Gazette.

I was very grateful for Stuart's help. He had maintained regular contact with the relevant government bodies and had supported the award of the work permit.

Stuart was informed of the good news as soon as the Employment and Equal Opportunities Department had made their decision and faxed it to the Boro. Stuart made sure that I was next in line to hear the info.

Boro were not keen to comment on the news, insisting that they could not do so until the results of Juninho's medicals were known. However I knew, also, that Boro officials needed more time to scrutinise the minute details of Juninho's contract, especially bearing in mind the problems which could be incurred from its translation from Spanish to English.

There was more good news on the South American front for Boro. I discovered that Carlos Marinelli had arrived on Teesside last night. Unfortunately Juninho was no longer in Europe. He had flown out to Brazil, and it was uncertain exactly when he would be back on Teesside. Wonderful!

The Juninho work permit situation contributed to a very hectic day. Both my morning and afternoon were packed solidly with writing news stories and features. I was doubly whacked by the end of the day.

Late on, I fitted in a call to Shaun Keogh, from the Middlesbrough Supporters South. He revealed that he had reached an agreement with Newboulds for them to send him 100 of their famous pies for the MSS Christmas bash in London in November. It was a lovely tale, and would give me a good story closer to the time of the party.

Friday, September 17

JUNINHO made his official entrance at Rockliffe Park today following his brief business trip back to Brazil. The midfielder trained with the team for the first time.

I was waiting outside the training headquarters when he arrived with his father Osvaldo. Juninho's sudden emergence left Boro TV hastily setting up their camera.

I asked Juninho for a quick interview.

"I eat first," he said, rubbing his stomach, while Osvaldo came over to me and shook my hand again.

"Just a quick interview," I insisted.

"I'm very hungry," said Juninho, still edging away from me.

"Just five questions," I said.

"Two questions," said Juninho.

The interview went well, and we fitted in our five questions. It was important to get some early Juninho quotes to pass on to the fans. It also helped to take a bit of pressure off the club's PR department because Juninho's comments were lifted from the Evening Gazette later by the rest of the media.

Boro had been planning a press conference to unveil Juninho to the world again, but there were problems with the minor details of his contract. Boro did not want to make an official public announcement until everything was in the bag. The club's official line was that there was a delay with the international clearance papers, which was true, though it was the hard work going on behind the scenes to settle every minor detail of the contract which was delaying Boro's request for the international papers.

The delay meant that Juninho would not be available to play in Sunday's Premier League game at Leeds United.

I was rather pleased that there was no press conference. I already had my story in the bag, and it saved a second trip to Hurworth.

Carlos Marinelli also arrived at Rockliffe Park shortly after Juninho. The Argentinian teenager had been collected from his hotel by John Barry, head of education and welfare at the Boro Academy. Carlos probably needed to learn a few words of English before I could make an attempt to interview him.

Inside the training headquarters, PR officer Louise Wanless had been desperately fiddling with her mobile phone. She was paying the price for having loaned it to Christian Ziege yesterday.

"Christian asked to borrow my phone," said Louise, "And when he gave me it back, all the instructions were in German. I asked him to change them so he did."

The instructions on Louise's mobile phone were now all in Russian!

When we went into Bryan Robson's office, the manager patiently dealt with a host of questions, ranging from Juninho to Sunday's game at Leeds, and to Andy Townsend, whose move to West Bromwich was completed.

Robbo indicated that Boro had no intentions of putting Juninho on a pedestal, which had happened on the previous occasion he was with Boro.

"Juninho will be part of the team and will play as part of the team," he stressed.

It had been a fruitful morning. My only problem came when I tried to phone over my story to the Evening Gazette. I had mistakenly left the phone switched on in my pocket since the Chesterfield match. The battery went dead after I had sent over only the first two paragraphs of my story. It wasn't the best of situations, with my deadline just 20 minutes away.

Fortunately Gordon Cox from the Boro website helped me out of the mess by loaning me his phone. Aaaahhh. That's what friends are for.

Sunday, September 19

THE weather turned today. We were treated to blustery winds and heavy rain on our arrival at Leeds United.

Fortunately the journey to Leeds is a simple one. It's almost like a home game, taking less than an hour's drive, It was even easier today, because the Sunday traffic in the city centre was very light. We parked up on the area which had previously been two training pitches, behind the main stand at Elland Road. My raincoat, which I had packed in my briefcase as a precaution, saved me from a soaking as I walked towards the press entrance.

I was hungry, so coffee and biscuits in the new press lounge were most welcome. Bernie Slaven was sitting preparing some pointed questions for an interview with Brian Clough which was taking place in Derby later in the week, so I helped him out with a few suggestions.

Freelance writer John Donoghue and John Richardson from the Daily Mail quizzed me for a few Boro stats as we built up towards the kick-off.

The Leeds press box is a luxurious, fully enclosed affair, and most enjoyable to sit in to watch games in January and February. However the temperature was still relatively high outside, despite the rain, and I would have preferred to be sitting outside with the crowd to soak up the atmosphere.

I may have been comfortable, but at half-time I was absolutely starving. So I dashed down to the press room for the food. Leeds is the best club in the country for looking after the press, and once again they did not disappoint me. This time the fayre was pizza and chips.

The chips in particular were absolutely delicious, so I was none too happy when Bernie pinched a few off my plate.

In previous years the meals at Leeds have included chicken fricassee, roast beef and Yorkshire pud and also pasta verde. I will look forward to next year's visit with a dripping tongue.

However the hot food did not make up for the disappointment of losing another game at Elland Road. Boro were OK, but not good enough, and went down by 2-0.

The game was hanging on a knife-edge with Leeds leading 1-0 in the 64th minute and Boro pressing strongly. But an underhit backpass from Colin Cooper led to Leeds' clinching goal.

After the managerial press conference, I approached Coops for a quote about the second goal. My friendship with Coops goes back a long, long way, but when he said "Don't even ask", I got the message!

Gary Pallister, sporting four stitches in a gashed eye, stopped to answer a few questions, and I also had a brief chat with Gianluca Festa.

Pally had been caught by Harry Kewell's elbow, though the ref took no action. "The ref was five yards away, so he must have been unsighted," said Pally, derisively.

My travelling companions in the car had been on a corporate freebie at Leeds, with a meal and drinks thrown into the bargain. Afterwards we popped into the Old Peacock for a few more drinks before leaving. I was the chauffeur, so I was restricted to a single cola and no alcohol. At least the journey back was a doddle. It was 9.30pm when I arrived home.

Monday, September 20

ALL working days are busy. Some are busier than others. Today I had to make two journies to Rockliffe Park, because a Juninho press conference was called for 2pm. It was all rather hectic.

The press conference came as a bit of a surprise, because on the morning it was clear that Boro still had not settled the finer points of Juninho's contract.

Juninho had arrived for training with his father Osvaldo and I assumed that further talks were planned with Boro chief executive Keith Lamb.

However, Bryan Robson insisted that Juninho would be playing against Chesterfield tomorrow, despite all the problems, so I filed the story accordingly.

Robbo also announced that Paul Ince was to be the new club captain in place of Andy Townsend. Judging by Ince's outstanding and inspirational performance at Leeds, it was a good choice. It would be popular with the fans, because Ince had won them over from virtually his first kick for the club.

I watched Carlos Marinelli arrive with his father and wondered how long it would take the Argentine teenager to break into the first team. Not long at all, I imagined. There was already a buzz around Rockliffe Park that Carlos had been brilliant in training.

Afterwards I carried out an interview with Keith O'Neill, along with Alastair Brownlee and Gordon Cox. Keith, just back from injury, admitted that he had found the going hard at Leeds, but could not wait to get another 90 minutes under his belt. I filed today's story from the car, before returning to the building to interview Dave Parnaby for the Boro youth scene round-up.

Dave revealed that his son Stuart, one of the most promising lads at the Academy, had not suffered the very bad knee injury which had first been feared. In fact he would be out for only ten weeks or so. It was good news all round.

It was 11.40am before I arrived back at the Evening Gazette. I popped out for a sandwich just before one o'clock, then returned to the office to discover that the Juninho contract problems must have been solved. Louise Wanless, the Rockliffe Park PR officer, had phoned to say that a press conference had been called at Hurworth.

I could have done without it, bearing in mind my heavy workload. But I had no choice. So I jumped into an office car and met up with Evening Gazette photographer Terry Reed at the training headquarters. All of the national newspaper lads were there, plus Tyne Tees, BBC and local radio.

However, this was a lot different to the first Juninho press conference which was held at the Riverside Stadium four years ago. On that occasion the world's sporting press were in attendance. The cameramen, reporters and radio people had been piled several rows deep, and you couldn't move without tripping over electric leads. Then when the questioning started, virtually every question was in Portuguese. I can remember ending up with little substance in my notebook.

Fortunately this press conference was all in English, and quite productive, even if it did take a huge slice out of my afternoon. Juninho did very well in answering a barrage of questions, though it was clear that he had lost a little bit of his knowledge of English. Juninho needed to ask club interpreter Zelia Knight to translate a couple of questions. However, I suspected that he would need little time to settle in again.

By the time I stormed back along the A66 and returned to the Evening Gazette, I had only enough time to make a series of outstanding calls and carry out a few odds and bobs before leaving for home. The life of a local reporter doesn't get any easier!

Tuesday, September 21

JUNINHO made his debut tonight - but only just.

The Brazilian's international clearance papers arrived from Spain just eight minutes before the 5.30pm deadline which had been set by the Football Association.

Had those vital papers failed to arrive in time, there would have been a lot of disappointed people at the Riverside Stadium. In fact there could have been a riot! Anyone wearing a club blazer would have been lynched. After all, more than 20,000 supporters had queued for several hours to buy tickets purely to celebrate Juninho's return in the Frank Worthington Cup decider with Chesterfield.

I knew there was something wrong when I phoned the club early in the morning to check whether the international clearance had been received. It had not. And some members of staff were already in an advanced state of panic.

I did not manage to speak directly to chief executive Keith Lamb nor secretary Karen Nelson. But then they had other things on their mind than answering press calls. I did not envy them their nerve-wracking battle against time. It was hardly any easier for the club's PR department, who were besieged by calls from press and fans alike.

However, misleading reports in the morning papers and on radio that Juninho had definitely received his clearance did not help matters. If they had known the truth, many fans probably would not have bothered queuing for tickets.

Clem, from Radio Cleveland's Red Balls on Fire, phoned me on the afternoon and was rather shocked to discover that Juninho was not yet cleared to play. Clem had queued patiently for two and a half hours to buy a seat in the West Stand. I took advantage of the situation to pull his leg. Clem could take a joke, but not on this occasion.

The same applied to thousands of other fans, who had stood outside the stadium for a similar length of time. When they returned to their cars with their tickets, they switched on their radios and were now being informed that Juninho's clearance had not yet been granted. Not surprisingly, they wanted to know what on earth was going on. So the Evening Gazette switchboard was besieged.

Juninho was big news everywhere. National radio stations were particularly keen for interviews. I was interviewed on Talk Radio at the same time as the Evening Gazette assistant editor sports, Allan Boughey, was talking to Radio Five Live in their mobile radio car which was parked in the Gazette car park. Tony Lockwood, who had devoted an afternoon's sports programme on Talk Radio to Juninho, was not amused when I told his listeners that Juninho might be sitting this one out.

As Juninho's deadline neared, I phoned the FA. Still no news. Oh dear. I made plans to hire a false beard and moustache for the evening. Then I discovered that Rob Nichols from Fly Me To The Moon actually owned a false beard. Don't ask me why. Ask him. But it could have proved useful, because some fans vent their frustration in such times as much on the Evening Gazette as they do on the club.

However, Rob's false hair was not needed. After much hard work, sweat and nervous tension, Boro finally received Juninho's clearance papers at 5.22pm, with only eight minutes of the FA's extended deadline remaining. It had been too close for comfort.

There was a buzz about the place when I arrived at the Riverside. Brilliant! Everybody had a smile on their face. You could almost smell the anticipation. In the event the whole night was superb. Juninho ran around, passed and probed, and looked just as he always did, despite tiring in the second half. He played a great part in Boro's 2-1 victory, and was involved in the build up to both goals scored by Paul Ince and Steve Vickers.

Afterwards Bryan Robson gave a glowly testimony to Juninho's performance. So, too, did Chesterfield manager John Duncan, whose team had played very well. "You are never going to keep Juninho quiet," he admitted, "So we concentrated on trying to lessen his effectiveness."

I wanted a player's reaction as well, so I chatted to Steve Vickers outside the players' lounge. He was full of praise for the Brazilian's contribution. The fans were happy too. I chatted to Simon Bolton, secretary of the Boro Official Supporters Club, on our way across the car park afterwards. He couldn't believe how good Juninho had been. Neither could I.

The start of a new era? I hope so. I arrived home at about 11.15pm, but delayed going to bed, such was the heavy flow of adrenaline in my veins.

Wednesday, September 22

JUNINHO was big business again. After I had written up all my reports for tonight's Evening Gazette, a Sky TV crew turned up to talk to me about the impact that the Brazilian had already made on the town.

I spoke to Sky reporter Dave Roberts and his cameraman colleague in the warm sunshine of the Evening Gazette car park. Then they accompanied me to the print room above the press hall, where they filmed the newspaper under production.

I spent the afternoon desperately trying to catch up on the mound of work which was increasing on my desk, but it was impossible. Juninho's return had created so much extra work this week. I had spent several extra hours on the phone alone.

There were more stories to produce, as well. I usually knock together my column for the Herald and Post on a Monday. But my article which had appeared in the early Middlesbrough edition of the weekly newspaper was now out of date, following Juninho's debut. So I had to compile a new article for the East Cleveland edition of the Herald and Post. It was an example of how my workload had suddenly burgeoned.

In fact the whole day was rather hectic. The evening was spent discussing the format of this book with my colleague John Wilson from Juniper Publishing. I had been religiously keeping this book up to date every evening, though we needed to discuss size, design and costings so that I could work towards an agreed format. We also laid down initial plans for the next Evening Gazette sponsored book, which would hopefully be published following this one. It had been tentatively titled Teesside's Sporting Greats. There's no rest for the wicked.

But then I'm a workaholic. I couldn't imagine it any other way. I get bored doing nothing, and find most TV dull and tiresome. I just want to research stories and write them, whether at work or at play. John's the same. We have a great understanding and good working relationship. It means that we can collectively channel our spare time into producing meaningful books all the year round.

Thursday, September 23

LIKE most of the fans, I was eating, sleeping and dreaming about Juninho. But I was keen to write a non-Juninho story today for a change. So I broached the subject of Hamilton Ricard with Bryan Robson.

The amiable Colombian had not been playing well and the goals had dried up. I wanted to know what was behind his apparent loss of form.

Robbo was happy to talk about the striker and stressed that Ricard had not enjoyed a rest from football for more than two years, having spent the two previous summers playing in the World Cup and the Copa America.

The manager stressed that Hamilton would be given as much rest as possible to try to re-ignite the spark.

Maybe the arrival of Juninho had given Robbo the opportunity to rest Ricard. In answer to the old chestnut question, 'Can you play Gazza and Juninho in the same side?", Bryan inferred that he was considering a striker's role for the Brazilian. I didn't think this was a particularly good idea, but I could see that Robbo was trying to find a way of getting all of his best players in the team at the same time.

We spoke in the press room at Rockliffe Park, shortly before the manager carried out his regular Robbo's Replies session for Boro TV.

Alastair Brownlee was bright and bubbly following his visit with Bernie Slaven to see Brian Clough in Derby yesterday. "Cloughie was brilliant," said Alastair. "He talked from twelve o'clock until half past three and he was still talking when we came away."

Must have been one of those rare moments when Alastair failed to get a word in edgeways!

Saturday, September 25

ANOTHER bad day at Black Rock. Boro went down 1-0 at home to Chelsea and never managed a single shot on target.

Most of the big guns were there to witness Juninho's Premier League return. Henry Winter from the Daily Telegraph and Martin Samuels from the Daily Express swelled the numbers in the press room before the game. Mike Walters from the Daily Mirror had taken advantage of the long haul North to visit his mother in law in Hartlepool on the morning.

The build up to the match was great. The match was disappointing. Juninho was subdued by Dennis Wise, referee Paul Alcock's embarrassingly weak handling of the game ruined it for many fans and Paul Gascoigne was dismissed in the last minute for swearing at a linesman.

Bryan Robson had solved the Juninho-Gazza question by leaving

Gazza on the bench and bringing him on for the final 18 minutes. Gazza was incredibly hyped up but unfortunately his energy was channelled into the wrong area at the final whistle. It was a sending off Boro could have done without.

Robbo slated the ref afterwards, particularly for his failure to award Boro two first half penalties. He repeated his comments for the BBC TV cameras. I suspected Robbo was heading for yet another FA disciplinary hearing.

But my major thoughts were for the team. Three home defeats out of five was not good enough. There were major problems to solve.

Gianluca Vialli did not appear for the press conference because Chelsea were zooming off to catch a flight to London from Teesside Airport. There was a strange feeling of emptiness after the game.

Monday, September 27

IT was raining heavily when I drove up to Rockliffe Park in the office Corsa. The weather more or less summed up the current mood. The 18-mile journey seemed to take a lot longer than usual.

I knew that the first team were on day off, but I had been led to believe that Bryan Robson was coming in. I needed to chat with him about several issues, including a Sunday paper report that Aberdeen were planning an £800,000 bid for Andy Campbell. In addition, I needed to check on the injury situation.

However, after sitting and waiting for a while with Alastair Brownlee, it was clear that Robbo was not coming in. Hopefully he was trying to sign a new striker, because Boro had serious problems up front.

There was another absentee. Gordon Cox relayed the news that he would not arriving because he was having problems with a back joint. He was laid up in bed. It must have been a real problem for him, because Coxy is normally hyper-active. It made me feel glad to be up and about, despite the rain.

Paul Gascoigne arrived looking distinctly under the weather following his sending off on Saturday. However, he still raised a smile and an exchange of pleasantries with Alastair and myself.

Ray Train, Boro's chief scout, also came past and we discussed Boro's pairing with Watford in the Frank Worthington Cup. Ray is a regular traveller on the road, visiting other Premier League grounds to run the rule over Boro's future opponents and produce detailed dossiers for the Boro coaches. There's not a lot he doesn't know about opposition players, and teams' playing systems.

I suggested that the fans would be happy with the draw against

Watford. But Ray was quick to stress his point. "They are very, very strong at the back," he insisted. It was the comment of a man with genuine inside knowledge. It made me realise that Boro's task was not going to be as easy as some fans were hoping. At least there was no chance of Boro under-estimating their opponents.

I desperately needed a fresh story for the back page, so I railroaded Boro physio Bob Ward for a chat about Juninho and Paul Ince, both of whom had left the field through injury on Saturday. Bob came up with the relevant facts and I had a story, though Bob did stress that I should say that Juninho was doubtful for next weekend's derby at Newcastle, even though he added off the record that he was hopeful the Brazilian would be fit. I was happy to go along with that, especially as I could write that Juninho was fighting a fitness battle, which was true. Ince was a genuine doubt, having been sent for a scan on his groin strain.

I braved the rain to phone over the story from the car and then returned to have a chat with Juninho's father Osvaldo, and Carlos Marinelli's dad Hector. The duo were keeping each other company while their boys were having treatment and training respectively. Both guys are very friendly, though Osvaldo still needed to stoke up on his English a little more. Hector spoke virtually no English at all, but nodded regularly and seemed to understand some of the things that I was saying.

A quick chat with Academy director Dave Parnaby followed, and then I zoomed back to Middlesbrough to catch up on my desk work.

Tuesday, September 28

THERE was still an air of frustration in the air at Rockliffe Park when the squad returned following a day off. Bryan Robson was berating the ref, still very unhappy about the three points which he believed had been taken away from the team by the official's incompetence.

"If we had been given the penalty for handball after four minutes, there's no way we would have lost that game." he insisted.

Robbo talked positively about his squad, and stressed that he was certain his strikers would start to score goals again.

However, Robbo admitted that he had been on the trail of a top striker for almost a year, and was planning to watch him again tonight. I probed with a couple of questions to try to work out who this guy might be, but Bryan was giving nothing away. I suspected that his target was playing in a Champions League game on the Continent.

I asked Bryan about Andy Campbell, who was being linked with a handful of clubs. "Andy is staying here," he said. "I want to give him more time to realise his potential."

By the end of the interview, Bryan was smiling again. He told me that Viv Anderson had met up with Sheffield Wednesday boss Danny Wilson the previous night for a chat. The two were good friends following their days together at Hillsborough and at Barnsley.

Danny had told Viv that Bobby Robson had approached him immediately following the Owls' 8-0 drubbing by Newcastle and said: "Don't worry, it only takes one win, Dave."

It was Bobby Robson all over. No doubt the story would soon be helping to lift the Boro players before training.

Once I returned to reception, I was interviewed myself. Total Football were present at Rockliffe Park to research a feature for their magazine. I was approached for my views by a reporter called Jeremy. I am a bit wary about magazine reporters. They always seem to have strange lop-sided smiles. They promise to address a story from a certain slant, and then write something totally different. However, Jeremy seemed to be a decent guy and I suspected he would not sell anybody short. So I agreed to do it. Then I walked out to the car to phone over my own story. When I returned to the main building, Jeremy was interviewing Gary Pallister.

I managed to slip away from Rockliffe Park just in time to avoid a coachload of hyped-up German teenagers, who had arrived to watch training. I imagined that PR officer Louise Wanless faced a rather trying time ahead.

Wednesday, September 29

THERE may be more good than bad to come from the home defeat by Chelsea.

I climbed the stairs to see Bryan Robson in his office at Rockliffe Park and he was still angry about the non-penalty decisions.

So, too, apparently, were the players.

"We had a training session yesterday and the lads were arguing and yelling at each other all the way through it," said Robbo. "Gordon McQueen remarked that they hadn't been like this for ages."

Now Robson was planning to make sure that the players unleashed their pent-up frustration on Newcastle on Sunday.

I had arrived early at Rockliffe Park. So Bryan had plenty of time for a general chat about football. We discussed the Champions League, and Robbo pointed out that Manchester United could make £18m from this season's competition. The big clubs were getting bigger.

It had increased Robson's determination to ensure that Boro were not left behind.

He said: "The gap is getting wider so we have to try to close it as soon as possible, because it could be too late in a few years' time."

I had to rush back to the Evening Gazette afterwards because I was in charge of the Sports Desk, which is the usual procedure when my boss Allan Boughey is on his day off on a Wednesday.

I needed to pick up another interview for the Sports Gazette, and I remembered that it would be difficult to grab somebody tomorrow because the first team players were on day off. So I rang Colin Cooper for a chat in late afternoon. I could tell that Coops had his hands full with his young family, but fortunately he was happy to spare me the time for an interview.

Coops had been back to his best against Chelsea last Saturday and fancied the team's chances at Newcastle. "We really need to win there, and I believe we can," he insisted.

Ironically Coops would be one of the few North-east lads playing in the game. He pointed out that the 'derby' side of the battle would mean more to the fans than some of the players. I realised what he meant. Of the definite starters, Alan Shearer was the only other one born in the North-east.

Thursday, September 30

IT had been a very quiet week in the build-up to the Tyne-Tees derby as far as stories were concerned, though it probably suited Bryan Robson. I found that I was treading water with my questions in our morning meeting, trying to avoid writing a derby showdown story too early. However Robbo was bright and helpful and provided plenty of positive answers.

Before phoning over my story to the Evening Gazette, I took part in a photo shoot. It was an official session to launch the start of the Teesside Sports Awards, which are sponsored by Northumbria Water. I accompanied Robbo and Graham Neave, executive director of Northumbria Water, to the gym at Rockliffe Park, where I ended up sitting astride a weights machine. Unfortunately I was the victim who was selected to pull on the weights for the picture. It was a bit early in the day for physical work. Gazette photographer Michelle Maddison took the photos of the three of us together. Her prints were to be used in the Evening Gazette to kick start the prestigious awards.

Before I left the training headquarters, Paul Gascoigne arrived and exchanged pleasantries. He still looked a bit down following Saturday's red card, but had turned up for training on a day when the rest of the first team were on day off. It was a good sign and once again indicated his level of commitment.

Chapter Three

OCTOBER

Sunday, October 3

ONE of the facts of life of working on a busy sports desk is that it is impossible to take all my annual holidays in the summer because we have to work to a rota.

In fact it suits the sports desk for me to take most of my holidays during the football season, as it means that I can use my experience to pick up back page leads every night during the three months of the summer when everything is otherwise rather quiet. Writing back page leads is very much a specialist job in the summer, bearing in mind there is nobody at the club to interview. The staff and players are all catching up on their holidays themselves. And, before anybody suggests otherwise: No, I don't make up the stories!

So, two months into the football season, I was off on holiday. There I was, merrily chugging up and down the sun-baked northern coast of Corfu in a small-engined boat on the very day that Boro were in North-east derby action against Newcastle United at St James's Park.

I'm a poor spectator at derbies, mainly because the pressure of losing is so great. So, if I had to miss a particular game, I would have selected this one.

However, by the same argument, it's difficult to concentrate fully on a day out when you know that Boro are involved in such a big game at the same time.

Not surprisingly, my mind kept wondering towards thoughts of the derby. I suspect I may have made far too many references regarding the subject to the other occupants of the boat. My better half, being a season ticket holder, was just as keen as I was. However, our new friends from Swindon, David and Barbara Jenkins, who we had met just 48 hours earlier, must have wondered what the fuss was all about.

David and Barbara were regular attenders at the County Ground a few years ago when Swindon won promotion to the Premier League, but were not allowed to go up because of alleged illegal payments and other financial irregularities. So it was interesting to hear their tales. But, Swindon's fortunes having waned in recent years, they now spent their weekends sailing on a nearby reservoir.

As we cruised in and out of the beautiful coves between Barbati and Kassiopi, I realised that it could be a long time before we received any information about Boro's derby performance. Greek time is two hours ahead of British Summer Time, so it would be seven o'clock before I could phone home for the result.

In the event, we arrived back at our local bar just as Chelsea and Manchester United were kicking off in a live Sky TV match. Gustavo Poyet had put Chelsea ahead before I'd had the chance to work out where the game was being played.

Boro had kicked off an hour earlier and we were suddenly informed by the commentator that Alan Shearer had scored his second goal for Newcastle. What a bummer.

We needed a couple of drinks to settle our nerves as we sat out the first half of the Chelsea game, and awaited news of the Boro with some trepidation. After the adverts, we were informed that Boro had suffered a 2-1 defeat, and were shown Brian Deane's late consolation goal.

When we returned to our apartment, I used the Evening Gazette's Cellnet-sponsored mobile phone to ring home for the full run-down from my son Matthew. He told me that Gary Pallister had been accidentally punched on the head by Mark Schwarzer after only ten minutes and was stretchered off with concussion. Boro had apparently played very badly in the first half before chasing the game after the interval. I got the picture, because I had seen it all before in recent weeks.

However, never let a derby defeat spoil a holiday. With local wine at £3 a litre, it was a little easier to forget about the game during the rest of the week.

Monday, October 11

BORO needed a few new ideas, 100 per cent commitment and a change of luck to turn their season around.

They didn't receive any luck from England's game against Belgium at Sunderland yesterday. It was revealed that Paul Ince, back in the international side after a ridiculously long gap, was suffering from a hernia problem which needed an operation.

Paul had been the Boro's most influential player this season and he would be sorely missed during his five weeks' rehabilitation following the op.

However there was an added problem. With England now involved in the Euro 2000 play-offs in early November, any plans which Boro held for going ahead with Ince's operation at that time had to be shelved.

There was some promising news. Boro had a new player in their ranks when Brazilian striker Frank Andre Pizzolatto turned up to start a trial with the club.

I was standing in reception at Rockliffe Park when he arrived with his agent. Both men walked across and immediately shook my hand. How friendly! I suspected they did not know I was the local hack. Maybe they were confusing me with some high ranking official at the club. No doubt it's easily done!

Pizzolatto had been recommended to Bryan Robson by Brazilian star Edinho. When Robbo was in Argentina completing the signing of Carlos Marinelli, he had gone out for lunch with Edinho. Bryan had asked Edinho to keep him informed any any potential players who would be suited to the English game, and Pizzolatto was the first player sent across. Fingers crossed! Boro had a dire need for a successful striker.

With just one win from the last six Premier League games, and with some fans already on his back, I suspected that Robbo was starting to feel a bit of pressure.

Bryan was already looking ahead to future fixtures and stressing that they must be won. This was not his usual style. It indicated that he was as keen as the rest of us to see the team record a couple of quick wins. I had a quick chat afterwards with a few players outside the training headquarters, including goalkeeper Marlon Beresford, who was pleased to see his former club Burnley at the top of the Second Division.

Once my story was phoned in to the Evening Gazette, I carried out my regular Monday interview with Academy director Dave Parnaby and then headed back to start work on my advance features. I was singing loudly in the car on the way back to Middlesbrough. It's that back to work feeling!

Tuesday, October 12

ALASTAIR Brownlee was propping up the reception desk at Rockliffe Park when I arrived. It was good to see him again, and a pleasant surprise when he handed me a copy of his new book Tales From The Red Settee, which had been co-written with Bernie Slaven and put together by Boro's PR officer Chris Kershaw.

I was grateful to receive a copy and keen to compare it to this book, which was progressing nicely. When I opened up Tales From The Red Settee, Ali had signed it personally, and so too had Bernie and Juninho, who had taken part in a joint signing session at Boro's new superstore in the Captain Cook Centre last night. It was a nice touch, and good to see that Bernie and Juninho were getting on well together. Bernie had not been too complimentary with his comments when talk first surfaced that Juninho might be returning to Teesside.

Ali and I climbed the stairs to interview Bryan Robson in his office to pick up his comments on tomorrow's Frank Worthington Cuptie against Watford.

Robbo was concerned that there might be a low attendance. I told him that I could put 10,000 on the gate by putting big headlines of the back page of the Gazette if Carlos Marinelli was named in the squad. The fans wanted something to excite them and this Argentine teenager was apparently an entertainer.

However, when Robbo checked, the lad's clearance papers had still not arrived. The problem of completing the many minor details which would lead to the clearance papers being released was not Bryan's territory. However, I was a little surprised that the teenager was still unable to play competitive football for the club.

Afterwards, Ali and I chatted outside to Alun Armstrong who, we had been tipped off by Robbo, was definitely playing against the Hornets. Alun was chatty and gave plenty of positive replies to our questions. He would be hoping to grab a goal or two to try to force himself into the side on a regular basis.

We also interviewed Mark Schwarzer, who was still cleaning up in his sporting bets with Alastair. "Eventually I will find a sport at which England are better than Australia," Ali insisted.

When Juninho arrived, Alastair asked the Brazilian if he had read his copy of Tales From The Red Settee.

"I didn't get a copy," said Juninho.

"Do you want to buy one?" I asked, removing my own copy from my own pocket and thrusting it in the air.

Juninho laughed out loud. He had soon picked up the British sense of humour again.

I phoned over my story to the Evening Gazette from the car. As I spoke on my mobile phone, I found myself in competition with the wailing alarm on Ben Roberts' car, which seemed to have activated all by itself. As soon as I had finished sending over my report, the alarm stopped.

Wednesday, October 13

BORO beat Watford by 1-0 in the Frank Worthington Cup tonight, but the match was played in front of the lowest ever crowd of 8,843 at the BT Cellnet Riverside Stadium.

Boro have attracted many much smaller crowds in their history, of course, but the sight of fewer than 10,000 fans in the stadium for a competitive match turns the stomach.

Many fans had stayed away because of the team's poor run of results. They were frustrated by the apparent lack of passion and the low entertainment value. It was a protest with which I could sympathise.

Many others were absent because the pricing structure was the same as it was for Premier League games. Fans were not prepared, or in many cases were simply incapable, of paying up to £25 to watch Watford in the Worthington Cup.

I could see both sides of the argument. I knew that club officials had deliberated for a long time over the prices. They decided not to drop them because Boro were playing Premier League opposition. If they lowered the prices, it might set a precedent which could cause problems in the future. It turned out afterwards that Arsenal were to be Boro's next round opponents. If Boro had reduced the prices against Watford, many fans might have insisted that the prices should again be lowered against the Gunners because the level of opposition was the same and so was the competition. It would lead to future friction.

I sympathised with the club greatly before the game, but when I took my seat and stared around the empty spaces in the stadium, I realised that the wrong decision had been made. A gamble should have been taken, and the prices should have been reduced.

It was a relatively dull game. Despite the lack of atmosphere, Boro worked hard and won the tie thanks to Juninho's first goal since his return to Teesside. But it was a magnificent save by Mark Schwarzer, from a Peter Kennedy penalty, which ensured that Boro settled the issue without the tie going into unwanted extra-time.

As soon as the final whistle had sounded, match announcer and DJ Mark Page played the disc "It Don't Impress Me Much" by Shania Twain. It was a most appropriate choice.

Watford boss Graham Taylor was a disappointed man afterwards but acknowledged that his side's lack of a cutting edge had cost them dear. However he did not say: Do I Not Like That! The former England boss was doing well with a relatively small squad at Watford, and never stopped smiling during the press conference.

I can remember seeing Taylor during his time at the helm at Wolves, when he always looked strained and under pressure. This time he was a different man. I could tell he was thoroughly enjoying his work back at Watford, which was his spiritual home.

Bryan Robson was both relieved by the victory and happy at the prospect of entertaining Arsenal in the fourth round. Even better, the top half of the cup draw was looking wide open. If Boro could beat the Gunners, there was a genuine chance of going all the way to the final again.

"Hopefully Arsenal will send a weakened side up here, in keeping with the way that the big clubs operate in this competition," said Robbo. I couldn't agree more.

However it was impertinent of my colleague Ken Daley to remind me afterwards that Arsenal had won all four previous visits to the Riverside.

After the press conference, I managed to grab Gary Pallister for a few words. The big defender had conceded the penalty, though only in the eyes of referee Alan Wiley, because Pally's alleged foul tackle on Michel Ngonge had been a perfectly good one. Pally was obviously keen to sound off about the decision.

As the players filed past us out of the players' lounge, they had a smile on their faces. That was better!

Thursday, October 14

WHAT a peaceful day! Boro were in for warm-down training at Rockliffe Park today but there was no need for me to drive up to Hurworth for interviews. I had picked up all my stories last night.

It gave me the opportunity to spend a productive day in front of the computer screen getting most of my work up to date. I had compiled my match facts sheet last night, so that the Evening Gazette's match graphic could be prepared for publication as soon as I arrived at the office at 7.15am. But I needed to write up my match report as quickly as possible.

I followed up by writing the back page lead, the bulk of which consisted of quotes about Boro's home tie with Arsenal in the next round of the Frank Worthington Cup. With today's paper completed, I got stuck into outstanding advance features. There were frequent interruptions by phonecalls, as ever, but not as many as I would have received had Boro lost last night.

However, any hopes of a quick getaway from the office disappeared when I returned to my car at the end of the afternoon to discover I was blocked in by another car. There was a woman bottle-feeding a baby in the offending vehicle, and she indicated that she was waiting for somebody to come out of the nearby doctor's surgery. She signalled that they would be no more than a couple of minutes.

So I waited, and I waited. Eventually a man appeared, with an old woman. He helped the woman slowly across the road and into the back seat of the car. In the meantime the first woman had completed her feeding of the baby and was helping to bring up its wind. I continued to sit patiently while the guy spent more extra minutes rummaging around in the boot before finally getting into the car - in the back seat. Before you could say 'Road Rage', the woman who had been feeding the baby suddenly jumped from one front seat to the other, turned on the ignition and drove away! I was flabbergasted. She could have moved the damn car in the first place 15 minutes earlier. These Newcastle fans get everywhere.

Friday, October 15

DAY off, but there's no rest for the wicked. I drove through to the Linthorpe Bed Centre in Middlesbrough, where Gary Pallister was taking delivery of a seven foot bed. Pally is a big lad, and the bed had been specially made to his requirements. It was seven feet by seven feet, and had strengthened springs in the mattress.

Pally was delighted with the bed, and spent some time lying on the bed in different positions to test the springs while other customers in the shop watched him with interest. I chatted to Pally and also manager Sean Fay, who revealed that Robbie Mustoe and Alun Armstrong had previously bought beds there.

Chief photographer Doug Moody from the Evening Gazette was on the spot to take pictures and suggested I got on the bed with Pally for one of the snaps. In bed with Pally. Now there's a new one.

Sunday, October 17

MY lucky tie notched a double when Boro put on an exhilarating show for the Sky TV cameras beating West Ham United 2-0 to make it two wins and no goals conceded in five days.

Bryan Robson moved Christian Ziege into midfield and the switch made a big difference. Brian Deane and substitute Alun Armstrong scored the goals.

Hamilton Ricard was in tears when he was substituted and needed to be consoled by both Viv Anderson and Robson. The Colombian had missed some glorious chances. But his overall performance had been much improved, which should give him some consolation at least.

Gordon Cox from the Boro Website was back on duty after being sidelined for some time with a bad back, and it was good to see him around again. There was a mixed bag in the press room, but only a couple of London reporters.

Hammers boss Harry Redknapp was first into the press room afterwards. He was seething that referee Uriah Rennie had failed to award his team a justifiable penalty after only ten minutes. Not only was the penalty for a foul by Gary Pallister turned down, but Mr Rennie booked Paolo Di Canio for diving.

Redknapp blamed Arsene Wenger, stressing that the Arsenal boss had publicly claimed that Di Canio had dived two weeks ago and put the idea into referees' heads that the Italian was a diver. "I told everybody in the club that Di Canio would be booked for diving in his very next match, and I was proved absolutely right," raged Redknapp. "Yet Di Canio does not dive."

Redknapp's quotes provided a good story for the tabloids, but I was more interested in the Boro side of things. Robbo followed the Hammers boss into the press room and admitted they had escaped over the penalty. He was naturally delighted with the win, and insisted that Boro must build on it to get a run going. Too true.

Afterwards I managed to grab Brian Deane for a chat. It would give me a good feature story for the next Sports Gazette.

Monday, October 18

BORO were on day off today, so I was able to write up my Evening Gazette articles without too much pressure.

Academy director Dave Parnaby rang me while I was compiling the back page lead. "You don't bother to come up to Hurworth to see me when the manager is not here," he teased. Dave was perfectly right, I had to admit.

On the evening I phoned Boro fan John Brookes, who had been featured on TV in the Channel Five 'Footie Shorts' programme yesterday.

John, who lives in Hartburn, is well known because he is the fan who paid £100 for the "Wembley 256 Miles" sign which had once hung outside the Riverside Stadium. However John had been featured on Channel Five because he had worn the same Adidas Samba trainers to every Boro home match for the past 14 years. Remarkably, the trainers were still in one piece, even if they did pong a bit.

"I bought them from Willie Maddren's shop in Norton Road," said John. "When the club was saved from liquidation in 1986, I knew immediately that they were lucky shoes. So I promised that I would wear them for every match in the future."

John has been true to his word. I hope he never stops wearing the trainers, or the club may go to the wall again.

Tuesday, October 19

I HAD just arrived at Rockliffe Park when Boro physio Bob Ward popped over to tell me that Carlos Marinelli had twisted his ankle in training and would not be fit to make his debut in the reserve match against Sheffield Wednesday at the Riverside Stadium tomorrow, as had been planned.

I couldn't believe it, especially as I was all keyed up to write about the Argentine teenager's long awaited first game in a Boro shirt.

PR officer Louise Wanless couldn't believe it either. Louise had spent the last few days along with the rest of the members of the Boro press office preparing the way for a Family Fun Night to coincide with the reserve match. They had been planning on attracting a crowd of around 15,000 or more to witness Marinelli's debut. Now the plans were in tatters.

The news that Marinelli was injured still gave me a story, but I had been robbed of the chance of a follow-up on Thursday. I was as frustrated as the fans would be when they read the story in the Evening Gazette. This Marinelli saga was just dragging on and on.

Viv Anderson confirmed the injury news. "There's nothing we can do about it," he admitted. "It's a pity because Carlos has looked good in the two games he has played behind closed doors. He is desperate to start playing."

I retired to the canteen at Rockliffe Park with Louise and Alastair Brownlee. We were in a state of depression. Carlos didn't look any happier. He was sitting by himself eating his breakfast.

Phil Stamp was quite shocked to discover that Marinelli was injured. "All my pals were coming along to watch him tomorrow," he revealed. "They won't be bothering now."

I suspected many fans would feel the same way, which was a shame, because all the other young lads in the reserves would have been boosted by the support of a noisy crowd behind them.

Wednesday, October 20

I HAD a chat with Gianluca Festa to discuss his on-going problems with his hamstring problem. The Italian defender had just returned from a trip to Milan, where he had been to see a specialist.

Festa was very keen to avoid an operation, and the first thing he said to me was: "The specialist said that I don't need an operation."

Instead, Gianluca was hoping to solve the problem with a series of concentrated exercises, in addition to further treatment.

However, Bryan Robson was not so positive when I went up to see him in his office at the training headquarters. As far as the manager was concerned, this was the last chance saloon for Gianluca, especially as an experienced English specialist was insisting that an operation was the only lasting solution.

Robbo said: "Gianluca is desperate to avoid an operation, but if this doesn't work, then he will have to have it. We know what needs doing. We can't wait for ever."

Gianluca had originally suffered the hamstring injury in April and, despite a long battle, had so far failed to shake it off.

Another headache for Robbo was the Carlos Marinelli saga. The teenager was unable to make his debut for the reserves tonight because of injury. However an added problem was that Boro were still awaiting the Argentine's international clearance papers.

I spoke to secretary Karen Nelson in her office at the other end of the corridor. "We are just putting together another strong fax now," she revealed. "The problem is at the Argentine end. Their FA won't release Marinelli's papers because Boca Juniors have some unpaid bills to settle first. But that's not our problem and we will be demanding the release of the papers."

I phoned over the story and then raced back to the Evening Gazette along the A66. Our office Corsa was off the road because the engine was clanking, so I had a smart Escort under my control. It fairly zipped along. I needed to be back in Middlesbrough sharply because I had a lot of work to get through if I wanted to take a day off tomorrow.

However, progress with my workload on the afternoon was badly hampered by a works experience girl, of all things. Most people who arrive on works experience are quiet. In fact very quiet. We try to find work for them, but it is not always easy.

If we don't have any jobs for the works experience people, they normally trawl quietly through the Press Association directories reading the news and sport as it arrives on our screens. However this particular girl, who was a pupil at a Teesside school, was different. Totally different. For a start she never stopped talking. She wanted to know what I was doing every minute of the time. There was a rugby international on TV between England and Fiji, which one of the reporters was watching to compile a match report for our City Late edition. This girl wanted to know the score every minute.

She insisted on making a pot of tea when we didn't want one. She wouldn't allow anybody else to answer the phones. And she ran around the office like a headless chicken, speaking casually to different members of staff, before running back to the sports desk. She criticised other journalists, often to their faces. And she gave them nicknames. When she swore at the Fijian rugby players on TV, using a rather rude word, she apologised. "I'm sorry about my swearing," she said. "Journalists don't swear do they?" I don't know about that. This one was about to swear quite violently.

Friday, October 22

I WALKED down to Radio Cleveland to record the Red Balls On Fire programme, which was hosted by Clem and Fischer.

Both guys have bubbly, outgoing personalities and make you feel at home immediately. Red Balls On Fire is cleverly put together; the only drawback being that it is not broadcast at the best of times on Friday evenings and Saturday lunchtimes.

The recording went well, with the biggest talking point being the growing concern that attendances at the Riverside could implode. I was in full agreement with the two guys that the situation was dodgy, even though the Boro had started to win again.

We discussed the minimum fan base. Fischer felt it could be as low as the 9,000 which Boro had attracted for the Watford game in the Frank Worthington Cup. I thought it was probably much higher, but couldn't be confident.

Boro did need to prove something to a lot of people this season. The problem was that I wasn't sure what they had to prove. Even when the team was winning some fans were not happy. Maybe only another trip to Wembley would restore all-round confidence.

Earlier in the day I drove up to Rockliffe Park to see Bryan Robson. Alastair Brownlee and Gordon Cox were also there. We discussed the fact that Boro had been charged by the FA for allowing Gazza to play in Sir Alex Ferguson's testimonial, when he was suspended. Robbo was not happy about the situation, and was prepared to accept responsibility. "I'll offer to pay the fine, if there is one," he said. A brave decision indeed!

Outside, we interviewed Phil Stamp, who was back after yet another injury. "Do you think you've been unlucky with injuries," asked Alastair? "I've been very unlucky," said Stampy. A true understatement.

Then we stopped Mark Schwarzer for a chat. Australia were due to play Wales in the Rugby World Cup tomorrow but Alastair was reluctant to enter into one of his famous losing wagers with Schwarz. "No bets," Ali insisted. "Anyway, I can't work out which of the teams I want to win least."

Sunday, October 24

I BATTLED my way through virtual non-stop rain on the M1 to watch Boro's live Sky TV match at Watford this afternoon. While us fans struggled on the roads, the team enjoyed the luxury of flying south.

However it was well worth the soaking because Boro won 3-1, with the added bonus being a wonderful ongoing altercation between members of the Watford crowd, which happened right in front of the press box.

No sooner had Mark Williams headed Boro in front with an own goal after only three minutes, than the aggro started.

Two Watford yobs, clearly angry to see their side fall behind, were upsetting their fellow fans in the family area right in front of me. Their language was extremely blue, and their manners were appalling. It would have made great TV.

One hapless woman fan got up from her seat, stormed down the gangway and out of the ground with the match only five minutes old. Another guy, in his efforts to escape the wrath of the yobs, found a seat three rows away. He was almost carried into it by supportive fans around him. Other fans, unable to get away from the area, were in regular conversation with the yobs, absorbing regular mouthfuls of abuse. By this time the yobs were sprawled over three seats apiece.

An ageing steward was called, but did not fancy the confrontation. Then Juninho put Boro two-up. Another steward arrived, slightly younger than the first, and looked no more capable of handling the difficult situation. It was left to one of the previously silent fans, a big strapping guy who might have been Superman in disguise, to finally intervene. When he threatened the obnoxious duo, at last there was a cowardly response. Finally, the yobs accepted defeat, and accompanied the relieved steward out of the stand, no doubt to find seats elsewhere in the stadium.

So it was back to the football for the press. Tommy Smith pulled a goal back for Watford shortly after the interval, but Paul Ince grabbed a late clincher for Boro and it all made for a good day out all-round.

I had travelled through the rain down the M1 with Len Shepherd and Nigel Gibb, plus a guest passenger. He was a guy named Bruce, who had been visiting a pal in Yarm, only to find that his car had packed up during his stay and he could not get home.

Bruce lived in Hitchin, so we gave him a lift to Luton Airport, from where he intended to get a taxi. He was eternally grateful. Bruce's claim to fame was that he had been thrown out of the Tall Trees on Friday, for allegedly throwing a bottle at a bouncer. At the time he was rather annoyed: "Why the hell would I want to throw a bottle at anybody?"

insisted Bruce, who was 30 and respectable. However in retrospect, he was now something of a folk hero among his pals and it had all been worth it. "Nobody EVER gets thrown out of the Tall Trees," they told him.

When I arrived at Watford and we parked up in the hospital car park, I decided to wear my woolly hat to prevent my head from getting saturated by the constant downpour on the way to Vicarage Road. It worked well. Outside I met regular fans Gary Stevenson and Gary Thornburn and had a bit of a chin-wag.

Once inside the stadium, I felt it was safe to remove my hat. However I discovered soon afterwards that I needed to make a 20-metre walk across an open area to reach the press room. I decided to brave it without my hat, only to be drenched by huge droplets of water which were cascading from the stand roof. Sod's law.

With dripping hair, I entered into pre-match conversation with Barry Parnell, who was working for Century Radio, and then Martin Lipton from the Daily Mail and Nick Wood from the Northern Echo.

Martin is not a particular fan of Paul Gascoigne, nor Boro. But he is always good to talk to and I tried to convince him that Boro were a much better team than he believed.

Martin is a Spurs fan and was enthusing about his team's defeat of Manchester United yesterday. However he said: "I'll do you a straight swap now, trading Chris Armstrong for Brian Deane." It wasn't my decision to make.

After the match a saturated Bryan Robson entered the press room and answered a few questions, mainly from the southern press about Gazza, who had not travelled with the squad. Then I raced off to the players' tunnel, joining an interview that Gary Gill from Radio Cleveland was carrying out with Curtis Fleming, before grabbing man of the match Mark Schwarzer along with Nick Wood. Mark was upbeat following a great display and was happy to answer all questions.

I drove the car back from Watford because the lads had enjoyed a welcome couple of pints. Despite hold-ups from four sets of frustrating roadworks on the motorway, and constant showers and spray, I arrived back home at five minutes to midnight. I resisted the temptation to go straight to bed, sitting down to enjoy a hot cup of tea and read the Sunday Telegraph for half an hour.

Monday, October 25

UP at 6.30am after six hours in bed, and then off to work. At least the rain had stopped. I phoned Boro secretary Karen Nelson to quiz her on the latest developments regarding Carlos Marinelli, and she revealed that Boca Juniors had promised the release of his international clearance papers tomorrow.

It was good news, especially as Boro had switched their reserve game against Barnsley on Wednesday from Billingham Synthonia to the Riverside Stadium, in the likelihood that Marinelli's anticipated debut might attract a decent crowd.

I spent the morning writing up my reports, sent across my weekly feature for the Herald and Post, before getting down to work on advance features after lunch.

I also found time to be interviewed. Seventeen years old Paul Belbin from Thornaby popped in to grill me for his B Tech in Communications at Cleveland College of Art and Design. He did a very good job with his questioning. I hope he passed his exams.

Tuesday, October 26

PAUL Gascoigne had a bit of moral support from the family as he battled to shake off his niggling thigh strain.

Son Regan was following dad around at Rockliffe Park as Gazza prepared to go back on the treatment table. Regan was thoroughly at home, and no doubt he had enjoyed playing with all the computer games and mod cons which had been installed in the back of Gazza's new £50,000 four wheel drive, complete with number plate spelling his son's name.

I had a bit of a panic when my trusty notebook disappeared. It eventually appeared in Gordon Cox's pocket. It's not only players who play silly jokes on each other from time to time. But I would like to thank Colin Cooper for waiting very patiently to be interviewed while I searched desperately around for my book.

Earlier we had interviewed Bryan Robson in the press room. He was upbeat about recent results. I had heard that Boro were considering a tour to New Zealand next summer and asked Robbo about it. He confirmed the details.

Wednesday, October 27

DAY off, but again no rest for the wicked. Anthony Vickers phoned from the Evening Gazette to say that Carlos Marinelli's international clearance had arrived and the Argentine was playing for the reserves at home to Barnsley tonight.

I was more relieved than anything else. The long running saga was finally over. I drove through to the BT Cellnet Riverside Stadium and made my way up to the top tier of the West Stand, which was deserted but for a packed directors' box. The near 7,000 Boro fans were housed in the East Stand, and behind the North Stand goal.

Carlos did not let down the fans who had made the effort, scoring the only goal of the night from a stunning left footed free kick. But he was clearly rusty and I felt that it was impossible to judge him on the strength of this one performance. I knew that there was a lot more to come, and would reserve final judgement. The new Maradona? No. The best player on the pitch? Undoubtedly.

Thursday, October 28

THE Boro coaching staff were buoyant at Rockliffe Park following Carlos Marinelli's debut. I was pleased they had seen what they wanted to see.

Bryan Robson told me that Marinelli would be brought along slowly, but I suspected that circumstances would eventually dictate otherwise. Once the 17-year-old was fully fit, I could not see him benefitting from a prolonged spell in the reserves.

Outside in the sunshine, I interviewed Keith O'Neill, along with Gordon Cox and Chris Kershaw from the Riverside Red matchday programme. Keith had just been named in the Republic of Ireland squad for the forthcoming Euro 2000 play-offs against Turkey. He talked positively, but knew it would be tough for the Irish. This especially applied to the second leg. The Turks had deliberately switched the game away from their main stadia, leaving the Irish lads facing a four-hour coach journey after they had alighted from the plane. It already smelled of dirty tricks. After phoning over my story, I returned to talk to Dave Parnaby for an article on the youth scene for the Sports Gazette. After lunch I wrote up this story, in addition to a main feature on Marinelli. I had made a note of the lad's every kick last night, and the summarised results - plus quotes from Bryan Robson which I had saved - made for a balanced all-round piece.

Friday, October 29

IT was Yes, Prime Minister day at Rockliffe Park today and everybody was gearing up for the visit of Tony Blair to officially open the training headquarters.

The PM had been due to open the building some time ago, but the no small matter of the start of the bombing campaign against Yugoslavia put paid to that. It was bad timing from Boro's point of view, because the plaque which the club had commissioned to commemorate the official opening was already hanging on the wall in the reception area. Naturally they had to commission a new one after the PM scrapped his initial visit. However, I did raise the curtain to check the plaque and make sure that Boro had not simply scratched out the old date and inscribed a new one on top! It turned out to be a brand new plaque.

I did not bother attending the official function. It was not my cup of tea. In any case, I had met the PM some years earlier, not that he would remember. He and I were guests at the same wedding reception.

Boro's security men and stewards were in place very early in the morning, even though the official opening was not taking place until the afternoon. Fortunately my face was well known and I was not expected to provide identification documents in order to enter the training headquarters.

Bryan Robson was already resplendent in his best suit at nine o'clock. However, at that time he was more interested in tomorrow's home match against Everton than the visit of the PM. Robbo was looking forward to the game, as well he should. Even Alastair Brownlee was wearing a smart collar and tie. However, as the tie resembled something which the leader of the 37th Middlesbrough Scout Troop might wear, Ali received a few negative comments.

The Boro players were not due to arrive for training until the afternoon, in order to meet the PM at the same time. So Ali and I made a quick getaway.

It suited me, because I did not need a second interview. I was already planning to ring Grangetown's world boxing champion Cornelius Carr to talk about Sunday's title defence in order to write a back page story for the Evening Gazette for tomorrow.

I rang Cornelius, or John, to give him his real first name, at lunchtime. John and I go back a long way. I used to interview him when he was a talented teenage amateur boxer, so he is always friendly and amenable when I contact him - even with a WBF middleweight title defence just 48 hours away.

John was putting his crown on the line against South African Dingaan Thobela at Raynes Park in London. The Teessider was already mentally hyped up for the defence. On paper, Thobela looked a difficult opponent because he was a former double world lightweight champion. But the South African had since moved up two weights and I suspected immediately that he would be no match for Carr's power punches.

As ever, I wished John well, though I suspected he was well in control and did not need to rely on good fortune. The WBF is not a particularly well respected boxing organisation, but I hoped that John would win well and go on to earn the big pay-day he deserved.

Saturday, October 30

ANOTHER great day at the BT Cellnet Riverside Stadium as Boro beat Everton by 2-1 with two excellent goals. Christian Ziege hammered in a free kick, while Brian Deane powered home a strong header from Phil Stamp's cross.

It was Boro's fourth win in a row and everybody was in a buoyant mood.

Before the match I had a brief chat with freelance Dave Taylor and Bob Moncur from Century Radio in the press room. Bob insists that I have an infatuation with Juninho, but it isn't true. The reason why I wrote so many Juninho stories in the opening weeks of the season was purely because I got them first. Now I was writing a host of Carlos Marinelli stories!

At half-time I chatted with Peter Ferguson from the Daily Mail. He's a very friendly guy, but only an occasional visitor to Teesside. However on this occasion he could not understand what he was doing at the Riverside, because the Mail had doubled booked and sent Doug Weatherall to report on the match as well. I left it to them to sort out who was going to write the match report.

After the game, Everton boss Walter Smith was first into the press room. He rubbed his fingers up and down the sides of a glass of water, waiting for the first question from the Scouse reporters, which didn't come. So, in the end, Walter began answering imaginary questions. He was very honest, and admitted that Boro had deserved to win.

Bryan Robson was upbeat again and so, too, were Gary Pallister and Steve Vickers when I interviewed them afterwards. Steve had been making his 250th appearance for Boro, and was doubly delighted. Even the heavy blustery rain which provided a soaking for everybody leaving the stadium, failed to dampen our high spirits.

Chapter Four

NOVEMBER

Monday, November 1

BRIAN Deane was the man of the moment. Another winning goal on Saturday, despite suffering a cut eye which needed three stitches.

Many fans had raised their eyebrows when Bryan Robson forked out £3m to sign Deane from Benfica just over 12 months ago. But Robbo stressed today that Deane had saved him a lot of dosh.

"At the time of signing Brian, I was being quoted £8m for Duncan Ferguson," said Robbo. "That was the asking price for similar players, yet we got Brian for a lot less and he has done a great job for us."

I stopped Brian on the staircase to the Rockliffe Park restaurant. He was naturally upbeat after scoring his sixth goal of the season, and insisted that it should be seven. "I'm claiming the goal at Watford which was put down as an own goal by Mark Williams," he said. "It went into the net off him, but I got the first touch."

Gordon Cox from the Boro Website was at Rockliffe Park too, and we chatted to Phil Stamp, following his superb cross which led to Deane's winner. However, Stampy accepted that even this valuable contribution did not guarantee him a place in Saturday's derby against Sunderland. The battle was on.

Afterwards we spoke to Mark Schwarzer, who had agreed recently to return to the Australian squad from his self-imposed exile, only to be left out of the squad for the forthcoming matches against Brazil because he was not guaranteed a game. However Schwarz was very happy with the situation. It was the arrangement he had agreed with Aussie boss Frank Farina.

This was a happy time for the Boro keeper. Australia had just reached the final of the Rugby World Cup and won Mark a few wagers, not to mention the fact that he and his wife Paloma had celebrated the arrival of their first child last week.

All these interviews take up valuable time. I was late in ringing in my story to the Evening Gazette, but just made it. Then I went back to interview Dave Parnaby for the latest news from the Academy.

Tuesday, November 2

I WAS interviewed myself today, by Bernie Slaven. It was something that I would not have believed ten years ago, when he was the club's hotshot. But now Bernie was doing very well indeed as a TV and radio summariser.

Bernie arrived with the Boro TV team, including Alastair Brownlee, and we crowded into the editor's office for a bit of privacy. Fortunately the editor was on a day off. It would have been virtually impossible to conduct the interview on the editorial floor. Nobody else at the Gazette would have been able to get any work done.

Bernie had prepared well for the interview, with a series of questions written out on an A4 sheet of paper. I'm always nervous whenever the camera starts to roll, but I warmed to the experience, and in the end was disappointed when the questions ended. We talked for 29 minutes. The edited version on Boro TV was to last only eight minutes.

The Boro TV crew told me afterwards that Alan Moore and Keith O'Neill had both been involved in a rumpus at Club M at the Tall Trees on Saturday night. Apparently the Boro duo had been in a disagreement with other parties when they were leaving the club.

Alan in particular had been badly beaten around the face, while Keith had gone to hospital today for an X-ray. I needed to check this one out before I could even consider printing it, because it was potentially very political from my point of view. It was the kind of story which gets local sports reporters banned from clubs!

Earlier, I knew nothing of the rumpus when I drove up to Rockliffe Park to see Bryan Robson. One of my prepared questions concerned an alleged sighting of Robbo and Aston Villa striker Dion Dublin in a pub in Wynyard, which was the result of a tip off from an anonymous fan.

I put all such questions to Robbo, however unlikely they may seem, and am not surprised when most of them turn out to be wrong. But, blow me, this one was right. Trouble was, Robbo and Dublin had not planned to meet up in the pub. Robbo had walked in with his wife for a bar-meal, only to bump into Gary Pallister, Dublin and their wives. Apparently Pally and Dublin are great pals following their days together at Manchester United, and meet up regularly.

Robbo said: "It was a chance meeting. I phoned Steve Bruce at Huddersfield because he told me that he had once had a great meal at Wynyard, and I fancied seeing what it was like. When I found the restaurant, the last person I expected to see was Dion Dublin. But then any fans expecting a signing should not raise their hopes. I know that Dion is very settled at Villa."

Another question, when I enquired whether Watford had made an attempt to sign Paul Gascoigne, was denied by Robbo. There was clearly no truth in the story, so it wasn't even worth officially denying in the Evening Gazette.

Afterwards, Gordon Cox and I talked to Robbie Mustoe in reception. The Boro midfielder had made a successful comeback for the reserves last night in a friendly game at Billingham Town, despite sporting two stitches in a cut just above his left eye. The eye apart, Robbie's comeback following a knee injury had gone well.

Then I walked out into the warm sunshine and waited for Dean Gordon. He arrived wearing a baseball cap with a rather long peak. I spoke to him about his latest venture as a DJ. Deano was apparently in big demand, and was due to perform at the Empire in Middlesbrough on Friday. He was clearly enjoying this musical sideline, though stressed that his main ambition was to get back from injury as soon as possible. The news was good concerning his rehabilitation. Deano was hoping to start training again by January, which would be ahead of schedule.

Wednesday, November 3

THE Moore-O'Neill story broke in the Daily Star today. Damn! The incident must have been witnessed by a few nightclub revellers, and spread quickly.

Once a story is out in Middlesbrough, it doesn't gather dust. There are fringe media people hanging around who are ready to sell the club down the river for thirty pieces of silver. They are quickly on to the phone to the Star and the Sun whenever they hear a juicy titbit. Don't bother checking the facts; just flog the story.

Unfortunately the Boro are completely naive over how the system operates, and how much money can be involved for good tip-offs. The non-stop flow of Gazza-knocking stories is the perfect example of how the club is being sold short by certain people.

Neither do Boro help themselves at times. When it comes down to punches being thrown at a nightclub, the only way for the Boro to beat eventual embarrassment is to issue a formal statement to me, at the Evening Gazette, post haste. But Boro often try to roll things under the carpet in these, and similar, circumstances and are at risk of having to pay the price in the end.

Fortunately, in this case, I thought that the Star dealt with the story very sensitively and professionally, which was something of a surprise.

I was running the Gazette sports department today while sports editor

Allan Boughey enjoyed his day off. So I had my hands full, even though Robbo and the players were all on a day off as well. It was left to chief reporter Peter Harris to check the facts and write up the Moore-O'Neill story as a front page lead for the Evening Gazette. I provided him with a few background facts and some useful telephone numbers. While the Gazette had been beaten to the story by the Star, the saving grace was that there were not many Star readers in Middlesbrough and, for most Boro fans, this would be the first time they had been made aware of the story.

The revelations had come at a bad time. Yesterday, before entertaining Boro TV, I had grafted away to compile a two-page feature on Keith O'Neill for the Sports Gazette. He had talked about the Republic of Ireland's forthcoming Euro 2000 qualifiers against Turkey and provided me with some excellent quotes. It made for a fine feature.

Unfortunately, the news arrived this morning that O'Neill was not included in the shortened Irish squad for the Euro qualifiers.

It meant that I had to scrap the whole two-page feature, and write another one in its place. I had a Gary Pallister interview in my notebook which I planned to write up as my second regular Sports Gazette feature. So I hastily searched through my book to put together a series of Mark Schwarzer quotes from separate interviews and compile a feature large enough to replace the doomed O'Neill one. By the time that I had finished writing both features late in the afternoon, my eyeballs were sinking deep into my head.

Friday, November 5

KEITH O'Neill was thankfully none the worse for the effects of the incident at the Tall Trees and was in a bubbly mood in the reception area at Rockliffe Park. He had already been passed fully fit for tomorrow's mega game against Sunderland, after an X-ray on his jaw showed no problems.

It was good news, and helped lift a potential veil off the team with such a big game now just over 24 hours away. The nightclub fracas was put to rest when chief executive Keith Lamb stopped me outside secretary Karen Nelson's office to say that he would shortly be giving me a press statement on the matter.

The statement had been agreed jointly between the Boro and the Tall Trees, and stressed that the matter was now over and done with as far as all parties were concerned. I phoned the statement to the Evening Gazette immediately, and left it up to the news desk to write up the story.

Then I spoke to Gianluca Festa, along with Gordon Cox. The Italian defender's quotes about his battle for fitness gave me a good story for Saturday's back page. The programme of exercises which Festa had undertaken over the past two weeks seemed to have solved his six-months hamstring problem, though the big test would come when he started playing again.

Earlier I had gone in to see Bryan Robson, who revealed that Festa was back in the squad against the Wearsiders. However he stressed that Festa would be 17th man, and would not be involved. With O'Neill fine, the injury situation at the Boro was better than it had been all season. Robbo said: "We had so many players in training yesterday that I didn't know where to place everybody."

I had arranged to talk to Carlos Marinelli this morning, with the help of interpreter Zelia Knight, but I was informed on my arrival that Robbo had pulled the plug on the interview. He wanted the Argentine lad to stay out of the limelight as much as possible. I wasn't too happy, because I felt that my questions would have been sensible and sensitive. But I had to go along with the manager's wishes.

Charles Porter, the chairman of Robbie Mustoe's testimonial committee, rang me on the afternoon to reel out the remarkable number of exclusive items which the committee had acquired for auction at Robbie's testimonial dinner.

They included several items donated by Paul Gascoigne, notably the much treasured shirt in which he scored his memorable goal for England against Scotland in the Euro 96 game. This shirt was truly a one-off in football terms. Gazza had also donated a special Gazza fruit machine, which was one of only ten manufactured, and was reputed to be worth £10,000.

It's one of the sad facts of life that Paul is criticised heavily in the media, both by pressmen and football fans. Yet the real Gazza, one of the game's true nice guys, never fills a single column inch. I can't remember any player ever helping another during a testimonial year in the way that Gazza has helped Robbie.

Saturday, November 6

BORO were held at home by Sunderland in a blood and thunder 1-1 draw. Both sets of fans were great and the atmosphere was electric throughout. Just like the old days.

But Boro really should have won it, especially as the Wearsiders went down to ten men in the 32nd minute when Chris Makin was sent off.

Hamilton Ricard scored his first goal for ages to fire Boro ahead with only 14 minutes left, but Phil Stamp collided with Niall Quinn in the penalty area soon afterwards and Sunderland were awarded a penalty. Mark Schwarzer made a truly magnificent save from Kevin Phillips' spot kick, but Michael Reddy fired home the loose ball. Despite all the adrenaline and excitement, the final result left an empty feeling. I could have happily gone home and not written another word on the match.

The press room was packed afterwards, most of them new faces from the various media organisations on Wearside and Tyneside. Bryan Robson was in first and resisted becoming involved in a discussion about an elbow by Brian Deane on Paul Butler, early in the game, which had been missed by the referee. If Deano had gone off at that stage, it could have been Boro who faced a backs to the wall battle.

Afterwards, Sunderland boss Peter Reid was very forthright, but when asked if Deane should be tried by TV, said: "No. I wouldn't want to go along that road." I fully agreed with him.

I wanted to catch Stampy afterwards to discuss the penalty decision, but as I walked into the area outside the players' lounge, he was just disappearing into the lift to go and receive an award in the sponsors' lounges.

I waited patiently for his return, but Stampy must have got a flier. There were not too many players around by this time, so it was a relief when Colin Cooper appeared to give an interview to myself and Gary Gill from Radio Cleveland.

Monday, November 8

NO need to head off for Rockliffe Park today. The Boro players and senior coaches all flew out to Marbella last night for a few days' break with the sun on their backs, and a bit of light training to boot.

I was still concentrating on the biggest talking point of the weekend, which was Brian Deane's elbow on Paul Butler during the derby match against Sunderland. So I rang Adrian Bevington at the FA for the latest update.

Adrian, Middlesbrough born and bred, had attended the derby game. When I rang him on his mobile, he was sitting on the train on his way back to Lancaster Gate. I asked him for an official FA comment on the Deane incident, which he gave me, and we also chatted about things in general.

On the record, he told me that nothing would be done until the referee's report was received. Off the record, he suspected that FA officials would want to look at the video of the game. I suspected that, too.

Afterwards I rang Boro reserve team coach David Geddis at the training headquarters. David was in charge this week in the absence of Bryan Robson and Co, and I needed to know which players had stayed behind, especially as there was a reserve game tomorrow night.

David revealed that Paul Gascoigne was among the senior players who had not travelled to Spain. Gazza would be playing against Blackburn reserves tomorrow, though David asked me to ring him again later when he had finalised the team.

Academy director Dave Parnaby rang with the news of the junior teams. He was delighted that both the Boro under-19s and under-17s had won in their home games against Bolton Wanderers on Saturday. It was the first time this season that both teams had won on the same day.

We received a few e-mails at the Evening Gazette today following the derby battle. Once, in particular, made us all chuckle on the sports desk. It was from a Sunderland supporter, who was heavily criticising the Boro players for dirty play during the game. We planned to print this letter in the Sports Gazette at the weekend, and it should lead to dozens of scathing replies from irate Boro fans.

The truth was that both sides were very committed in the derby, and it was silly to suggest that one team was a lot more physical than the other.

Later in the day I phoned Shaun Keogh at Middlesbrough Supporters South to confirm with him that he had arranged for H Newbould Ltd to send down 100 of their succulent pies for the MSS annual Christmas bash. It was all sorted. Shaun's only problem was that he had not yet organised transport to London for such valuable foodstuff. However he was working on it. Should be the highlight of the night for those pie-starved Boro exiles.

Tuesday, November 9

I TELEPHONED the Irish FA today to check on a report that Curtis Fleming had been called up as a late addition to the Irish squad, and ended up giving the Irish official more information than he gave me.

It proved to be true that Curtis had been called up by manager Mick McCarthy for the Euro 2000 play-offs against Turkey, but the guy at the Irish FA was surprised to hear that the Boro defender was currently in Spain with his teammates.

Curtis was in Marbella, and only a few miles from Malaga Airport, from where he could get a flight direct to Dublin. So I put the Irish FA official's mind at rest.

Then I rang Boro secretary Karen Nelson to check that Curtis had been informed of Ireland's needs. He had. I could just imagine him hastily throwing his kit and toothbrush into his bag, with a view to catching the next flight out.

Afterwards I contacted David Geddis on his mobile, and the Boro coach gave me the line-up for tonight's reserve fixture at Blackburn. Paul Gascoigne was playing, as expected. So, too, was Carlos Marinelli, while teenage wing-back Adam McMahon was making his first start at reserve level.

I spoke to Adrian Bevington again at the English FA, and he confirmed that the disciplinary committee were indeed planning to look at the video of Saturday's game against Sunderland, to inspect the elbowing incident. I was disappointed to hear that the committee intended to look purely at the Brian Deane incident, and not some of the other instances when the laws of the game were breached.

A fan called Mr Webb, who rang me, was similarly disappointed. He felt that Deane was being unfairly singled out, and I agreed with every word he said. Mr Webb stressed that the club should be doing more to support Deane. I hoped they would do just that when, as expected, Brian was charged and accepted the opportunity for a personal hearing.

It had been a busy morning, but a successful one. I had enough stories to keep me going for the next two days. The rest of the day was equally productive. I wrote up my Paylor on Wednesday column, and then hammered out a two-page look-back at the derby battle for the Sports Gazette, through the eyes of Colin Cooper. Up to date at 4.30pm! Boro should go away to Spain more often.

Friday, November 12

ROBBIE Mustoe hosted his testimonial dinner in the Tall Trees in Yarm, and a good night was had by all, even if it did go on until almost two o'clock in the morning. Three speakers, including the excellent Paul Fletcher, and an extensive auction of signed shirts and memorabilia helped to drag out the event. I reckoned that the proceeds of the auction and the raffle would have earned Robbie just over £20,000, in addition to a small profit which may have been made on the dinner tickets. The highlight of the night was the auction of Paul Gascoigne's shirt which he had worn when scoring the memorable goal against Scotland in Euro 96. Unfortunately the shirt wasn't on view at the Tall Trees. Gazza had brought along the wrong one by mistake. The shirt on display was the grey shirt he wore against Germany.

However the 700-strong guests were promised that they could have their pick of the two shirts. It was clear from the outset that it was the

England v Scotland shirt which was the major attraction. Gordon Cox did a great job running the auction and the packed hall was on tenterhooks as the price just kept on rising by £100 at a time.

Finally there were just two bidders left, and it was Middlesbrough Football Club who eventually won the battle, paying £6,400 for the shirt. The proceeds were to be donated to North-east children's charities, so it was a worthwhile exercise all-round.

I did have a major problem afterwards, when testimonial committee chairman Charles Porter informed me that Boro chairman Steve Gibson had requested that the name of the buyer remained secret. I could not accept that. Most people in the hall were aware that the winning bid had come from a Boro FC table, while the auction had also been filmed.

When I told Charles that I would have to print the outcome of the auction regardless of any requests to the contrary, he asked me to have a chat with Steve first, which I did. I put my case and, as usual, the chairman was very amenable. "Eric, we are not that sensitive," he shouted, trying to drown out the male vocalist who had suddenly started prancing around to a backing track which was belting out on the stage. I knew immediately that there would be no problems printing the story and took my leave, along with everybody else, as we flooded out to try to get away from the turn.

I had spent the evening at the Tall Trees sitting at a table which included former Boro player Chris Morris on my right, and Sky TV reporter Dave Roberts on my left. Chris is always good for a chat. He has settled on Teesside and has bought a season ticket at the Riverside Stadium to watch the Boro. Chris invested his own testimonial cash wisely and his businesses are doing very well. I didn't doubt that Robbie would be just as sensible with his cash.

Chris was enjoying a couple of drinks during the evening, though Dave and I were on the wagon. I was driving, mainly because I live over 20 miles from the Tall Trees and any other form of travel would have been very expensive or very difficult. I was interested to hear Dave claim he was now tee-total, following a particularly bad bender. I'll see how long it lasts! However Dave did stick to drinking cola all night. It was just as well because he faced around only four hours in bed. He had to catch the 7.15am train from Darlington to travel to Glasgow to report on the Scotland-England Euro play-off first leg for Sky.

Monday, November 15

I discovered today that Keith O'Neill had bought three of the items in teammate Robbie Mustoe's testimonial auction at the Tall Trees, including the limited edition Gazza one-armed bandit - which set him back a cool £5,600.

Keith had also bought a signed AC Milan shirt for £1,900 and a signed Ronaldo Inter Milan shirt for £2,100. It left him with rather a large cheque to write out at the end of a night-out.

I stopped Keith on the staircase at Rockliffe Park. He was very upbeat about his triple purchase, as well he might be. "These are for the future, when I stop playing," he stressed. It had been estimated before the testimonial dinner that the Gazza slot machine was worth in the region of £10,000 to a serious collector. So Keith's sound bidding had given him a decent investment, not to mention an immediate profit should he ever decide to sell.

On the afternoon, Ray Robertson, the chairman of the North-east branch of the Football Writers Association, phoned to say that Willie Maddren had been awarded a trophy at the FWA annual dinner for his contribution to football and his courage in fighting motor neurone disease. I was happy to publicise the fact, and also that the FWA had auctioned two shirts in aid of Willie's MND fund. I was rather taken aback to discover that one of the shirts was a signed Ronaldo Inter Milan shirt, which had been bought by former Hartlepool United chairman John Smart for £700. It was considerably less than Keith O'Neill had forked out on Friday, and I did not have the heart to break the news to Keith. However, he would not be perturbed because the cash was for a cause.

Paul Gascoigne arrived with the England shirt which he wore in the Euro 96 clash against Scotland, which had been bought by the club on Friday for £6,400. There was already some disagreement about the validity of this shirt, especially as Bradford midfielder Stuart McCall was claiming that he owned the real shirt. McCall insisted he had swapped with Gazza at the end of the game. There are, however, two shirts issued for every international appearance, and Boro had just purchased the second one.

Bryan Robson had not travelled with the team to Marbella. Instead he had enjoyed a family break in Dubai. He was, therefore, rather shocked when he walked into the training headquarters and I broke the news that O'Neill was suspended for Saturday's trip to Arsenal. The confirmation had arrived from the FA during the previous week. With Christian Ziege also suspended, Robbo was perfectly right when he declared that he didn't have a great deal to select from on the left-hand side.

On the way out of the training headquarters, Gordon Cox and I spoke to Colin Cooper, to pick up a few words about the trip to Highbury. Coops was positive about Boro's prospects. It gave me a ready-made interview for my Herald and Post article.

I returned a call to Dave Parnaby late in the evening and he gave me the low-down on the club's teenage squadron. Dave was really buzzing because Boro Under-19s had won 2-0 at Sunderland on Saturday, and the Wearsiders were runaway leaders at the top of the league. The lads had done really well.

Tuesday, November 16

I TOOK the inaugural Evening Gazette Millennium Memories book with me to Rockliffe Park today. Several similar books were being circulated throughout Teesside for people to sign and commemorate the Millennium.

Bryan Robson was the first very to write down his special Millennium message and he looked forward to bringing home the club's first trophy at the same time as Middlesbrough became a city. Paul Gascoigne and Keith O'Neill repeated similar hopes afterwards, and were pictured by Gazette photographer Steve Elliott recording their personal messages. There was anger at the training headquarters because Gazza had been pilloried in the Daily Star today. The pictures had been taken at Robbie Mustoe's testimonial dinner without permission. However the guy who had sold the pictures to the newspaper was by-lined. He was well known to the club. A letter was sent off that very day banning him from all future club activities.

Outside, Gordon Cox and I chatted to Mark Schwarzer about the fact that he had missed out on an Australian international cap against Brazil. Mark Bosnich, who had been injured in the first of two friendly games Down Under against Brazil, was unable to keep goal for the second match. If Mark had been part of the Aussie squad he would have been called up to play.

However, Mark was not fazed. He was happy to be at home with his family, especially following the birth of his son last month, and was looking forward to Saturday's game against Arsenal.

It gave me a useful piece for Paylor on Wednesday, though I had to finish the column very quickly because I was heading off at lunchtime. I accompanied Evening Gazette assistant editor sports Allan Boughey to Whitaker's in Corporation Road, where we met up with Dave Allan, head of Boro's PR.

We had several subjects to discuss, including potential newspaper coverage of Boro's under-19 and under-17 games. It was a fruitful meeting, while the smoked salmon, halibut and prawn meal was sublime. I spent much of the afternoon writing up Bryan Robson's comments on the first round of the voting for the Cellnet player of the year. Skipper Paul Ince was already miles ahead. Not exactly much of a surprise!

Wednesday, November 17

MORE Millennium Memories. I took the Evening Gazette's inaugural book back up to Rockliffe Park and asked Gianluca Festa and Robbie Mustoe to sign it in order to complete the first page.

Both players spent some time composing their messages. Gianluca worked on his on a spare piece of paper, before writing it in Italian into the book. I asked club interpreter Zelia Knight to translate it. It was an appealing message. Thankfully no swear words!

Robbie was a good choice to complete the first page because he was celebrating his testimonial year. The five football club messages would make good reading when the books were retrieved many years into the future.

Bryan Robson was attending a funeral, so Viv Anderson was in charge today. He was flicking through the latest Teletext football news when PR officer Louise Wanless and I entered his room. Teletext is a regular media avenue used by football coaches to keep in touch with the comings and goings in the game.

Viv had watched Boro reserves' 3-1 win at Bolton last night. Andy Campbell scored all three goals and also hit a post, while Carlos Marinelli had apparently produced a storming first half performance.

There wasn't a great deal happening elsewhere, though Viv was quick to respond when I reminded him that Boro hadn't won at Arsenal for 61 years. "Since Bryan and I came to to the club our record at Arsenal is quite good," he insisted, and then proceeded to run through each game. They have amazing memories, football coaches. I had to admit that Viv was right, though it would still be good to end the bogey on Saturday.

Downstairs, I grabbed Robbie Mustoe again for an interview. We spoke about his testimonial year, and the fresh battle he faced to regain his first team place. Robbie pointed out that the current midfield trio of Juninho, Christian Ziege and Paul Ince had not been at the club last season when Robbie, Paul Gascoigne and Andy Townsend ruled the roost. It summed up the strength of the increased competition, but I was still ready to back Robbie to see plenty of the action this season.

I wrote up the Mustoe feature on the afternoon and also spent some time talking to a reporter from the Daily Telegraph, who was planning to write a big feature on the Boro. I had never heard of the guy, called Mark Palmer, but I was happy to answer all of his questions.

Mark needed background information on the club and I knew that my answers would influence the tone of his piece. In discussing the ups and downs of the past five years, I stressed that Robbo was a rookie manager when he arrived on Teesside in 1994 and had made many mistakes as part of his learning curve, particularly in buying top quality flair players before the team had some foundations.

However, the club had stuck by Robbo and, after guiding Boro back on track with the inspirational signing of Paul Merson, I suggested that the club's ambitions were in stronger hands than before. Maybe last season's ninth place supported that fact. Mr Palmer gobbled up the facts and figures. I suspected he would not be writing the usual infuriating knocking piece which reporters who know nothing about the club normally produce.

Thursday, November 18

DAY off but, after spending all day working flat out on my forthcoming Teesside's Sporting Greats book on my trusty PC, I had to drive through to the Blue Bell Hotel after tea for the official launch of Fly Me To The Moon's official Millannual.

It had been a foul day, with constant sleet showers, and it was a foul evening. But weather like that doesn't stop football people from crossing their doorsteps.

There was a very good turn-out at the Blue Bell, including George Hardwick and his wife Jennifer. It was good to see them again. George looked great, especially for a 79-year-old guy who had just undergone two major operations. He's a fighter in every aspect of his life.

Alastair Brownlee and Gordon Cox were there, plus familiar faces like Alex Wilson, Neil Robinson from Waterstones, Anthony Vickers from the Evening Gazette and most of the contributors to the annual, including its editor, Rob Nichols. Since being approached by John Wilson from Juniper Publishing to compile the annual, Rob and his team had worked wonders to produce so much copy that another 16 pages had been added to the planned pagination.

The book looked fine. It was the first ever hardback annual produced by a fanzine and hopefully would create a bit of national interest. Fly Me To The Moon was the longest running fanzine and, with the publication of this annual, continued to be a pacesetter.

Clem and Fischer from Red Balls on Fire were among the guests. Clem revealed that the duo had been offered the chance to produce an hour-long pilot programme for Radio Five Live with a view to it possibly becoming a regular weekly event. It was a huge opportunity for the lads, and I could tell they were nervous. But they were doing a great job on Red Balls on Fire and, if they could convert their unique Radio Cleveland concept from a local into a national one, there was no reason why they couldn't make it. They were currently working hard on the pilot, and Clem promised to ring me with the full story next week.

Saturday, November 20

ONE of the problems of travelling long distances to away games is that you never know what you are going to come up against on the way. We like to think we always allow plenty of time to get there, but at times you are in the lap of the gods.

So it was not very pleasant to suddenly come up against huge slow-moving queues on the M1, on the way to Arsenal today, and then be informed on the radio that the motorway was closed further south because of an accident.

You can do two things in these situations: panic, or try to get out of the mess. We always panic first, and then later take the second option. I took my life in my own hands to jump out of the car on the M1 and hastily search out the road atlas in the boot. Then I had to repeat the exercise when we discovered I had left Lennie's coat hanging half in and half out of the boot.

According to the radio, traffic was being diverted off the M1 at junction nine, so we came off at No.10 - along with hundreds of other vehicles. Within a couple of minutes we found we had left one queue to join another. We were locked solid on a minor road leading to Harpenden. It was all rather stressful. To make matters worse, it was now after one o'clock and Highbury was many miles away.

Drastic situations need drastic measures. We decided to turn off on to a farm track and take a tour of the pleasant country roads of Hertfordshire. Within seconds we were bombing around narrow lanes rather haphazardly. But all mud things come to an end. Eventually we found a truck road, and used it to find our way across to the A1M.

Even so it was touch and go whether I would see the kick off at Highbury. There was plenty of Christmas traffic when we reached London and we made very slow progress through the capital.

When we arrived somewhere close to the ground, there were no parking spots to be had. Eventually we found one, at least a mile away from Highbury. I had to leave the lads and run all the way to the stadium. When, breathing heavily, I entered the stadium at last, and walked into the cramped Arsenal press box, Tim Rich from the Newcastle Journal was talking on the phone to my workmate Martin Neal at the Evening Gazette. Tim was telling Martin that he would have to do the running report for the Sports Gazette because I had not arrived. Not until I tapped Tim on the shoulder, of course. I was grateful to know that Tim was ready to help out, especially if I ever needed to call on him in the future.

On the drive down to London, I was accompanied by regular passengers Len Shepherd and Nigel Gibb, plus Gazette journalist Mike McGeary, who was watching the game and then going on to the Middlesbrough Supporters South party at the Strand Palace Hotel. Mike had asked me, in the car, who would be the star man today. Without hesitation, I told him that it would be Mark Schwarzer by a mile.

Funny how I seem to know these things. Boro were absolutely battered, went down 5-1, and were grateful for some brilliant saves from Schwarzer for preventing a much worse defeat. I think Mark was also helped by my lucky tie. Without a combination of the two, Boro could have conceded twice as many goals.

Bryan Robson was subdued in the sumptuous press interview room afterwards, but made few excuses. Arsene Wenger described the performance as Arsenal's best of the season. But Boro had played badly, and only a superb goal from Hamilton Ricard made the trip worthwhile.

I vented my frustration in the press box in an interview on Clem and Fischer's live show on Radio Cleveland. The Red Balls on Fire duo were shivering in the intense cold. I sensed they would be stocked up with thermals next time. Highbury is traditionally a very cold stadium. I was wearing so many T-shirts I had difficulty breathing.

It was 6.15pm when we drove away from Highbury without Mike McGeary, who was representing the Gazette editorial department at the supporters' party. I would have loved to have gone, but I could not spare the time, especially with reports to write up on the Sunday and a family visit arranged.

I had left Mike sitting forlornly in the press room at Highbury with Paul Armstrong from the BBC, who was a big Boro fan and attended as many matches as possible. He, too, was going to the supporters bash. "Won't be much of a party now," he said. I suspected the mood would change for all the fans after a few bevvies.

I drove all the way back from Highbury. I couldn't believe how clear the roads were. It was a dream journey. And I was back in the house before midnight - though only just.

WHEN you are writing several thousand words a week about one club and its players, it's inevitable that you will upset somebody occasionally.

I never ever deliberately write anything malicious or sarcastic about anybody at the Boro, and am genuinely disappointed when I cause personal offence. Players expect to be criticised for poor performances and mistakes they may make during games, but they have a right to expect a fair crack of the whip otherwise.

Mark Schwarzer had a few strong words to say to me today over something I had written last week. I appreciated his concern, and I apologised. To make matters worse, the offensive article had referred to something in his private life. He felt I had betrayed a confidence. I could not argue against the valid points he made, and could only hope that it would not affect our relationship.

It's a long time since I have had a really bad fall-out with a player, but you are always walking the tightrope. Not all members of the Boro squad read the Evening Gazette, but any maligned player would immediately be made aware of any dodgy article by his teammates. And, if I was to lose the confidence of one player, I would lose them all. I have seen it happen in the past to other reporters elsewhere. That's why local hacks must always be honest and careful, but never spiteful, in their reporting.

After interviewing Bryan Robson, Gordon Cox and I chatted to Gianluca Festa and Curtis Fleming. Festa talked in depth about the Arsenal game, and especially the disputed penalty which he had conceded. The ball had innocently hit Gianluca on the arm inside the box and he said: "I say to the referee, how can I walk around without my arms. I did not know where the ball was."

Curtis looked back in vivid detail at the horrendous travelling that the Republic of Ireland squad had been forced to endure on their trip to Turkey last week. He gave an eye-witness account of the angry scenes after the match which could have led to a nasty incident. Both interviews gave me good stories for later in the week.

Paul Gascoigne arrived at Rockliffe Park having once again been dragged through the mire in the media, this time in the Sun. I don't know how he copes with the non-stop personal tirade from the tabloids, and neither do the rest of the squad. I know that his fellow players are just as sickened as he must be by all the sleaze which is constantly blasted in his direction.

Clearly upset by this latest 'exclusive', Gazza went straight upstairs for a chat with Robbo. Afterwards he was talking on the phone to his agent

Mel Stein from the car park. But Gazza still broke off to exchange pleasantries with me as I made my way to the car to phone over my stories.

Tuesday, November 23

BRYAN Robson was in a surprisingly buoyant mood, despite Boro's drubbing at Arsenal on Saturday. He was thinking positively. Robbo made it absolutely clear that he wanted to put the match behind everybody, and concentrate on the important games coming up in the next month. I agreed with him, though I did not want to see three points ever conceded as easily again as they had been at Highbury. Over a cup of tea, along with PR officer Louise Wanless, we looked back at the match and dissected it. On reflection, Robbo admitted that he should not have tampered with his defence so much, while stressing that Arsenal would probably still have won the game regardless.

Robbo had exchanged several words with the fourth official during the match. "When he picked up the board at the end of the game to show the added minutes I pleaded with him if he could put up 'none'," joked the Boro boss. "If it was four or five minutes we might have conceded another couple of goals. Fortunately it was only one."

Christian Ziege was back today after helping his wife to recover from an operation, though Paul Ince had been told to rest for a couple of days following his exertions of the last couple of weeks.

I grabbed Jason Gavin for a chat. The Irish teenager was sporting a black eye which carried four stitches. However he was in good heart and, having been praised by Robbo for his performance on Saturday, was keeping his fingers crossed that he was in the side to meet Wimbledon on Saturday. I felt he deserved another chance. Most of the Boro squad were enjoying a day off tomorrow, so Jason's quotes would give me a story for tomorrow's back page.

Afterwards I raced back to the Evening Gazette to start work on my Paylor on Wednesday column, but it turned out to be a long drawn out affair. I was awaiting information from the Worthington Cup press people about the green bus they were planning to send around Teesside, with John Hendrie aboard, over the weekend. It held up the completion of the column until early afternoon. Once I was sorted, and had traced the photo of the bus, there was just enough time to squeeze in the writing of a Gianluca Festa article for the Sports Gazette before racing home for a late tea.

Friday, November 26

I HAD a brief chat with Christian Ziege today for a general piece for tomorrow's Evening Gazette. He was looking ahead to the Frank Worthington Cuptie against Arsenal on Tuesday, believing that Boro could avenge last week's hammering at Highbury.

It was good to see Christian at Rockliffe Park, never mind talking positively about football. He revealed that his wife was still in hospital in Germany, having had a serious operation at the end of the previous week.

Christian had flown back to England at the beginning of this week and committed himself in training, while his wife was in hospital. I'm sure that she was being well looked after and receiving plenty of visitors, but I can think of a few Boro players of the past who might have found a reason for staying away from the club in such a situation.

I thought it was a tremendous act of loyal dedication by Christian, though I suspected that deep down he would still be finding it very difficult to concentrate wholeheartedly on his football.

Even agreeing to take part in the interview would have had some nuisance value for him at this difficult time, so I was grateful that he answered a few questions. He was likely to play against Wimbledon tomorrow and Arsenal three days later without making a return to Germany.

Bryan Robson was looking forward to the game. He was confidently expecting a much improved performance against Wimbledon, especially as Ziege and Keith O'Neill were back after suspension. I was surprised and disappointed to see there was no Jason Gavin listed when he handed me his squad. Robbo revealed that he had deliberately named a scaled down 17-man party because some of the squad players were training on Saturday, with the Arsenal match in mind.

Paul Gascoigne had a spring in his step despite the horrendous battering he had received at the hands of the Sun, and in a TV programme on Wednesday night. I asked him if he had put his foot through the TV. Certainly I had been tempted to do likewise. However Gazza was succinct. "I didn't watch it," he insisted. A wise decision.

Clem and Fischer from Red Balls on Fire were surprise visitors to Rockliffe Park this morning. They had arranged to interview Juninho as part of their preparations for their pilot programme for Radio Five Live. Dave Roberts from Sky TV also breezed in and out. "Still on the wagon?" I asked him. "Yeah, but the big test is coming up at Christmas," he replied. The trick will be not to unwrap those long thin presents.

Saturday, November 27

OH dear. Boro were quite dreadful at home to Wimbledon and avoided defeat only because the Dons strikers were so incompetent in front of goal.

I had to compile a running report on this match for the Sports Gazette. Not easy! I had to draw deep on all the skill and experience I had gathered during the last 15 years in order to fill my column inches on this awful goalless draw.

At half-time I chatted to Roger Tames, from Tyne Tees who, despite his rather unfair Teesside nickname Roger Tyne, always talks positively about the Boro. Roger is a southerner by birth and I have never detected him favouring one North-east club above another in general conversation. The only team I'll warrant that he dislikes is Tottenham. Nuff said on the subject.

As we tucked into quiche and coffee in the press room, Roger was as perplexed as I was by the Boro's ineptness. "Boro are making Wimbledon look like Brazil," he remarked.

If we thought the first half was bad, the second half was worse. Then Bryan Robson added to the agony by substituting Juninho after an hour. The Brazilian was the only player who was bringing any excitement and hope to the game, so the decision was very loudly booed. In fact the North Stand chanted: "You don't know what you're doing."

The method in Robbo's madness was to try to preserve a point, because Boro looked like losing the game. At the final whistle, I was approached by several angry fans.

"Print the truth," one insisted.

I always do.

"Say that Robson should be sacked," said another.

I would, if I felt he should be sacked. But I believe that you should only sack somebody if you know that you can replace them adequately. Bearing in mind the high expectations on Teesside, I couldn't imagine where Boro could find a manager who could guarantee to keep them in the Premier League, never mind bring the title to the town next season. However Robbo had clearly made mistakes in his tactics in both of Boro's last two games, and the fans had every right to be angry. Nobody can ever guarantee that a team will win, but the fans deserved much better than this.

Afterwards the manager steadfastly defended his decision to take off Juninho, though his suggestion that the Brazilian had not been playing better than anybody else would not go down well with the fans.

Dons boss Egil Olsen entered the press room without his famous wellies. He had sympathy for Boro. "I don't know how Boro have played before but I can't imagine they have ever created so few chances, which shows we played well defensively." he said.

I didn't hang around afterwards. I had to find my way to Low Mill in Farndale to review a concert by Chicago-based husband and wife duo The Handsome Family for the Evening Gazette. The journey as far as Kirkbymoorside was fine, but then the trip across the moors was horrendous. Dark and scary, just like The Handsome Family.

My wife and I were rather shocked to discover that the show was being held in a small wooden 1940s-type hut, which did not have a bar. Not even for soft drinks. We were in strange territory, among strange people. However we thoroughly enjoyed the show and I even bought a T-shirt. And when I finally stumbled across the car in the pitch-black at half past eleven, I had a smile on my face at last. But it had been a long tiring day.

Tuesday, November 30

I'VE never been a particular lover of corporate hospitality at football grounds. It's one of the contributory factors towards football changing dramatically over the last decade, and with it has come increased prices and the gradual disappearance of many ordinary fans from the clubs they love.

However, 'Hypocrisy' was my middle name tonight when my wife and I accepted a kind offer from Cellnet to be their guests for Boro's Worthington Cup fourth round clash at home to Arsenal.

Having had little choice but to take my final week's holiday of the year, or risk losing it, this was a good opportunity to escape from the daily hum-drum Christmas shopping trips and see how the other half lived in the modern world of football.

In the event, the hospitality was great and I discovered it was an ideal way to watch the game. It was just a pity that every fan didn't have the same opportunity.

We were wined and dined before the match, at half-time and after the final whistle. There was a choice of meals before the game started, a tray of sandwiches always on hand and a free bar. You could not take drinks out into the seats, but no doubt any fans who preferred to watch their football from their armchairs could remain in the box, watch the game on the TV and drink to their hearts' content.

The seats outside the box were excellent, at the back of the West Stand Lower, and in fact it was great to be able to watch a match from close quarters, instead of having to strain my eyes up in the gods in the press box. I could not be accused of being at a different match to everybody else on this occasion.

The only letdown was the match itself. I was disappointed to see that Arsenal had fielded a team which was little better than their Football Combination side, and even more disappointed to see Boro struggle to beat them. In many respects I was pleased that I did not have to report on this one.

Thierry Henry, Davor Suker and Ray Parlour were the best players on the pitch, and if it had not been for Henry's totally unnecessary handball a few minutes from time, Boro would have lost it.

Boro were understandably nervous, following two bad performances, and no doubt this contributed towards their disjointed display. However, Hamilton Ricard grabbed two good goals, including one from the penalty spot, and Boro would probably have won it in extra-time if the ref had awarded a penalty in Juninho's favour as he should have done. So, we were treated to the first ever penalty shoot-out at the Riverside Stadium. It was very tense, but maybe more so for Bryan Robson and his players, because they had a lot to lose on the night. In the event Boro strolled it. I took advantage of being outside the dignified confines of the press box to jump around like a lunatic when Mark Schwarzer ensured Boro of a quarter-final spot by making his second superb penalty save. Damn good things, these hospitality boxes!

Chapter Five

DECEMBER

Sunday, December 5

I DROVE through to WH Smith in Middlesbrough's Cleveland Centre for an official signing session for Gordon Cox's book Charlton's Champions.

I tried to park in the car park above the centre, but became gridlocked with dozens of other cars looking for spaces which didn't exist. Did all these people really need to be Christmas shopping at lunchtime on a Sunday? I doubted it, but was left with no choice but to drive up to the Evening Gazette to park, once I had freed myself from the bumper to bumper madness.

I was the first one to arrive in WH Smith and was slightly worried, especially as a large queue of customers had already formed. However, John Hickton and his wife Rosemary soon turned up. It was good to see them again. Such a friendly couple. Big John never turns down the opportunity to come back to his cultural home and sign a few books.

The Hicktons were soon followed by Charlton's skipper Stuart Boam, then Jim Platt, Malcolm Smith, Peter Creamer, John Craggs and the author.

Coxy apart, they all played for the favourite Boro team of my generation. Coxy was still learning to tie his shoelaces at the time. The players formed an imposing sight around the table and proceeded to sign as many books as possible, while chatting away happily among themselves and to the customers. Thanks to the help of Alastair Brownlee's promotional messages over the centre's Tannoy system, the queue never diminished over a hectic 90-minute period. Fortunately Smiths had enough books to cope.

Monday, December 6

STEVE Gibson rang me on my mobile at Rockliffe Park this morning and told me he would like to see me and my Evening Gazette colleague Anthony Vickers. We arranged to meet in the Bulkhaul offices at Riverside Park at 12.30pm.

It's always an important matter when one receives a call from the chairman, and this occasion was no different. Steve welcomed us into his office and got straight down to the point once we had settled comfortably on to his sumptuous red leather suite.

With several million pounds worth of planned investment shortly going into the club, Steve was very worried about the negative vibes currently flying around Teesside. There was heavy criticism of the team and particularly manager Bryan Robson, despite the fact that Boro had lost just one of their last nine games. The chairman had first hand experience of the extent of the problem. Both Gibson and Robson had recently been personally abused by fans.

Steve also showed me a shocking cutting from a national newspaper last week which claimed, without any foundation, that a rift had developed with Gibson and Robson. This kind of rubbish did not help the Boro one iota.

Steve was very concerned about the lies which were being fed to the fans, and asked for our support in trying to prevent the malingerers from prejudicing the view of the more loyal supporters, who were still in the majority. We told him that the Evening Gazette always supported what we felt was right.

I asked Steve to give me a story, in which he could stress again exactly what the club was trying to achieve. But the chairman was reluctant. The time had to be right, especially if criticism of some fans was implied. He knew it was important that no wedge was struck between the club and those fans who were leading the dissensions. Steve pointed out, quite rightly, that a string of good results over the next two weeks would solve the problem, especially as Boro could reach the Worthington Cup semi-finals, FA Cup fourth round and seventh position in the Premier League.

The chairman added that he would review the situation if Boro had a disastrous time before Christmas. So we left without a story, as such, but were left in no doubt that Steve's ambitions were as strong as ever. He made it clear that he believed that Robbo was still crucially important to the club. I realised that many fans did not fully appreciate that Gibson believed that Robson was just as important to the club as he was. A Boro without Robson was unthinkable to the chairman.

Earlier, Robbo had been in a forthright and positive mood, despite the current crop of injuries at the club. I waited for the outcome of a hospital trip by Curtis Fleming for an X-ray on his ribcage. Later I was informed by Gordon McQueen that Curtis had torn rib cartilages and would be sidelined for up to six weeks.

It was a blow for Curtis, but it gave me a fresh story for tonight. I also chatted to Robbie Mustoe, along with Alastair Brownlee and Gordon Cox, about the forthcoming FA Cuptie at Wrexham, which would provide a story for Wednesday.

This was my first day back at work following my week off and any hopes of making progress on the afternoon floundered. I received several elongated phonecalls from Wrexham-based journalists, all wanting details of Boro's current form, and this all took time to dictate. But these guys were also useful to me in providing a rundown on the Welsh club.

Then Gary Thornburn phoned to give me details of the official launch of Gianluca Festa's new football boots in Middlesbrough on Thursday. Festa's Cagliari-based company had been producing the boots for only three weeks, but already many of the Boro players are wearing them. Gary, who is well known to the Boro players and was acting as PR for the enterprise, stressed that 150 other players around the leagues were trying out the boots, including Gustavo Poyet at Chelsea.

Tuesday, December 7

GIANLUCA Festa was delighted to talk about his new football boots today. The Italian is occasionally a little frustrated about his own failure to express himself in English exactly as he would want to, but still did enough to get his points across.

Festa stressed that his Colombian teammate Hamilton Ricard had started wearing the boots, and had scored five goals in five games.

"Maybe they are magic," he said.

It was a great advertisement.

Judging by the strong interest in the boots from around the country, Gianluca could be on a winner. The boots are made primarily of kangaroo leather, which no doubt gives players an extra spring in their step. Pun intended.

Festa insisted: "When you use new boots, you have blisters. Nobody has blisters with my boots. They are very light, and very, very comfortable." Then Gianluca's sales pitch improved. He added: "I think Christmastime is a good chance for people to buy good presents for the children." Right on.

Gordon Cox and I also chatted to Steve Vickers about Boro's forthcoming trip to Tranmere Rovers in the Frank Worthington Cup.

Steve was a member of the lowly Tranmere side which humiliated First Division Boro back in 1988, and scored a cracking goal when Rovers drew 1-1 at Ayresome Park in the league cup two years later.

Some Boro fans were expecting an easy game next week, but Steve warned: "Tranmere have nothing to lose, and in the past they have been known as giant-killers. This will be a very tough game and we must prepare properly."

We also chatted to Neil Maddison, who had failed to win a regular place this season. He admitted: "It had crossed my mind to ask for a move but I couldn't have done it. I can't see any club being bigger than this one."

Genuine quotes and I could think of a couple of recent games where Neil's attitude and battling qualities were sorely missed.

Bryan Robson was still hopeful of having most of his players fit, despite revealing that Hamilton Ricard had been sent for an X-ray on a swollen toe. "We had eight senior players for training yesterday," he revealed. "I had to bring in some of the younger lads to make up the numbers."

It had been a busy morning at Rockliffe, but it was even busier back at the Evening Gazette. I struggled to complete my normal workload.

Paylor on Wednesday had to be truncated, while a non stop flow of phonecalls prevented me from making progress in other areas. One of the calls was from John McEvoy from the Wrexham Mail, who supplied me with a phone number I had been requesting. It was of Dave Smallman, who had scored the Wrexham winner on the last occasion Boro visited the Racecourse Ground in the FA Cup. I handed the number over to my colleague Andrew Wilkinson. It would make a good back page story for Thursday, when I was on day off.

I also had an appointment with Phil Harris, from Britannia Miniatures, who had produced a model of Ayresome Park, only eight inches by six. I was quite impressed. He had done a good job. The model was two years in the making, and had been designed purely from photographs.

However I noticed that the players' tunnel in the main stand did not correspond with the half-way line. Phil was a bit perplexed as well, especially as the models were selling like hot cakes and he had sold the first batch of 50 Ayresome Parks in only 24 hours. However a quick check in the Ayresome Park Memories book, when I arrived home, showed that Phil's model was perfect. It's funny how your mind can play tricks on you after only a few years away from the old stadium.

Friday, December 10

BRYAN Robson looked a tired man this morning, as well he might. His wife had been involved in a nasty car accident the previous evening which left her needing hospital treatment for three broken ribs.

Robbo had lost a lot of sleep as a result of his wife's accident, but he was at his desk before I arrived at Rockliffe Park at 9am and was happy to carry out the press interviews.

The manager, relieved that most of his injured players were fit again, revealed that Carlos Marinelli would almost certainly be on the bench for the first time in tomorrow's FA Cup third round clash at Wrexham.

Robbo denied reports that he was on the verge of signing David Johnson from Ipswich and David May from Manchester United, but marked my card by revealing that he was looking closely at the Swedish striker Matt Svensson at Crystal Palace.

Once back in reception, I joined Gordon Cox and Alastair Brownlee in a chat with Mark Schwarzer. The Aussie goalkeeper's interview was regularly interrupted by noisy comments from passing players, notably Christian Ziege and Paul Gascoigne, while Gianluca Festa was singing "Roma, Roma" constantly in the background. Roma had knocked Newcastle United out of the UEFA Cup last night.

When I returned to the Evening Gazette, I received a regular flow of inquisitive calls from Wrexham-based journalists. I could not give away too much team news, especially as I had realised some time ago that this game was very high profile in the North-west. So I merely passed on the 18 names in Boro's travelling squad.

Saturday, December 11

ANOTHER day of unmitigated Boro disaster to be forever recorded in the annuls of time. Boro lost 2-1 in the third round of the FA Cup at Wrexham without barely lifting a finger of resistance. It was a shocking defeat.

I have seen it happen several times in the past. Grimsby, Cardiff, Swansea and now Wrexham. They all seem to roll off the tongue.

I wouldn't say I was blase at the final whistle at the Racecourse Ground, but I was neither angry nor suicidal. I have been in the game long enough to know that these things happen.

They shouldn't happen of course. Leading 1-0 at half-time thanks to a good finish from Brian Deane, Boro had the tie in the bag. But they failed to cope with Wrexham's resurgence in the second half and were humiliated.

After the game I waited for the players to emerge from the dressing room. They were all red-faced. They had received their second battering of the afternoon in the dressing room. I stopped Robbie Mustoe, who was captain for the day, to ascertain his feelings. He was absolutely shellshocked.

But Robbie was honest and open about the defeat, and made no attempt to make any excuses. He admitted that Boro had thrown it away. Bryan Robson did not try to hide either. I thought he carried out his press conference with a lot of dignity, and answered every question fairly.

Nobody likes to be booted out of the Cup by a struggling side. The reporter sitting next to me in the press box had remarked rather critically before the game: "This lot look like a non-league side."

I had to agree with him. Wrexham were struggling badly, too, having failed to win a league game since September 18. All the more embarrassing to lose the game, though Wrexham fully deserved their success.

This Cuptie defeat was only a single hiccup. It would fade in the memory if Boro were to win their Worthington Cup quarter-final at Tranmere Rovers on Tuesday. Suddenly the trip to Prenton Park had gained new proportions.

This had been my first visit to Wrexham and I had a dream journey to North Wales, arriving at 12.45pm. First impressions of the Racecourse Ground were excellent. There were two new stands which gave a modern effect, though there was still a surviving bank of terracing which brought back many warming memories. If only all stadia retained some of their terracing.

The first person I saw when entering the stadium was Billy Ashcroft. He looked very fit and well. When he was introduced to the fans at half-time, Big Billy received a bigger welcome from the Boro fans than he did from the home supporters.

There was no press room as such, but a kindly lady provided myself, my travelling companion Nick Wood from the Northern Echo, and Alastair Brownlee, Bernie Slaven and Gary Gill with a welcome warm cup of coffee. The press box was perfectly adequate, but continuous rain blew in all afternoon, and I had to operate with my notepad on my knee. My mobile phone and stopwatch were left on the bench top to suffer the elements. It was not easy writing in the darkness, especially when my hands began to grow numb with the increasing cold.

It was impossible to even consider struggling through the packed main stand to try to grab a cuppa at half-time. But I was disappointed that there was no food nor drink available for the press at full-time. A cup of tea would have sufficed.

"Any chance of getting something to eat?" I asked a passing steward. He simply shrugged his shoulders. It was not exactly the welcome that I would have hoped for from Welsh Wales.

Later, I was interviewed myself, by Clem and Fischer, for their Radio Cleveland show. I was forthright with my comments, though I was more hungry than angry. Radio Cleveland were receiving a regular flow of calls from listeners battering Bryan Robson, and so, too, were Century Radio. As manager, Robbo had to take the flak for the defeat, though the players had let him down very badly. Everybody at the game could see that. I felt that the radio stations were doing the Boro a dis-service by allowing all these people who had not been to the game to jump on the bandwagon and further drag down the image of the club.

I was absolutely starving and hyper-ventilating when I arrived back at the car at 6pm.

But I put my hunger and thirst on hold during the journey. I had expected to encounter difficult driving conditions on the way back to Teesside, but I seemed to sail through the North-west motorway network. I was back in the house for 9.15pm, whereupon I gulped down three chocolate biscuits for my combined lunch, tea and supper.

Pity about the result, but one of the better journies, whatever my stomach might think.

Monday, December 13

BRYAN Robson was remarkably cool and collected for a man under fire. He made no attempts to deflect the heavy criticism currently coming his way. He merely pointed out that the fans had a right to vent their feelings.

But, for the first time, I sensed that Robbo was aware that the whole thing could end in tears. The pressure was building up. When the Boro fans put the knife in, they turn it several times before withdrawing it.

However, Bryan talked positively, mainly about the need for the team to bounce back in tomorrow's Frank Worthington Cup quarter-final at Tranmere. Even so, with key men like Gary Pallister and Colin Cooper injured, he admitted that Boro's task was tougher than he would have liked.

Afterwards, I interviewed Keith O'Neill, along with Alastair Brownlee and Gordon Cox. Keith was likely to return to the side after injury tomorrow. Having got to know Keith well over the past few months, I had learned that he had a very positive approach to his football. When he said he wanted to win, he really meant it. He provided some very aggressive, honest and determined quotes for tomorrow's back page lead in the Evening Gazette.

Tuesday, December 14

TIME to don the hard helmets! Boro's season went horribly pear shaped when they were knocked out of the Worthington Cup quarter-final by 2-1 at Tranmere. It was the team's second cup defeat in four days by lesser league opposition.

The pressure from fuming fans was now lying heavily on the shoulders of Bryan Robson, though he did not shirk his responsibility after the game. As the media crowded into the narrow corridors around the Prenton Park dressing rooms, Robson emerged to undertake all requested interviews.

He spoke to Sky TV, then Tyne Tees TV, followed by the newspaper men. When asked how he felt the fans would react to this latest setback, he merely replied that he was glad the game had been broadcast live on TV, because it gave the fans the opportunity to see that the players had tried their hearts out.

They did, but they had no luck. Dreadful refereeing by our old friend David Elleray didn't help, but Boro were also slightly lacking in confidence and often took the wrong options. They still deserved to win, but didn't. Christian Ziege scored the goal.

It was a truly depressing journey home to Teesside, but basically I was relieved to make it back. When we had left Yarm in the early afternoon, it was hailstoning and sleeting. There was a slushy covering all over the local roads and along the A19 and it didn't look promising.

Nigel Gibb, one of my travelling companions, did nothing to relieve the tension.

"These are the worst conditions I have ever known when setting off for a match," he revealed.

And Nigel had been travelling to away games for more years than he would care to remember.

Once we reached the A19, I was relieved to see the weather improve. The roads stayed clear. However, there was plenty of snow to be seen going over the top of the Pennines. It was a weird and eerie sight driving across the all-white Saddleworth Moor. There's a guy lives in an old farmhouse which is sandwiched between the east and west lanes of the M62 on Saddleworth Moor. How he can stomach this kind of weather for three or four months of the year, I can hardly imagine.

Despite the regular bumper to bumper traffic jams near Manchester, especially around the M60, we reached Prenton Park at 6.15pm. When I emerged stiff legged from the car, I was blasted by the elements. It took my breath away. I could not remember anything worse before a match. It was bitterly, bitterly cold with a blustery wind, and biting rain. Three T-shirts, a shirt, a jumper, a jacket and an overcoat would afford me some protection, but this still promised to be one of the coldest ever games.

I found my way to the warm press area inside the ground and sat alongside a few national newspaper journalists before the game. I managed to soft-talk a cup of tea for myself from the ladies in the kitchen. Ian Ross from the Guardian was quite positive about the outcome. "Don't be fooled by Tranmere's results," he said. "Tranmere are not a good side. Boro will win this."

Then Ian became rather negative when I told him about the bad weather in the North-east. "Oh, you won't get home after the game." he added.

I discovered that I had been given a ticket for a seat in the main stand, instead of the press box. I could not even find the seat when I went to check it out. So I linked up with Clive Hetherington from the Northern Echo and we found two seats together in the bustling press box. Then we donned our silly woolly hats to keep out the cold.

I thought we had got away with it until two fresh-faced lads turned up five minutes into the game. "You're in our seats," said one, wearing a Radio City jacket. "I have to sit here because I need the ISDN point."

Clive was using a lap top computer and needed a flat surface. "I'll get up," I said. "But he can't."

Negotiations were brief. I conceded my seat, but Clive sat firm. I stood up with the other young radio lad at the back of the box. He didn't need a seat anyway. He wasn't working. He was on a freebie which many football clubs are fooled into giving away to "journalists", particularly those from some radio stations.

So, I spent the whole game standing up. Simon O'Rourke from Tyne Tees did offer me his seat, but I declined. The problem was, because of low lights in the press box, the pitch looked dark and it was difficult to make out the Tranmere shirt numbers. But I got through it, and was grateful for the fact that it was a helluva lot milder at the back of the stand than I could have imagined.

Afterwards I made my way to the dressing room area. Once the managers had been interviewed, I took down a few quotes as Gary Gill from Radio Cleveland interviewed Robbie Stockdale.

I wanted to talk to Juninho, and I had a brief conversation with Boro chief scout Ray Train while I waited. Ray reckoned that Tranmere had played even better against Boro than they did when he watched them knock West Ham out of the FA Cup on Saturday.

When Juninho emerged, so did several other national hacks, including the amiable John Richardson from the Daily Mail. I had no choice but to share the interview. Juninho was open, and honest, and we were given some useful comments. The bonus was that the national hacks would be unable to use the Juninho quotes until Thursday because they were already past their deadlines. I could use them tomorrow.

I was becoming edgy about the long journey back to Teesside, even though my colleague Gordon Cox was driving. On the way down to Tranmere, a radio announcer had revealed that all roads around Harrogate were blocked by snow.

However we encountered very few problems coming home. There was compacted snow on the A19 between Thirsk and Northallerton and we were forced to slow down to 30mph for several miles, but we made it. It was still a rather stressful journey, though it had nothing to do with the weather. A warning light suddenly appeared on the dashboard of the car, when we were still on the M1, to warn Coxy that we were running out of petrol. "I'll get some at the next service station." he promised.

The problem was, every petrol station we passed going northbound was closed. As the miles slowly flew by, the light seemed to glow more brightly. I was certain that we would not make it, and I envisaged us having to trudge for miles through the snow and hailstorms. Bed was a long way off.

Even the normally unmovable Coxy was unsettled, and was reduced to driving at 50mph on the run-in to Yarm to conserve valuable stocks of fuel. I counted the miles as we ticked them off one by one. In the event we made it back to Yarm, but only just. We must have travelled around 60 miles with the warning light on. It was one of the achievements of the season, and only Coxy could have done it.

By the time I arrived home, it was 2.10am. Four lovely hours in bed to come!

Wednesday, December 15

THE fans were very, very angry. I knew that my telephone at the Evening Gazette would be red-hot all day with supporters ringing to tell me that Bryan Robson should be sacked immediately, but I had no choice but to instruct the rest of the sports desk staff to deflect all calls. I simply had too much work to get through, especially as I was in charge of the desk.

I arrived at the sports desk at 7.15am and spent almost 45 minutes in the morning editorial conference, which was over-lorded by editor Ranald Allan. He quizzed me about the stories I had picked up last night, and we agreed that Juninho's quotes would be used on the front page.

I had filled in my match facts sheet at Prenton Park, but I needed to write up my match report in between organising the Evening Gazette sports pages.

Next came another editorial conference, and then I hammered out the Juninho story for the news desk. It was after 9am by this stage and the calls were beginning to come in thick and fast from enraged fans. I could hear my colleagues around me speaking to callers. I always talk to fans whenever possible, but on this occasion it was impossible. They had to vent their frustrations elsewhere.

I was hard pressed to write up a story for the back page before the newspaper's deadline. As a fan and a paying season ticket holder, I did not believe that Bryan Robson should be sacked, because I was certain it would lead to a concertina of events which would pitch the club into chaos. So I wrote up my back page story, speaking as a Robson supporter on this occasion. To back up my claims I was forced to touch on some of the things which Steve Gibson had hinted at during our tete-a-tete last week.

I knew this was betraying some of the chairman's confidences, but I felt that I was doing right by the club and by the supporters. This was a serious situation and anything which might lead to the club's demise needed to be prevented at all costs.

I worked on completing Friday's Boro v Tottenham head to head graphic before noon, but there was no time for lunch. My colleague Philip Tallentire went out to buy me a tasty baguette from Goodbody's, for which my stomach was eternally grateful.

However, for a spell, I was exposed, alone in the office over lunchtime. The phones were still ringing continuously and I had to take a couple of calls from fans. One caller was fine, but the other took some placating. I had not time to argue. In any case I agreed with most of the things he said. I'm sure he felt better as a result of our chat, but I can never understand why I have to provide this counselling. Why don't these disgruntled fans phone the club first? Then again, maybe they do.

After lunch I agreed to undertake a Talk Radio interview for my old pal Tony Lockwood, but turned down a similar request from Sky TV. I did not feel that I owed the reporter who phoned me any favours. In any case, with the setting up of the cameras etc, it would have taken up at least an hour of my valuable time.

In between working generally on the sports pages on the afternoon, I wrote up a feature for the Sports Gazette, stressing that the time had now come for change. One of my plans was for Robson, Gibson, Paul Ince and a Boro PR executive to take part in a series of fans forums at local social clubs. I felt that it was crucial that the club tried to close the widening gap between themselves and the fans.

It was 5.15pm when I left the office. Except for four hours sleep, I had been working non-stop since 7.15am the previous morning. I might have escaped from the office earlier, but as soon as I was the only one left on the sports desk, I had to answer the ever-ringing phone again.

I received a couple of rather nasty faxes from fans who had read my back page story. They were spitting blood. One fan wrote to tell me that once they had forced Robbo out, they would get me out too. However two phone callers were complimentary, and both used the word 'excellent' when they described my back page story. One of them said he had previously wanted Robbo out, but had now changed his mind since reading my piece. So I left the office shattered, but on a high rather than a low.

Friday, December 17

IT'S a funny old world. After being blasted by some fans for claiming in Wednesday's Evening Gazette that Bryan Robson should stay at the Boro, I received several negative comments when I turned up at Rockliffe Park today.

Some of the staff at the training headquarters had translated my article into believing that I was calling for Robbo's head. I was flabbergasted. I had declared quite clearly in the story that the best option was to leave Robbo at the helm. If nothing else, this little misunderstanding indicated to me how difficult it was for the man in the middle in these situations. It doesn't matter what you write, people read what they want to read, as my colleague Andrew Wilkinson has told me many times.

"Robbo's after your blood," I was told at Rockliffe. Maybe this particular statement was a wind-up, but I was half expecting to become embroiled in a stand-up argument with Bryan. However he had to attend to other business before arriving at the training headquarters, and it was Viv Anderson who hosted the morning press briefing. Viv was his usual outgoing self, harbouring no complaints about any of the week's press stories, and he answered all the relevant questions about the current situation.

I also asked Viv about Paul Gascoigne. More and more stories were appearing in the tabloids claiming that Gazza would soon be on his way from Teesside. I did not want to miss out on the story, if there was any truth in it. But Viv insisted again that the subject of Gazza leaving the Boro had never been mentioned.

As I left Viv's office, Robbo was just unlocking the door to his own office. He wished me good morning. I didn't get the scent of any aggro at all.

When I returned to the Evening Gazette office, a former colleague Stuart Beagrie rang up for a chat. He told me that he had heard on the grapevine that Emerson might be returning to Boro when the Spanish transfer window opened next month. It was one to check up on.

Saturday, December 18

THERE was a feeling that the lads were wearing "We're Backing Robbo" badges on their hearts as they produced a stirring and thoroughly entertaining performance to beat Spurs by 2-1 at the Riverside.

If ever a team effort was designed to stress that all the players were fully behind the manager, then this was it. However Boro did things the hard way, conceding an early goal in a nervous opening15 minute spell but then gaining in stature to take the points with goals from Christian Ziege and Brian Deane.

It was just a pity that Bryan didn't turn up at the post-match press conference to accept the plaudits. Once again the Boro boss decided to take a back seat. The conference was hosted by Viv, who was breathing heavily after apparently rushing non-stop up the two flights of stairs at the Riverside.

George Graham had been first manager into the press room after the game. He was his usual self, quite open, but still giving the impression he was holding something back.

He was critical of a challenge by Hamilton Ricard on Spurs goalkeeper Ian Walker, and initially claimed that Walker had been 'attacked'. However, he later withdrew the word 'attacked' for something less controversial.

Most hacks usually simply accept managers' comments without recourse. However, it was interesting to see John Sadler from The Sun make a stance and accuse Graham's players of whingeing. The Spurs boss did not want to get involved in this argument.

Viv was brief when he followed George into the room, praising the players, and stressing that Bryan had not felt the pressure any more than normal during the week.

Afterwards I joined Gordon Cox in attempting to grab a player interview, but nobody was biting. In fact all the lads looked shattered. They had clearly put a tremendous amount of effort into their performance.

Juninho had been outstanding; his best performance by far since returning to Teesside. I shook hands with both him and his father Osvaldo before they entered the lift to leave the stadium. I could see that they were buoyant.

Eventually chief coach Gordon McQueen stopped for an interview. Gordon supported Viv's comment, saying: "Not a lot fazes Bryan."

Afterwards I waited alongside the national lads for reporter Martin Booth to reappear with some player quotes. He had been given special permission to go down to the dressing room area in order to get some exclusive quotes for the "non-Sunday" newspapers, for use on

Monday. He returned at 6.10pm, having spoken to Robbie Mustoe and Ian Walker.

There were controversial quotes from Walker, as might be expected. He accused Hamilton Ricard of having elbowed him twice in the face, though when I studied Walker's wording I realised that he had never once used the word 'deliberate' to describe the alleged elbowing.

Even so, Walker left the Riverside with a huge lump at the bridge of his nose which suggested a break. It would give the national guys something to get their teeth into on Monday.

Sunday, December 19

I WAS shocked to arrive at the Boro Disabled Supporters Association Christmas bash at the Riverside to discover that the room was only half empty.

When I spoke to Paddy Cronesberry, the hard working chairman of the association, I discovered that ticket sales had gone badly this year.

The reason was not obvious. "Maybe it's because of the Millennium," he suggested.

However the association would not lose money. The room was provided free of charge by the club, while there was still a profit to be made on every ticket sold.

It was a half decent evening, despite the lack of numbers, thanks partly to the vocal contribution of Alastair Brownlee, who spent half the night on the karaoke, along with his pal Barry Parnell. Barry's rendition of Puff the Magic Dragon brought the house down. Paddy is also a bit of a crooner, not unlike Elvis himself, and was quick to take the stage and sing a couple of songs. I would have loved to get up, too, but my singing voice is even worse than than my speaking voice.

Dean Gordon arrived to accept the player of the year award, while Jason Gavin was there to receive the young player award. Robbie Mustoe also attended and was handed a special award as part of his testimonial year.

There was also a nice touch when Alastair was presented with a specially inscribed memento by Paddy for his contribution in helping to raise £30,000 for the disabled supporters' new mini-bus.

Earlier in the day I had spent some time on my lap top computer writing up my match report from yesterday, only to discover that when I pressed the button to e-mail the report to the Evening Gazette, the story simply disappeared off the screen. All that blasted work for nothing. I did not have the strength of mind to write it all again, so I decided to go into the office even earlier in the morning to knock it up again.

What does Paylor know about football? He's never played the game. Wrong. Spot the Stan Bowles lookalike in the Hartlepool Mail side of the 1970s.

*Just like every other Boro supporter, matchdays fill me with a
great sense of anticipation.*

Ready to cover another Boro away game from the pressbox.

Paylor's lucky tie. I'm just as superstitious as the next fan.

*All set to broadcast from the Dell are the popular - so they say -
Century Radio team of Alastair Brownlee and Bernie Slaven,
with Rachel Whatley.*

In order to be first with the Boro news it's vital to have a good rapport with the managerial team. Above, I'm chatting to chief coach Gordon McQueen. Below, attending the morning press briefing at Rockliffe Park in the office of assistant manager Viv Anderson.

Both the exterior and interior design of Shab's MSV Superstore, on Portrack Lane Stockton, reflects his close association with Middlesbrough FC.

Keeping in trim with Robbo and Graham Neave, executive director of Northumbrian Water, at a promotion for the Teesside Sports Awards.

Former Boro Young Player of the Year, Craig Harrison, is now fully recovered from a serious illness and is ready to challenge for a first team place.

In my opinion Steve Vickers has played some of his best football for the Boro this season.

Next time I interview Mark Schwarzer, remind me to stand on a box.

In bed with Pally - not quite. Gary has just taken delivery of his custom made bed from Linthorpe Bedcentre.

There's no escape at Rockliffe Park from the local media's gruesome twosome, Alastair Brownlee and Gordon Cox, for Boro stars Keith O'Neill (above) and Robbie Stockdale.

Some of the journalistic colleagues I meet on my travels:

Nick " Biggles " Wood
of the Northern Echo,
minus his Dr Who
overcoat.

Jack Woodward,
left, of TFM and
John Murray of
5 Live radio.

Damian Spellman,
NE sportswriter for
the Press
Association.

At away games it's great to catch up on the news with Boro old boys like Stuart Ripley, above, and David Armstrong.

One of the most poignant memories of the season was the sad death of Boro all time great, " The Master " Wilf Mannion.

Robbie: " Paylor, if I don't get 3 stars for the next game, guess where I'm going to stick this?"

My long suffering travel companions to away games, left to right, Nigel Gibb, Andrew Shepherd and Lennie Shepherd.

Not the sort of car you'd want to hitch a lift in, as Alastair Brownlee, with passengers Gary Gill, (cool sunglasses), Bernie Slaven and Boro TV producer Simon Hanning hit the open road.

Standing outside the redeveloped Stamford Bridge only serves to reinforce that in the fifteen years I've been covering the Boro, the standard of the country's major stadiums has changed out of all recognition.

When I checked my inbox on the lap top, I discovered that 167k of Miss World photographs had arrived at the same time as I was trying to send my report, and I suspect it was too much for the machine to handle. Miss World photographs? From who? From where? Clearly it was some kind of a virus. I would just like to say thank you for nothing to the nutter who managed to send them to me. I suspect that it was my first experience with computer viruses, but not my last.

Monday, December 20

BRYAN Robson was at Rockliffe Park this morning, but again he left it to Viv Anderson to give the morning press briefing to myself, Alastair Brownlee and Gordon Cox.

It was all a little bit perplexing.

The furore surrounding Robbo's future seemed to have died down, especially following Boro's victory against Spurs on Saturday. I did speak to Bryan, simply to wish him 'good morning', but otherwise I did not see him again.

However, Viv was on top form. He provided a full run through of the weekend's events, and then dismissed a series of other questions which I had compiled from the Sunday papers, which linked Boro with half the players in the universe.

I still wondered whether something was amiss and kept my lugholes open during my stay at Hurworth, but everything else seemed to be shipshape.

Afterwards I spoke to Neil Maddison, along with Ali and Coxy, for a useful piece for tomorrow's Gazette. Neil had been making his first Premier League start of the season against Spurs, which was amazing, especially as he played so well.

Maddo admitted that it had crossed his mind to knock on the manager's door in the past, but he loved the club so much that he did not want to leave, and was prepared to continue battling for his place.

Paul Ince was back following his double hernia operation, and came into the training headquarters with Keith O'Neill, who had a back injury. The duo hobbled in like two old men, taking gentle steps. Incey would need another month to get fit, but hopefully Keith would be ready for Boxing Day.

When I returned to the Gazette I received a couple of calls from fans. One told me that he thought that my back page story last week had done more than anything to turn the tide in Robbo's favour. I was an interesting call, especially as several other people had clearly misunderstood the tone of the story.

I had a huge mailbag to deal with and there was no way that I could write individually to all the letter writers. So I decided to give over the Paylor on Wednesday column to replying to some of the more important points in the letters.

I finished writing the column at around 6.10pm, and then scampered over the road to the Indian restaurant to fill my face at editor Ranald Allan's annual Christmas bash for the Evening Gazette's heads of departments.

Tuesday, December 21

ANOTHER day, another night-out. This time it was the annual get-together of the local Middlesbrough sporting press, plus a few of our good friends. Gordon Cox had organised this year's bash, while Alastair Brownlee was among the gathering.

We kicked off in the Star and Garter and ended up in Joe Rigatoni's for an excellent meal. The only subject under discussion, as ever, was the Boro.

There's always a nice atmosphere in the restaurant, and we usually end up deep in conversation with the waiters, some of whom are originally from Italy. Last year they tried to convince us that Marco Branca had been much maligned by the Boro when his contract was terminated and the discussions dragged on until the early hours.

This time the only additional chat we had was with Steve Katz and the crew from VSI, who make the videos for the Boro. They were also enjoying a Christmas night-out at Joe Rigatoni's.

The lack of heated debate ensured that we were not detained all night, and I crawled into bed shortly after midnight. However, I was beginning to feel as if I desperately needed an early night.

Wednesday, December 22

VIV Anderson again hosted the early morning press briefing. I was beginning to become concerned about Bryan Robson's lack of involvement. I had not been in conversation with the manager for nine days.

I voiced my concerns to Viv, who insisted that nothing was brewing, and that Bryan was carrying on with his job as normal. Viv was clearly telling the truth, but something was not right as far as I was concerned. Downstairs, Gordon Cox, Alastair Brownlee and I stockpiled some interviews by talking to Robbie Stockdale, Gianluca Festa and Robbie Mustoe. Robbie was surprised to be dragged in front of the microphones and notebook again.

"Do you guys speak to anybody else?" he asked.

We do, but sometimes you cannot always catch the players who you want to talk to. It's those brave souls who risk walking through reception to go for an early morning cup of coffee who are more likely to be snared by the praying mantis of the press.

While we were waiting for players, Gazza's four wheel drive arrived. Gazza had an operation on Monday night to scrape out his knee. When he emerged from the vehicle, it looked as if he had been picked up directly from hospital by his good pal Jimmy Gardner. Gazza was wearing a three quarter length dressing gown, with bare legs and a pair of slippers. Gazza walked across the car park in this get-up. Unless I was mistaken, he was wearing a hospital dressing gown. He may even have left his clothes behind in the rush to escape. What commitment!

I was about to leave Rockliffe Park, intending to phone over today's story to the Evening Gazette, when I received a call from the boss. Bryan wanted to see myself, Cox and Brownlee.

I was not certain what to expect as we climbed the stairs again, but Bryan was fine. He was as bright and chatty as ever. When he is on TV, Robbo often comes across as a dour individual. He is much more outgoing away from the cameras.

Bryan apologised for not giving us interviews over the past few days, and stressed it was nothing personal. He said that he had decided to take a break from talking to the press for a few weeks. I questioned the wisdom of his decision, warning him that several members of the media might take advantage of the situation to have another go at him. But Bryan said that he was prepared to take that chance.

Robbo's decision was clearly the result of the battering he had taken in the national newspapers following the two cup defeats. Once they see the chance to have a pop at somebody, they come out with all barrels firing. If nothing else, Bryan was beginning to learn who his friends were.

I needed to discover how he was feeling in general, and quizzed him about his current thoughts on the job. He stressed that he had never once thought about quitting, and was determined to carry on. That was all I needed to know. It eased my mind that I was not about to miss a 'big story'.

Deep down, I also felt that Boro did not need a change of manager at this time. I have been reporting on the game long enough to know that there is no such thing as a perfect manager. I've seen lots of Achilles heels behind a string of managers' desks. Managers come and managers go, but the club carries on regardless.

However, in this particular case, if Robson was to leave Boro, I did not feel confident that the club was capable of attracting anybody better as a replacement. Surely Boro were safer in the hands of Robson, especially considering how far he had already taken the club.

The doubts over Robbo's future now dispersed, I wished him Merry Christmas and raced down to the car to send over my copy. I was just in time to meet first edition deadline.

Sunday, December 26

I ALWAYS wondered what it would feel like, if I ever caught the screaming ab-dabs at an away match. Today, in my 15th season of travelling, I found out. It was the worst football day of my life.

I was already suffering from a heavy cold which had ruined my Christmas Day and forced me to bed at 9pm. But I felt well enough to travel to Sheffield Wednesday and linked up with my travelling companions Nigel Gibb and the Shepherd family in Yarm.

We saw very little traffic on the way and arrived outside the stadium to find a good atmosphere, most of it created by the 5,500 Boro fans who had made the trip.

Having left the guys at a suitable pub, I made my way to the stadium. The press facilities at Hillsborough are OK, though I cannot understand the club's logic of having the press room at one end of the ground and the press box at the other. You have to force your way through the full length of the crowded concourse in the main stand to take your seat in the press box before the kick off.

Before the game I chatted to Keith Farnsworth from the Daily Telegraph and Ian Appleyard from the Yorkshire Post. Both men were keen to update their facts and figures and quizzed me about recent Boro results.

Then former Sheffield Wednesday defender Mel Sterland arrived. He was working for one of the local radio stations. When he surveyed the teamsheet he told me: "I think Wednesday will win today. I don't fancy this Middlesbrough team at all."

With six Boro players injured, I could understand Mel's view. However, with the travelling fans in good voice and Wednesday having won just one game all season, I could not see Boro losing this. Unfortunately Mel turned out to be right and I was wrong. The match was a big letdown. Boro lost 1-0, without creating a decent chance over the 90 minutes.

Afterwards, I began to feel ill while sitting in the press room, waiting for Viv Anderson to arrive. There had been a lock-in in the Boro dressing room and Viv did not materialise until 5.45pm.

Having gathered my quotes, I had to make a 20 minute walk back to the car, all of it uphill. When I met up with the lads again I was feeling dizzy. I was particularly grateful that I was not driving.

No sooner had we set off, than all hell let loose. We had to stop within 200 yards. I was so violently ill, outside the car, that I hardly knew where I was. I did not have a single ounce of energy in my body.

I spent some time lying on the floor of two or three grubby pub toilets. When some of my senses began to return, I could not envisage how we could possibly make it home. I knew it was not possible for us all to spend the night in a pub car park in Sheffield. I did not want them to leave me, but I couldn't ask them to wait all night.

Finally, we managed to make slight progress, hopping from one safe haven to another. I had to ask the lads to keep stopping at every pub and service station on the way back, as we undertook a rather varied and seedy toilet tour of South Yorkshire.

It was all very awkward, but the lads were very supportive. Gradually, I began to pull round. By the time we reached Wetherby, there was no need to stop any more, and we made it back to Yarm without mishap. When I jumped into my own car to drive home, I was feeling much better. I was totally drained, but my head was clear again. However it was an experience which I hope will never again be repeated. Not only by me, but by any fan, anywhere.

My next book, incidentally, will be entitled: A Guide to the Muckiest Toilets of Sheffield and South Yorkshire.

Monday, December 27

BRYAN Robson phoned me today. He wanted to know why I had failed to turn up for the morning press briefing.

The truth was that it was a Bank Holiday. We have to finish off the first edition of the Evening Gazette by nine o'clock, in order to maximise sales. I had arrived in the office for 7am and had worked flat out writing my match report and back page lead. I could not fit in a trip to Hurworth as well.

However Bryan, having trawled through the newspaper reports from yesterday's game at Sheffield Wednesday, was keen to address some of the points made. So we chatted over the phone.

Robbo was particularly disappointed that nothing had been written anywhere about the fact that Boro had six regular players out through injury.

As a result, he had prepared some statistics, and proceeded to give me a story for tomorrow's paper which detailed the full extent of the club's injury problem, and the effect it had had on the team's season. The Boro boss stressed that he did not want me to give the impression he was making excuses, which he wasn't. But he felt that enough was enough and one or two factors needed to be highlighted.

Wednesday, December 29

I HAD been labouring badly under the effects of my illness, which had developed into some kind of a flu-type viral infection over the past couple of days. I had hoped to carry on at work and report on tonight's home game against Coventry City, but was forced to give up the fight on the day of the match. I took to my bed.

I was particularly frustrated at the prospect of missing the match. It was with quite some pleasure, therefore, that I was told later that the match had been postponed because somebody had forgotten to put the cover on the pitch at the Riverside Stadium and the ground was frozen solid as a result. Divine intervention!

Chapter Six

JANUARY

Tuesday, January 11

FINALLY, I emerged from my sick bed this morning with bleary eyes and uncertain steps after suffering the worst viral attack of my life.

A 10 to 14 day viral infection, which was initially diagnosed two weeks ago, had turned into a chronic chest infection last week. The first illness was untreatable and required rest. Fortunately a second visit to the doctor's and a five-day course of antibiotics put paid to the chest problem. Now I was ready to rejoin the fray, like an emerging chrysalis. I was so excited about returning to work that I couldn't sleep, making it much more difficult to crawl out of bed at 6.30am instead of the 10.30am to which I had become recently accustomed.

Fortunately I was given an easy ride on my first day back in Civilisation. There was no need to go up to Rockliffe Park, because Boro were still in Ireland, where they had beaten Shelbourne by 3-2 in Dublin last night. Robbo's mobile phone was engaged, so in the end I rang Viv. I was pleased to discover that he remembered me.

I didn't need a blow-by-blow match report, because it was only a friendly game. But Viv filled me in with all the basic details and goalscorers. Then he announced the good news that both Gary Pallister and Paul Gascoigne had come through the 90 minutes unscathed after returning from injury.

Earlier I had rung David Geddis to pick up a report on the reserves' 2-0 defeat at Newcastle last night. David was relatively pleased with the team's performance, despite the result.

"I did a basic head count," he told me, "and worked out that the cost of Newcastle's team was £18.5m. So in the end our young lads didn't do too badly, especially as we had a chance of getting something from the game for a long time."

Back page report written, and it was time to attack Paylor on Wednesday. I hadn't missed compiling the weekly column despite my illness. However, I did need colleague Andrew Wilkinson's help in furnishing me with some Bryan Robson quotes from a recent interview, in order to complete the column.

Otherwise I made a few calls and put together the article before 1pm. I rang Dave Allan at the club, and he provided me with a couple of titbits, while my pal Len Shepherd came up with a juicy tale about former Boro player Pat Heard, who had become a professional stage hypnotist.

No time for lunch. I rang Dave Parnaby, who gave me the full run-down on the planned new intake of Boro scholars for next July, which made for a Sports Gazette piece.

Then, carrying on, I managed to fill in a full Boro day with a novel look ahead to the second half of the season for a two-page spread for the Sports. Exhausted but happy, I was back on the gravy train!

Wednesday, January 12

BACK up at Rockliffe Park today, and back in the old routine. Robbo remembered me, and I wished him happy birthday from yesterday.

The Boro boss had received a large mailbag of birthday cards, including several which arrive annually from a varied collection of female Manchester United fans. In fact Robbo stressed that he knew most of these fans personally, because they used to watch him train every day for United, in addition to attending games.

I blotted my copybook when we discussed a documentary which was shown on TV last night, featuring Posh Spice. I made the mistake of stressing that I had put my fingers down my throat and tried to vomit when the programme started. Then I remembered that both Victoria and David Beckham were personal friends of Robbo. In fact Robbo had even featured on the programme later, though by that time I was tucked up in bed. Definitely a faux pas on my part.

However Bryan was unmoved and gave me a good story about Keith O'Neill. The Irish international had flown to Germany to meet a specialist who could ascertain the full extent of his niggling back injury.

Before phoning over the story to the Gazette, I grabbed Neil Maddison in reception and he gave me a lively interview which would make a very readable piece for Saturday's Sports Gazette.

I spent the afternoon writing up features, but broke off to meet up with Boro fan Bill Smith, who brought me a photograph of what could be the first ever Boro shirt. It was white, with blue and white spotted silk trim. The picture was taken in the 1950s, and the shirt was 'modelled' by former Boro full-back Derek Stonehouse. The picture would give me a good 'Where is it now?' story.

Friday, January 14

BRYAN Robson revealed today that he was a lucky man to be at his desk. "I've just missed death by seconds," he said, as he downed a welcome cup of tea.

The Boro boss had only narrowly avoided a car accident in the pouring rain on the way to work. On a narrow country road, where vision was impaired by spray and rain, Robbo had been presented with the sudden sight of a lorry haring towards him, and a car trying to overtake it.

The Boro boss was forced to take desperate action to avoid a collision, and swerved off the road on to the grass verge.

"If I had been momentarily looking away, or operating the radio, I wouldn't be here now," he said. The lunatic in the other car had driven straight on.

Robbo gave me the lowdown on tomorrow's home game against Derby County, and then asked me if I had any latest information on the Rams' situation. I told the Boro boss that Derby County had three players suspended for tomorrow's game.

Bryan knew that two Derby players were banned but not three. I told him that the third one was Spencer Prior, and the Boro boss was surprised to hear it. He hadn't known that Prior was banned. As a result Boro secretary Karen Nelson checked my information with the FA, and discovered that Prior was not suspended after all.

It was a bit of bum information on my part, though I had passed it on in good faith, having been informed of the fact by my contact in Derby.

There was another birthday to celebrate this week. This time it was Gordon Cox, who had reached his 40th, allegedly. Maybe he was operating off an old diary. Amazingly, Coxy got away virtually Scot free over his birthday milestone, with only the gentlest of ribbing from coaches and players alike.

Back in reception, I chatted to Gianluca Festa along with Coxy and Alastair Brownlee, but I still needed a decent line for a Saturday story. So I was delighted to discover that Curtis Fleming was about to go into the restaurant business.

Curtis was buying a half share in the Mojo Cafe in Linthorpe Road. It seemed a good business move and was all about Curtis consolidating his future after football.

I waited around for Curtis and stopped him for an interview when he was on his way to breakfast. He was delighted to give me the details of his partnership with Tony Spensley and was clearly excited about the venture, which would ensure he would put roots down on Teesside at the end of his playing days.

"I've been here nine years and I've got a restaurant," he said proudly. "It would be great to think that I am talking to you again in nine years' time about a chain of restaurants."

I hope it works out that way for him.

After sending over today's back page story, I drove back to the Evening Gazette and wrote up the Curtis piece before lunch. I braved the rain at lunchtime to undertake a few messages. Funny how the Cleveland Centre seems to be empty when it is raining.

On the afternoon, I rang Teesside's top bowls star Norma Shaw, who had been dramatically left out of the England team for the international indoor championships.

I wondered whether she would be angry, after 23 years of international competition under her belt, but Norma took it in her stride. "I thought I had done enough to stay in the team, but the selectors felt otherwise and I'll just have to try to play well enough to get back in," she said.

Norma has been a great ambassador for Teesside over the years and was still at the forefront of her sport. She was currently building up towards a trip to Australia at the end of February for the world outdoor championships.

All in all, it made for another nice story for tomorrow's back page.

Saturday, January 15

TODAY was one of the low points of my 15 years covering the fortunes of the club. There've been many ups and downs, but a 4-1 home defeat at the hands of struggling Derby County was the pits.

Boro had no excuses. They had enjoyed the benefit of a winter break, and they had key players back from injury. But they did not play.

I felt no sympathy for the players or the management. This performance was totally unacceptable and everybody was to blame.

The supporters, desperate to try to make the club aware of their utter frustration, were calling for Bryan Robson's head again. The club would be wrong to take these chants lightly. There had to be some tangible action of some kind. Supporters always win in the end and the manager and players clearly needed to show that they could deliver over the next few weeks, or the pressure would become unsurmountable.

I expected a bit of abuse from some fans after the game, but it didn't come. They were probably just as sick as I was and just wanted to go home. In any case, the stadium was virtually empty at the final whistle. While we awaited the start of the press conference, I spoke to several other journalists, notably Clive Hetherington from the Northern Echo, Ian Murtagh from the Daily Star and Ken Lawrence from the Daily Mail.

Nobody could remember ever witnessing such a shambolic Boro performance under Robson's leadership

I also spoke to Gerald Mortimer from the Derby Evening Telegraph, who confirmed that Spencer Prior, who did not play, was definitely suspended. I was right after all, when I told Robbo yesterday that Prior was banned. I wondered how much Prior's absence had affected Boro's game plan, especially as he was a set piece specialist.

Robson was first to arrive at the conference and pulled no punches. He accepted that this had been Boro's worst ever performance under his management, and stressed that the fans had every right to voice their opinions.

He added: "I accept criticism when we put in a poor performance like that and get beat. But where were Middlesbrough when I joined them? I ask people to judge me on how we have moved forward."

Derby boss Jim Smith defended Robbo's record. He said: "I thought the criticism was a bit unfair. Middlesbrough worked tremendously hard. Bryan will turn it around. You have to ride the storm and hope that the chairman is a good bloke."

Skipper Paul Ince, who had done reasonably well on his return from a double hernia operation, was prepared to face the press.

And he was quick to jump to the manager's defence, as would be expected. He said: "I feel for Robbo. He is one of the main reasons why I came here in the first place. It hurts me probably more than anyone when I hear the fans giving him stick and saying he should go and all that.

"Sometimes it comes down to the players on the pitch. We are the ones who make the mistakes. We are the ones who don't pass the ball properly.

"I do know that Bryan is a winner. He always has been and always will be, so I hope the fans stick by him. He has done a lot for this football club."

Robson had some respite to look forward to, because the Boro were now facing a couple of away trips. It would be another month before they returned to the Riverside. But another home defeat like that horror show against Derby, and it was difficult to see how the manager could endure the heavy flak.

Monday, January 17

MY car refused to start yesterday. But I had to be thankful for small mercies. It was conked out on my drive, and not in an obscure car park miles from anywhere where it could have been wrecked.

I was grateful to my colleague Malcolm Pickering, the Evening Gazette's court reporter, for giving me a lift into work. I was also grateful for the woolly hat, scarf and gloves which helped to keep out the cold as I tramped up and down on the frosty pavement waiting for my lift to arrive.

I was carrying the match facts from Saturday's debacle against Derby in my case, plus the match report, which I had written up yesterday. I had written a hard hitting and damning report on the team's performance, which I believed was fully justified. Now it was important that I got through to work early doors in order that the report and match details could be processed.

Once at the Evening Gazette, I dropped into the 7.30am conference to discuss the current situation. Acting editor Alan Sims was looking for a fans' reaction piece for the back page, in response to the wealth of anger felt in the town over the weekend. This was duly organised once I had returned to the sports desk.

However, very soon, I was on the road again and heading up to Rockliffe Park. I wasn't sure what to expect from Bryan Robson. This had been the worst weekend for many years for everybody involved with the club. In the event, I found Robbo still exasperated but in reasonably good heart. Wisely, he had spent the weekend away from Teesside.

Without naming names, Robbo claimed that several players had let him down, and themselves down on Saturday and I agreed with him. The Boro boss was also concerned about the lack of talking on the pitch. He said that he intended to have personal chats with several players.

With regard to his own job, Robson insisted: "The time to judge me is at the end of the season. In any case, that's when I will decide whether I want to stay on at the club, depending on how we have performed."

On the face of it, they sounded strong words. But I knew that Robson believed that Boro would pick up in the second half of the season. So it would not come down to talking about staying or going.

Once downstairs again, I spoke to Dean Gordon about his current state of fitness. The popular wing-back, who had been out for five months following a cruciate ligament operation, was training with the first team again and was very upbeat. However he was slightly worried about a minor niggle which he was still feeling in the knee. He told me that he might need an arthroscope inserted to check it out.

After a chat with David Parnaby for the juniors column, I returned to the office and started working my way through the day's work. We had been deluged with letters and e-mails from angry fans, and made the decision to introduce a new Thursday feature in the Evening Gazette, called Paylor's Postbag.

It would be a way of enabling us to use some of the letters in the daily paper, as a taster for the main letters pages in the Sports Gazette. Despite the dozens of letters we received, I was surprised that I didn't have to deal with one single phonecall from an angry fan, though some of my colleagues did.

Tuesday, January 18

MY car was back on the road, thanks to my trusty mechanic pal who solved the problem yesterday. So everything was shipshape again.

I had to set off slightly early to arrive at the office before 7.10am in order to undertake a live interview for Talk Radio. I felt that the interview went OK, though not brilliant. Maybe it was down to tired questioning, so early in the morning.

I drove up to Rockliffe Park expecting to see Bryan Robson, but he had travelled to see the reserves win 2-1 at Manchester United last night and had decided to join the players on a day off today.

The Boro squad usually have a midweek break on a Wednesday, but they had been drafted in for extra training on Sunday, probably as a punishment for the Derby defeat. Robbo clearly felt that today was the best day for a break.

In the event, Gordon Cox and I spoke to reserve team coach David Geddis, who was very forthright about his side's performance last night.

I decided to race back to the Evening Gazette to write up the back page lead and finished the story with only a few minutes to spare before deadline. No sooner had I submitted the report than a story suddenly appeared on the national wire, from the Press Association, which contained quotes from Paul Merson slamming the Boro fans for calling for Robbo's head.

Merse's quotes provided a much stronger story than the one I had written about Colin Cooper's likely first team return on Saturday, so the original back page lead was hastily returned to me. It left me with literally two minutes to revamp the whole story in time for first edition, but I just about made it on time. I was not too happy that my name stayed at the head of the story, because it inferred to the readers that I had rung Merson to obtain the quotes. That's not my style, especially considering the acrimonious circumstances under which Merse left the club.

With the back page lead finally out of the way, I stayed in top gear for the rest of the day. I wrote up the rest of my Paylor on Wednesday column before dispensing with lunch in order to set about the Sports Gazette features.

The day ended on a very bright note. At 4pm, I was called upstairs to the boardroom to receive an Evening Gazette excellence award from managing director Neil Benson. It was a cheque for £50. I was very grateful for such a timely windfall. I was now in a position to pay off the bill for the car repairs!

Wednesday, January 19

STEVE Gibson returned my phonecall tonight and spoke positively about Bryan Robson's situation and the future of the club.

The Boro chairman had been away on business and had missed the Derby defeat. I advised him not to get hold of the video nasty of the game. However, while Steve provided me with some forthright yet diplomatic quotes, I could tell that there was an underlying factor involved.

The chairman had clearly not simply sat back and dismissed the defeat as just one of those things. He had already had a meeting with Robson and chief executive Keith Lamb, and with the coaching staff. I suspected that Gibson had made strong demands that improvements must be made.

It was also clear that the chairman was not going to sit quietly and back the manager regardless. There were indications that Robbo had to be seen to be producing the goods if he was to maintain the chairman's 100 per cent support. It killed off ridiculous suggestions from some areas that the chairman was in the manager's pocket.

Steve revealed that there was some money available for a new signing, though the money would have to be spent wisely, and only if the right man could be found at the right price. I sensed that maybe there was scope for an additional coach to come in as well to help the players on the training ground.

With a much needed day off looming for me tomorrow, I sat down and wrote up the Gibson interview for tomorrow's paper before heading off for my tea. I was home at 5.45pm.

Earlier, I had chatted with Robson for around half an hour about the overall situation at the club. The manager stressed again that he desperately needed his injured players back, particularly the three left-siders, in order to move into top gear. Only Colin Cooper was set to return to the fray at Liverpool on Saturday.

However, I suspected that Robson was determined to react strongly to the defeat. I knew that he had said some strong words to his current fit men, and that we would see a much more committed display at Anfield.

On the evening I did not manage to fit in the usual update on this diary, or the second book I was working on, Teesside's Sporting Greats. Instead I joined my Juniper Publishing colleague John Wilson to meet up with Roy Kelly, sports editor of the Hartlepool Mail, at the Staincliffe Hotel in Seaton Carew. Roy, who knows the Hartlepool sporting scene inside out, was interested in writing a Hartlepool's Sporting Greats book. Seems to be the start of a trend.

Friday, January 21

I HEADED off to Radio Cleveland this afternoon with my Evening Gazette colleague Anthony Vickers to record Red Balls On Fire.

I always try to accept the occasional invitation from Clem and Fischer to appear on their show whenever possible, especially as it offers a chance to get one's views across on a different medium.

The reason that Vic and I had been approached was because we had both written scathing pieces about the Boro this week. And, as the current state of the club was still on everybody's lips, Clem and Fischer wanted to take a critical look at the week's events.

Clem and Fischer do like a bit of a laugh when things are going well, and sometimes when things are not going so well. But few Boro fans were smiling at the moment, and the questions were all sensible and relevant. I thought the programme went well. Our discussion also left no doubts about the seriousness of the club's situation.

Earlier, I had chatted with Bryan Robson in his office, along with Alastair Brownlee and Gordon Cox. Bryan was upbeat about the team's chances at Anfield tomorrow. He talked meaningfully about the need to be tight and organised. Clearly the team had been working on a defensive system in training all week. This indicated that Bryan had taken deliberate steps to find a way of halting the slide. It was something the fans would want to hear.

I received a tip-off that Andy Campbell would be in the starting line-up following his Evening Gazette man of the match performance last week. So Ali, Coxy and I grabbed Andy outside the training headquarters for an interview.

I remember interviewing Andy a couple of years ago when he was clearly nervous and still very much a young lad. Now the Middlesbrough-born striker was maturing and he talked positively about his prospects. It was good to hear him express self-belief and I wished him well, because he would face a very, very difficult task against the Liverpool defence at Anfield.

Later in the day I had a pleasant chat with former Boro director Jack

Hatfield. It turned out that Jack was the owner of a Nineteenth Century Boro shirt which I had featured in Paylor on Wednesday during the week. I arranged to meet up with Jack on Monday and to organise a picture of him with the shirt.

Jack is still very much a devout Boro fan, and never misses a home game. He talked passionately about the team and the current dilemma facing the club. It was good to chat to Jack for another reason. I took the opportunity to delve in Jack's near photographic memory and quiz him about some of the stars of years ago for my Teesside's Sporting Greats book.

Saturday, January 22

TRIPS to Liverpool are usually anticipated with some trepidation. But I had positive vibes about this game as we left the North-east rain behind us and crossed the Pennines.

So it was to prove. Boro dug deep, battled their socks off and came away with a valuable point from a goalless draw. If only they had played with the same passion against Derby County last week.

But it was a good day out, and that's what you look for away from home. The car journey to Liverpool had been a dream, and we pulled up in a side street near Anfield at 12.35pm, with plenty of time to kill.

I made my way to the stadium at 1pm and was amazed to see hundreds of Liverpool fans already congregating outside the main entrance and awaiting the arrival of their heroes. I'm no particular lover of Liverpool, but the club obviously means one helluva lot to the fans who support it.

The press room is situated on the ground floor, close to the door which leads to the dressing rooms. I spent some time chatting to the ever-friendly Phil McNulty from the Liverpool Echo, who always has a few stories to tell. I was surprised to discover that his colleague Rick George, who has reported on the fortunes of Liverpool for a few years, had resigned and was now working on the Internet. I met up with Rick at half-time for a chinwag. He stressed that he was happy about his move.

Covering the fortunes of Liverpool for the local newspaper is one of the top media sporting positions in the whole country. No doubt the applications for Rick's job would run into hundreds.

Bearing in mind the large number of hacks already massing in the press room, I made an early move to commandeer a seat in Liverpool's cramped press box. You have to climb the staircase and mingle with the suits before finding the door which leads both to the directors' box and the press box.

I managed to squeeze past national newspaper reporters Paul Hetherington and Alan Nixon and settled down inside the box, with some difficulty, alongside Gordon Cox. This is by no means a reflection on Coxy's girth. But it's well worth the squeeze in the box. The view is top notch.

I was tight up against the wooden outer wall of the box, next to a host of Liverpool season ticket holders. Ironically the press box is raised slightly higher than the fans' seats, and it was a bit disconcerting to be asked by the nearest Liverpool fan to sit back in my seat when Boro were attacking. Apparently I was blocking his view and he couldn't see the far goal. I tried to oblige. After all, he had paid a lot of money for his seat. But I had a stiff back by the end of the game.

I enjoyed a friendly chat with the guy at half-time and there was no animosity. In fact he apologised for being a "shorthouse".

The match was stirring stuff and Boro ended up with a goalless draw. At the end of the match the fans were chanting "There's Only One Bryan Robson". I do believe that the travelling fans have a different attitude towards Robbo than some of those at the Riverside.

Liverpool always provide excellent hospitality. After eating my fill of pastries at half-time, I burned my mouth on a boiling hot cup of tea at the final whistle.

"Liverpool always put on a good cup of tea," Clive Hetherington from the Northern Echo reminded me as I sucked my scorched tongue.

Robson was first into the press conference. Amazingly he had only two questions to answer from the newspaper men, before going into a series of radio interviews.

Gordon Cox and I then bumped into Mark Summerbell in the corridor outside and began to interview him. After three or four questions we were interrupted by a steward, who told us it was more than his life was worth to allow us to continue with the interview in the corridor.

So Mark joined us in the press room, where the unfortunate Coxy had to start his interview all over again. When Gordon had finished, I wanted to ask Mark what it had been like waiting half a season for his chance, and how he had maintained his level of confidence.

As soon as Mark began to reply he was told to be quiet by a steward, because Liverpool boss Gerard Houllier had entered the press room. We tried to persevere with our interview, with Mark whispering his replies. But Houllier's comments were being made through a microphone, and in the end I gave up the interview as a bad job, while thanking Mark for his perseverance.

Houllier was reasonably complimentary towards Boro, making reference to their Italian-like performance. Gianluca Festa would be pleased.

Afterwards I did a quick interview for Clem and Fischer in the press box before heading off for the Flat Iron pub to meet up with the lads.

On the way to the pub, I bumped into Keith Lamb and Boro secretary Karen Nelson, and we chatted about the vastly improved display.

The journey home was a doddle, and I was in the McDonalds restaurant at Wolviston shortly after 9pm. However, as I was queueing, I could have done without the argument between a hapless customer and a snotty serving girl.

They normally say: "Can I take your order sir?"

But she wasn't interested. She was very aggressive and insisted on dealing with other customers ahead of him, even though he had been in the restaurant for longer. Then she refused to serve him at all when he queried her decision. Fortunately I had no such problems. And the delicious McChicken sandwich was worth waiting for.

Monday, January 24

COLIN Cooper was full of the joys of the forthcoming spring. Back in the side on Saturday after recovering from a knee injury, he had made a magnificent contribution towards Boro earning a rare away point at Liverpool.

Naturally Colin was a good choice for interview at Rockliffe Park, and he was happy to chat outside the players' entrance. For once, it wasn't raining. Gordon Cox, from the Boro website, also joined us and led off the questioning.

As ever, Coops was forthright with his comments. He praised the defensive work which had gone on in training last week to make Boro more solid, and insisted that the manager 'deserved a pat on the back' for the point at Anfield.

At the same time, Colin accepted that Boro were now a little too close to the relegation zone for comfort. He echoed everybody's sentiments by stressing that the quicker the next win came along the better.

Bryan Robson, while pleased with his players' commitment and work-rate at Liverpool, also talked about the need to ensure that Boro were not pulled into the dogfight.

After all the talk about the season being over a few weeks ago, suddenly it was alive again, if for unwanted reasons. Did we really believe that Boro could have a season which didn't go all the way down to the wire, usually for the wrong reasons?

On my way out of Rockliffe Park, I passed the crestfallen car of PR officer Louise Wanless. The car's spare wheel was lying on the tarmac underneath the car.

The wheel had come loose from its fixing as we were both driving into the training headquarters at 9am, no doubt thanks to the effects of the rather bouncy speed bumps which had recently been installed in the approach drive.

In fact the wheel had dropped from the car just inside the training headquarters compound. No doubt it gave chief scout Ray Train a few palpitations, when it caused him to take drastic evasive action in front of me.

It could have been much worse, of course, if the wheel had been deposited on one of the roads outside the headquarters. Fortunately there was no problem in this case, except for the one facing Louise, who continued to walk around with a smile on her face despite having the unenviable task of trying to re-attach the wheel under the car. Maybe she would ask one of the big strong lads to help her.

Later that day I spoke to Academy director Dave Parnaby, who enthused about Boro's 6-0 win against Crystal Palace, which put them in the last 16 of the FA Youth Cup.

I also received a call from former Boro director Jack Hatfield, who told me that he was at the family sports shop in Borough Road with the natty Boro shirt from the 1880s which I had featured last week. Evening Gazette photographer Terry Reed set off immediately to take a picture of Jack with the unique shirt.

On the afternoon I had to attend the annual Evening Gazette staff presentation, which took place in the Odeon Cinema. First time I had been to the pictures in ages. The presentation was informative and the questions which followed made for lively listening.

However the whole thing took one and three-quarter hours out of my working day, and I wondered how I would possibly make it up over the next three days. The first task was to work over for a while tonight. I arrived home just as tea was being deposited on the kitchen table.

Later on, I treated myself to a trip to the Staincliffe Hotel to link up with my brother in law Steve Collinson and nephew Ben to watch the Manchester United-Arsenal game live on Sky. In this case the cold Guinness was not the main attraction. It was a chance to run the rule over United, who Boro would be visiting on the coming Saturday.

In the event, United were awful in the first 60 minutes and were fortunate to grab a point. Arsenal were the better side, but United were rusty following their trip to Brazil for the world club championship and subsequent lay-off. I could not imagine that they would be a tenth as bad against Boro.

Tuesday, January 25

WITH Bryan Robson away on club business today, Viv Anderson hosted the press briefing at Rockliffe Park.

"I'm not telling you where Bryan has gone," Viv told us without any feelings of remorse. This was one to try to check out. It usually meant that Robbo had flown to the Continent to run the rule over a player. I needed to keep my lugholes wide open over the next few days.

Viv, however, did answer all the rest of my questions, and revealed that German international Christian Ziege was finally back in full training.

Before leaving, Gordon Cox and I spoke to Gianluca Festa. The Italian defender had enjoyed the battle at Anfield. I told him that Liverpool boss Gerard Houllier had described the game as being like an Italian match. Gianluca was impressed. It was home from home for him.

When I returned to the Evening Gazette, I wrote up the Festa quotes as the main item for Paylor on Wednesday before rattling off the rest of the column. No time for lunch. Just a quick visit to Marmaduke's for one of Beverley's delightful sandwiches.

I made great progress on the afternoon. I wrote up the Mark Summerbell interview for the Sports Gazette and then broke the back of a second feature. But time was tight again. I arrived home minutes before my pizza and chips were served. Phew!

Wednesday, January 26

A journalist from Edinburgh called Ken Steven, who I had never previously met, rang me today to tip me off that Hearts were very keen on Alun Armstrong. In fact the Scottish club's scouts were planning to watch him in tonight's reserve game at Barnsley. Ken even had a quote from Hearts boss Jim Jeffries.

Unfortunately I received the call from Ken after the deadline had passed for the main edition of the Evening Gazette, so I kept my fingers crossed that I could hold on to the story until tomorrow without the English tabloids getting wind of it. With Boro on a day off, I was unable to follow up the story at the Middlesbrough end.

Stuart Mathieson from the Manchester Evening News also rang me for a bit of statistical information about the Boro. He was interested in discovering Boro's record between them winning 3-2 at Old Trafford last December, and the end of the season.

I was happy to oblige. Stuart is my opposite number in Manchester, though I suspect that he doesn't have the same journalistic freedom if the stories I hear about United are true. Despite their size, United are reckoned by many pressmen to be the least publicity conscious club in the country. In fact they don't even have a public relations department. Maybe it's true when they say that United are not bothered whether they receive publicity in Manchester or not. Ironically, Manchester City are completely different on a day to day basis, so they tell me, and are delighted to deal with all press queries. But then the further you go down the ladder, the more open and frank clubs tend to be.

All in all, it makes me very grateful for Boro's friendliness. If ever I have a question, I can always find someone to listen, even if the reply is 'no comment'.

With Boro on a day off today, there was no trip to make to Hurworth. I wrote up Monday's interview with Colin Cooper as today's back page lead in the Gazette. Coops had provided me with plenty of strong quotes. In addition, I rang receptionist Catherine Keers at Rockliffe Park for the reserve team squad to complete the round-up.

After tea, it was time to put the world to rights. I headed off for the Castle and Anchor at Stockton to meet up with a few friends. It was the first Gordon Cox-organised Stockton Night Out of the year. Alastair Brownlee turned up after completing his Century radio show and we all relaxed with a few beers. Travelling companions Len Shepherd and Nigel Gibb were there, too.

We spent the evening discussing the ins and outs of the Boro, and got in an argument with a guy who insisted that it was virtually impossible to attract top players to Teesside because there were no decent night clubs here. It all became a little abusive. Must have been the alcohol. A few drinks normally loosen your mind and create a positive outlook. But I ended up feeling pretty depressed about the whole situation surrounding the club, despite the battling display at Anfield.

Friday, January 28

BRYAN Robson was a very frustrated man today. The injuries were piling up again and he would have at least eight members of his squad missing at Manchester United tomorrow, possibly nine.

"I think I'll ask Steve Gibson for a squad of 100 next season," he groaned.

As a result, Robbo was considering pitching Christian Ziege straight into his starting line-up at Old Trafford, even though he knew that the German international was not fully fit.

Despite the problems, the Boro boss was expecting another good show from his players tomorrow and was hopeful of a result.

Later, I chatted to Ben Roberts and discovered he was close to making his comeback. The Boro goalkeeper has had horrendous luck with injuries over the past couple of years and has just recovered from an operation to remove a blood clot from his back.

Ben described his recent experiences with injury as a nightmare, but revealed that he was now back in full training and was hoping to play a reserve game next month. It was good news, especially as Ben said his back had never felt better.

Ben's contract is up at the end of the year and I do not believe that he will stay with Boro. He certainly is good enough to command a regular spot somewhere and I expect him to move on to further his career ambitions.

Back at the Evening Gazette, we received a strong tip-off that Wilf Mannion was gravely ill. It came as a shock, especially as I had come to know Wilf very well over the last few years.

This was not the time to go overboard. We needed to check the story out and make sure that it was properly prepared and written sensitively before it appeared in the Gazette.

However it is a fact if life that newspapers must put together lengthy tributes and biographies of legends like Wilf when they hear that they are ill. These stories have to be written and then kept on hold, in case of bad news.

So I was forced to spend a large chunk of my afternoon poignantly writing up the story of Wilf's life. It was easy to compile. The Golden Boy was one of the greatest players of all time. But it wasn't a pleasant task, even though it meant that the the Gazette would be in a position to honour the great man properly, should the worst happen.

Saturday, January 29

IT always rains in Manchester. So you expect to get wet trudging in and out of Old Trafford.

However the miserable weather did not deter the Premier League's biggest ever crowd of 61,267 from turning up to watch the clash against the Boro.

Even so, I expected a bit more from the crowd. Old Trafford's newly built extra tier, which had provided 3,000 new seats, made the stadium look awesome. Old Trafford is by far my favourite stadium. But the atmosphere was not electric, as I had anticipated from such a huge gathering.

The United fans seemed to be waiting for something to happen. The longer the game continued goalless, the quieter they became. The only real noise coming from the home supporters was the constant booing of Paul Ince every time he touched the ball. The clearest and loudest singing came from the Boro fans on my right.

Despite the inclement weather, we had enjoyed a decent drive to the North-west and parked up in the car park of the Station at Sale pub. As its name indicates, the pub is next door to a station. So I left the lads in the bar and took the Metrolink from Sale to Old Trafford. It was three stops and took around five minutes. It was ideal. Maybe Middlesbrough Council should look at instigating talks with British Rail for Cargo Fleet station to be reopened as a halt. It could help to ease some of the congestion problems around the Riverside.

After arriving at Old Trafford station, I joined the rain-lashed throng of United fans in the 15-minute walk, past the cricket ground and along to the football stadium.

It was great to get out of the rain and into the press area, where the amiable guy who hands out the press tickets always has a smile and a friendly comment. If only everybody in the same position adopted a similar attitude.

The first people I saw upon entering the press room were Clem and Fischer. They are always good for a lively chat. But they were plenty of others to talk to, and over the course of the next hour I exchanged varied news and views with Tim Rich from The Journal, Clive Hetherington from the Northern Echo, Alam Khan from the Yorkshire Evening Post and Ray Robertson, formerly of the Northern Echo, in addition to brief words with some of the national boys.

The press facilities at Old Trafford are perfectly adequate, though not brilliant. The press room is fine, with tea and coffee flowing all the time, while the half-time pork pies are excellent. However, there aren't many of these tasty pies, and they disappear very quickly.

The press box is a little cramped by modern standards, and I could hardly move, specially as I was sitting between two hacks with huge lap tops. Thereby hangs a tale.

I can't for the life of me understand how these laps tops have begun to spring up in press boxes everywhere. I've got one myself, courtesy of the Evening Gazette, but I wouldn't possibly consider using it for a running match report.

The two guys on either side of me spent the whole game with their heads down, working away on their keyboards. Every time there was an incident on the pitch, they looked up too late to see it, and had to ask me what had happened.

It's ridiculous. These guys did not report on the game as they saw it, because they didn't see it. It wasn't their fault, but it's conning the public. Their match reports were written on hearsay.

This lap top innovation in press boxes is designed to save time in filing reports, and possibly save paying copy takers to sit on the other end of a phone to take down the report. Lap tops are very useful, but not for live reports. Reporters can't express personal opinions when they don't see major incidents. If this worrying new trend isn't nipped in the bud, then newspapers will take another step backwards in the media battle.

Fans who occasionally criticise my choice of man of the match, should at least concede that I am actually watching the game.

The match itself was excellent. Boro were defensively magnificent and could easily have won, despite having Christian Ziege sent off in the 60th minute.

Juninho had a penalty brilliantly saved by Mark Bosnich, but just when Boro looked set for a point, Mark Schwarzer failed to gather a harmless looking shot from David Beckham, which trickled into the net three minutes from time.

Afterwards I spoke to Tony Bugby from the Oldham Chronicle and Stuart Mathieson from the Manchester Evening News. They were full of praise for Boro's efforts.

So was Sir Alex Ferguson at the press conference. He was more keen to talk about Boro's battling efforts, than his own team. But it was all a little hollow to me. Another three points had gone begging.

Bryan Robson eventually turned up rather late at 5.45pm. Once again it was praise all-around, though Robbo declared that Ziege's sending off was a disgrace.

Afterwards I made my way through the drizzle to Old Trafford station. The roads around the stadium were still gridlocked with traffic, so it was a bonus not to have to try to drive through it. However, I had to wait some time for a train, unlike my incoming journey. After what seemed an eternity, standing in the cold and damp on the station platform, the lights of a train appeared in the distance, to great cheers from the frozen multitude around me.

I sat down behind two United fans, who were telling each other that their team was lucky to win. They also felt that Jaap Stam should have been sent off following the foul on Juninho which conceded the penalty. I wondered if they were saying the same thing at the time of the incident. Maybe not.

I arrived back at the pub at around 6.35pm and found the boys suitably inebriated. I wouldn't have minded a couple of pints myself. However it was out of the question. I drove us back, encountering few problems except for heavy spray on the M62. After a relatively uneventful visit to McDonald's at Wolviston, except when a female member of staff walked into the gents' toilet while I was washing my hands in readiness for my McChicken sandwich, I was home at 9.10pm.

Monday, January 31

I DISCOVERED this afternoon that Boro chairman Steve Gibson was now the controller of every single Boro share.

He had concluded a financial deal with ICI to buy out their 25 per cent shareholding, leaving him with 100 per cent.

It was an exclusive story and I was keen to try to keep things quiet so that the Evening Gazette had the story all to itself tomorrow.

I spoke to Steve, who said he could not comment on the financial details of the deal, nor the reasons for carrying it through. However he did stress that he was not a power-mad chairman who just wanted to control everything!

In fact Steve tipped me off that this shares deal was the prelude to a major new financial development involving the club. He could not give me details on or off the record, but promised that I would have the story within the month.

Next I phoned Terry Waldron, who deals with the press inquiries at ICI. Terry, a former colleague of mine at the Evening Gazette and himself a big Boro fan, was extremely helpful, as ever. He revealed that he had already compiled a two-page statement about the shares sale. In fact Terry was waiting for permission to fax me the statement.

This permission arrived at 4pm and Terry faxed his press release immediately. It contained almost everything I needed to know, except the value which had been placed on the shares. I rang Terry back for a bit more info and he did answer several other questions, though the price remained secret.

The press release revealed that Boro director George Cooke, who represented ICI's shareholding on the Boro board, was to be seconded to the club to oversee Boro's involvement in community initiatives, and initially would remain on the board.

The whole story was superb, and I wanted it fully written up before I left the office. So I was rather late in for tea.

Earlier I had driven up to Rockliffe Park and enjoyed having a chat with Anthony Ormerod, who had made his Premier League debut as a second half substitute at Old Trafford on Saturday.

It was great to see Ormerod given his chance again after spending so long waiting patiently for his chance at this level. It was clear that the experience of marking David Beckham in the final half hour had boosted his confidence no end. In fact Anth revealed that he had made a point of shaking Beckham's hand at the end of the match.

Ormerod was outgoing as usual, and I kept my fingers crossed for him that future chances would come along soon. I knew that several of the young lads were frustrated by their lack of opportunities, but I was also aware that those with good contracts were still very much in the manager's mind.

Bryan Robson was also upbeat following Saturday's battling display, and was interested to hear Sunday newspaper reports which claimed that Fabrizio Ravanelli wanted to return to the Boro.

"At least I've heard of Ravanelli," said Robbo. "All these Italians I keep being linked with are all new to me."

At the same time Robbo revealed that any Ravanelli return was unlikely to take place for several reasons, with the overall financial package being one of them. "I think some of my players would be waiting with boxing gloves if he came back," he added.

I also spoke with Christian Ziege, along with Gordon Cox from the Boro website. The German, who had been sent off on Saturday, stressed his innocence in the second incident involving Beckham which led to his dismissal.

Ziege also supported the strongly held view that United defender Jaap Stam should have been sent off for bringing down Juninho, which led to the Boro penalty.

Once back at the Gazette, I received a call from a woman fan, who did not want to give her name, who insisted that she and her family had been bullied by the police at the United match. She also claimed that the roof over the area which housed the Boro fans was dangerous. She felt so strongly about the incidents that she had already contacted the Boro, Manchester United and the FA to complain. But I could not write the story because she did not want to give me her name and address.

A couple of fans also rang to express their anger over the way in which several United players had harangued referee Andy D'Urso following the penalty award. I telephoned the FA for a comment, and to enquire whether they would be inspecting the video of the match and taking any action.

I received an official comment which implied there would probably be no action taken, because the ref had already dealt with the incident by booking Roy Keane at the time. However the FA spokesman did indicate that it was not a shut book, which suggested that the matter would be discussed further with a view to ensuring that no similar incidents happened again.

Chapter Seven

FEBRUARY

Tuesday, February 1

FEBRUARY had arrived. The accursed month. Boro had never won a single game in February in the Premier League, so far during Bryan Robson's reign.

Maybe things were about to change in the New Millennium. Assistant boss Viv Anderson was certainly full of smiles when he took the morning press briefing.

Despite the run of injuries, which seemed to crop up at this time of the season every year, there was a belief at Rockliffe Park that the corner had been turned.

Having written up today's back page lead last night, I did not need much fresh information. However Viv talked at length about the current problems facing players and referees in this country, before we got down to the nitty gritty of what was going on within the Boro camp. The player news was little different to yesterday, but I managed to get a fresh line on Hamilton Ricard to fill a short space which had been allotted on the back page alongside the Steve Gibson story.

Ronnie Reng telephoned after lunch. He's the London based German reporter who keeps close tabs on Christian Ziege's progress at Boro.

It's always pleasant to have a chat with Ronnie, especially as I can usually trade a few facts and figures. Ronnie gave me details of Ziege's likely next call-up for Germany, and stressed that the midfielder would not miss any Boro games as a result. It was good enough to give me a story for tomorrow.

After tea, I rang Albert Lanny at Redcar. Albert is a very close pal of Wilf Mannion, and keeps in regular contact with the Boro's Golden Boy. I had heard a disturbing rumour that all was not well with Wilf, and needed to check it out. Albert said that Wilf was poorly, but bearing up at this moment in time.

I was sorry to hear that Albert himself was not too well. He had been fitted with a new kneecap a few months ago, and it had not yet settled into place. I wished both Albert and his kneecap, and Wilf, well.

Wednesday, February 2

FROM one Boro old-timer, to another. I phoned George Hardwick early this morning to wish him a happy 80th birthday, and collect a few quotes for a back page story for the Evening Gazette.

George had already been rudely awoken from his golden slumbers by Gazette chief photographer Doug Moody, who was keen to organise a picture of George and his wife Jennifer for the day's edition.

When I called, George had just finished combing his hair to pose with Jennifer and a couple of glasses of champagne for Gazette deputy chief photographer Ian McIntyre.

"I haven't even had time to eat my breakfast yet," George groaned, no doubt with a smile on his face, when I demanded a few comments.

However, George was as accommodating and friendly as ever, and made it clear that he was enjoying life as much as ever, despite being deprived of his breakfast.

I also rang Boro reserve team coach David Geddis for tonight's reserve line-up. David filled me in with all the details and also talked about the progress being made by some of the club's younger professionals.

Tonight's game against Blackburn was being played at Billingham Synthonia and, while David felt that the players would have benefitted more from playing at the Riverside, his hands were tied and they had to get on with it.

I suspect that the reserve game might have been a bit more entertaining at the Riverside. It ended goalless and there was not a great deal to shout about.

Friday, February 4

BRYAN Robson tipped me off that Keith O'Neill would be in the Boro starting line-up at Leicester City tomorrow. So I chatted to Keith at Rockliffe Park, along with Alastair Brownlee, to pick up a story for Saturday's Evening Gazette.

Keith talked positively, as he always does. He talks the same way that he plays. He was desperate to get back into action and, after ten days of training, I suspected that he would have no problems as far as physical fitness was concerned, even though he had not played a competitive game since December 18.

"We are going to win at Leicester," he said with great conviction. I hoped he was right.

Keith's Irish teammate Curtis Fleming was also upbeat in another interview with me. He received a belated Century Radio man of the match bottle of champagne from Alastair and answered with one of his special "I am thrilled!" replies. Curtis's current level of commitment epitomised what the Boro fans were looking for from the team.

It was a rather hectic morning for Curtis. He was interviewed by a group of people from a community newspaper, and had his photo taken several times. I admired his patience and fortitude. He was still talking to them while most of the other players were preparing for training.

Robbo was also very positive in his pre-match comments. However he was none too pleased when I told him that Boro had not won a Premier League game in the month of February since he arrived on Teesside. However, with three home games in a row to come later in the month, things were hopeful. Watch this space.

The main talking point of the morning was Alastair's shirt, which everybody at the club agreed could not possibly have been ironed. One suggestion from somebody who shall remain nameless, was that there were more lines on Alastair's face than on the shirt. It did not go down too well.

Robbo revealed in general conversation that he did not know how to use an iron, or a washing machine. It was something which I had in common with the Boro boss. But Robbo did reveal that he was an excellent cook. His speciality? Apple crumble.

Back at the Evening Gazette, and we were informed that Wilf Mannion had been admitted to hospital. So I was forced to sit down after lunch and complete the feature which I had begun last week, telling the story of Wilf's life. It was added to the same file which contained the Queen Mother's biography, and we've had that one for several years! Hopefully it would be a long time before either of them were needed.

However I did enjoy finishing off the story. Wilf's remarkable story made for superb reading, except for the fact that he never made the kind of money from the game which his genius deserved.

Saturday, February 5

FOOD and drink is provided for free in the press rooms at Premier League grounds. But not at Leicester City. You must pay £1 for the privilege. However it's all in a good cause. The money is donated to charity, which is not a bad thing.

However, it already costs me enough of my own cash to report on Boro away games, so I don't want to see the outlay increasing. There are many times when I must put my hand in my pocket on my travels for items for which I can't possibly obtain receipts. So it costs me money to do my job.

I'm sure Leicester's pay-for-food idea could catch on at other stadia, which will bring more personal expense. And that's not complaining about the charity side of things. I already do my bit for charity. I have several direct debits in operation to charities of my own choice, and I also usually fork out every time that these charities make special appeals. I'm just a soft touch. So it's not a case of being tight. Not in this case, anyway.

Mind you, the food at Leicester is pretty good. Hot soup, chicken and steak pies and sandwiches are available all afternoon, while there are also cream cakes at half-time. Pretty good value for £1.

There is hot tea and coffee always on tap. I was deliberating whether to have a final cup of tea before leaving Filbert Street at 6pm when the press steward told me: "Don't worry. The tea is fine. It stays hot for seven hours." She was right. It was just as palatable as my first cup of tea at 1.30pm.

The journey to Leicester had been straight forward. Nick Wood from the Northern Echo joined Len Shepherd, Nigel Gibb and I on the trip down the M1. We stopped at Trowell Services on the way for a coffee. There were football shirts everywhere. Arsenal and Portsmouth colours were very prominent. We had to check our fixture lists to see where they were going.

Once we arrived in Leicester things became a bit difficult. We lost our way, and spent 20 minutes driving aimlessly around the town centre before a helpful soul sent us in the right direction.

Inside the stadium I met up with my German pal Ronnie Reng. He had travelled up from London to run the rule over Christian Ziege's performance, with a view to writing features for a German newspaper. A young Turkish reporter, who was there to watch Leicester's Muzzy Izzet, paced irritatingly up and down the concrete steps of the press box, occasionally sitting in different seats and then getting up again.

I sat alongside Jason Mellor from the Newcastle Journal and we chatted about North-east football in general. He was happy about having to miss today's Sunderland-Newcastle derby because it meant he would have a slightly less hectic working day tomorrow.

The view from the press box at Leicester is excellent, unlike the low pitch-level seats from which the Boro fans are forced to try to watch the game.

Before the kick off Boro had every chance of winning the game. Within 90 seconds they had none, when Keith O'Neill was very unfortunate to slice the ball into his own net.

Leicester effectively won the game at that stage. They were gifted another goal when Andy Impey was not picked up on the right, and

Mark Schwarzer parried his shot from an unbelievable angle into the net.

At half-time, as I trudged out alongside the collar and tie brigade in the executive suites, they were laughing and taking the mickey out of Boro. They pointed out, quite rightly, that their side were two goals up without having had a shot at goal. It was hard to stomach.

Boro did pull a goal back in the second half with a wonder strike from Andy Campbell, but Boro were awful on the day and Leicester cruised to the three points.

Leicester boss Martin O'Neill said very little in the press room afterwards, other than to express his relief at winning the game. Bryan Robson followed him into the press room, and was asked few questions.

In the concourse outside, Paul Ince delivered several strong comments about the fact that Boro now faced a relegation battle and had to battle their way out of the mess. He insisted, quite rightly, that Boro's next three home games in a row were cup finals.

Bill Anderson, the Leicester Mercury's amiable reporter, told me on the way out: "See you next season." I scowled.

"I mean it," he said. "You'll definitely be all right." I hoped he was correct.

As I was driving back up the M1 I was informed, by somebody who shall remain nameless: "Well it could turn out well for the diary of the season that you are writing. Boro could be relegated."

This may have been a pretty uneventful season so far, but the last thing I wanted was relegation. Diary, or no diary.

Monday, February 7

THERE were still a few smiles around at Rockliffe Park today. Maybe morale was higher than I had imagined, despite the gradual slide which now left the club teetering just four points above the Premier League relegation zone.

Bryan Robson was none too happy, however. He was still angry that the three points had been allowed to slip away so easily at Leicester on Saturday. The desperate overall situation was one which Robbo could not possibly have envisaged at the start of the season. Neither could anyone else.

However the situation was now very serious. Only one point had been taken from the last 15 and the team was giving the impression that it had forgotten how to win. The forthcoming three home games in a row were of huge importance.

"It's now a battle for survival," the manager admitted.

With Mark Schwarzer having jetted off to join up with the Australian squad in Chile, Robson revealed that Marlon Beresford would definitely be playing in next Monday's home game against Aston Villa. It would be Marlon's first Premier League outing for more than 12 months.

Gordon Cox, Alastair Brownlee and I managed to grab Marlon for an interview. He revealed that it had not been easy, spending so long in the reserves, but he was excited about the return to the front line. Amid a bit of friendly barracking from Paul Ince, Marlon also revealed that he was an Aston Villa fan as a lad. His father used to take him to Villa Park from their home in Lincoln.

I had a quick word with Robbie Mustoe, too. He was still struggling with his injured back, and I could see he was concerned about the problem. However Gazza was on the mend. He rushed off to get on the waiting bus for the reserves' friendly game at Huddersfield.

Before leaving, I fitted in a chat with Academy director Dave Parnaby, who was very disappointed that tomorrow's FA Youth Cuptie at West Ham had been postponed. The Hammers had informed the FA that they were suffering from a flu bug.

I bumped into Boro director George Cooke later in the day. He was shortly to leave ICI and join Boro on a full-time basis, working towards raising funds for the club's community academy at Eston.

George had been at Leicester on Saturday and, like me, was a worried man. Once again, we could only hope that the three home games would turn the tide.

Dave Allan, Boro's head of PR, rang me to give me a few interesting stories, including one telling me that couples would soon be able to get married at the Riverside. The club was expecting to be awarded a special licence very soon. It was a nice story, but I couldn't make my mind up whether it was a good or bad thing.

Tuesday, February 8

TALK of new signings was high on the agenda for Bryan Robson today. He was already formulating his list of targets. But the indications were that there would be no new faces on Teesside before the transfer deadline.

Robbo revealed that his South American contacts had informed him that the former Brazilian international star, Edmundo, was available for transfer. Edmundo was still banging in the goals at 33 and the Boro boss was very tempted.

However it was all a little complicated. Robson had received reports that Edmundo was facing potential problems with the law. It added too many dodgy scenarios to any proposed transfer deal. Robbo, rather reluctantly, felt that it was better to steer clear of this one.

The Boro boss was more upbeat today, partly because he had started to wade through a huge pile of correspondence which had been lying on his desk for a few days. He would also have been boosted by the fact that Hamilton Ricard had scored twice for the reserves at Huddersfield yesterday. These were the first goals that the Colombian striker had scored for some time. His loss of form had already led to him losing his place in his country's international side.

Robbo was worried about Boro's lack of goals, as well he might be. Boro had scored only twice since Christmas. Both of them were netted by Andy Campbell. Boro desperately needed to be creative again and start to put the ball in the onion bag. However, Bryan stressed that goalscorers didn't lose their touch permanently. He added that the players involved had to continue to work hard until their killer instinct returned.

Downstairs, Gordon Cox and I waited in vain for a chat with Andy Campbell. We wanted to chat to him following his wonder goal at Leicester. But the 20-year-old forward did not walk past us on the way for a bit of breakfast. Time began to run out, and eventually it was too late for us to send a message to the dressing room area, asking if Andy would give us an interview.

We spent much of the idle time listening to a wholehearted conversation on our left hand side. Christian Ziege, Gianluca Festa and Paul Ince were chatting away merrily in Italian. Very interesting.

The rest of the day was rather hectic. Paylor on Wednesday was hastily dashed out and then I started on a special report for the Sports Gazette looking at the importance of the timing of Robson's signings over the past five and a half years.

There was a break in the proceedings when Clem from Radio Cleveland rang for a chat. I think Clem was looking for me to make him feel better about the current situation at the Boro. We talked at length, but in the end we both felt a lot worse.

Wednesday, February 9

TIME to print all the names of the Boro potential targets that I had picked up in general conversation. All of them were French and, while I was not certain whether Boro had the ability to sign top players like David Trezeguet from Monaco, I felt it was only fair to the fans to publish the names.

To most fans, today's back page lead in the Evening Gazette would have read like a list of 'who-on-earth-is-he's'. Half a dozen French strikers, most of them newly arrived on their own first team scene, but all apparently possessing pace and the ability to put the ball in the net. In addition to keeping tabs on any developments in Italy, Bryan Robson had been concentrating his scouting efforts in France over the past 18 months or so. On the odd occasion when he had not been at Rockliffe Park this season, I was usually informed later that he had been to the Continent.

Clearly there was a great determination to strengthen the Boro attack in the summer, and it was no secret that the new men are unlikely to be English.

Friday, February 11

I RECEIVED a fax from Madrid today telling me that Boro had made a genuine attempt to try to open negotiations to buy free-scoring Dutch striker Jimmy Floyd Hasselbaink from Atletico Madrid.

I knew that the information was probably right, yet it was an amazing story. If nothing else, it indicated that Boro's ambition had not faded despite recent results, and also, that they might have some cash to spend in the near future.

I wrote up the article before leaving for Rockliffe Park, knowing that the story would stand up, even if Bryan Robson refused to comment. In the event, Robbo was happy to verify the tale, while at the same time stressing that Atletico had made it very clear to Boro that Hasselbaink would definitely not be leaving Madrid, despite all of their financial problems.

I phoned Evening Gazette sports supremo Allan Boughey with Robson's quotes, and he rewrote my early story before it appeared in the first edition.

Robbo had enjoyed a night at the centre of the universe in Seaton Carew last night. He was in the company of Sir Geoff Hurst at a sportsman's dinner. The Boro boss was bright and breezy today, and clearly looking forward to Monday's crunch clash with Aston Villa. He handed me the squad for the match, and indicated that Gazza was firing on all cylinders again and would be back in the starting line-up.

Outside, Alastair Brownlee, Gordon Cox and I began to interview Colin Cooper about the current state of affairs, and the desperate need to beat Villa. "Gazza's not around, is he? " asked Ali, checking the car park before switching on his mic.

Sure enough, no sooner had the interview started than Gazza arrived in his four wheel drive. Initially we were treated to the vehicle's horn being pressed constantly. Then this was replaced by a rendering of Status Quo's Down Down, which came blaring across the car park. Colin, who had seen it all before, was very patient.

Gazza's bubbly mood seemed to extend everywhere. I felt that the lads would be up for it on Monday. Even Gianluca Festa got in the act by pouring a cup of water over the top of the staircase, missing Coxy's priceless lap top by inches.

Once back at the Evening Gazette, I had to work to prepare several advance stories to cover for the fact that there was no Boro game tomorrow.

I received a call from a Midlands journalist who gave me quite a few interesting quotes from an interview which Paul Merson had recently given him. The best part was that Merse was apologising to the Boro fans and players for some of the things he had said about booze and betting at the time of his departure from Teesside to join Aston Villa. It was excellent stuff. Just what I needed to put together a special lead for tomorrow night's Sports Gazette.

Monday, February 14

PAUL Merson's much publicised return to the Riverside did not turn out to be the event which most Boro fans would have hoped for.

The Aston Villa midfielder had launched another scathing blast at Boro fans in the Sunday press yesterday, so it set the scene for what was expected to be a rather lively and noisy live televised match.

I had bumped into my pal Ronnie outside the Gazette when I arrived at 7.15am. "I'm going down to the stadium early tonight," he said, "So that I can hear them booing Merson when he gets off the team bus."

Later I discovered that many fans had done the same. I missed the arrival of the Villa coach, but heard the rest of the booing as Merson was catcalled every time he touched the ball during the game.

The only problem for the Boro fans was that Merson had the last laugh on the night, even if he was substituted reasonably early in the second half. Merse played well in a solid Villa side and Boro were worse than dreadful. Villa won 4-0.

Naturally there were calls for Bryan Robson's head during the match, including from the small following of around 300 Villa fans. But at the final whistle, the 12,000 or so hardy souls who were suffering to the bitter end were chanting in favour of Robbo.

I personally didn't feel a lot of sympathy for the manager after watching that shambles of a game, but it was a nice touch by the fans. Maybe these shivering supporters were the club's real hardcore following - the only section of the crowd certain to renew their season tickets in the summer.

There was a major incident during the game when Paul Gascoigne was stretchered off after breaking his left forearm following a rash challenge on Villa midfielder George Boateng. It was another bodyblow to Gazza, but food and drink for the tabloids. Never mind the score. They had a Gazza story.

The press room was packed, many news editors having sent extra working reporters in case Boro were beaten and Robson resigned or was sacked. The Newcastle Journal, for example, had sent both Tim Rich and Jason Mellor to cover for the possibility that Bryan might quit. If he did, there would be a lot of words to gather and write in time for their Middlesbrough edition. I didn't blame the newspapers. I knew what a panic they would have to meet edition times if the news came through that Robbo was no longer at the helm.

There was a touching moment immediately following the final whistle when Colin Cooper was interviewed on Sky TV and asked why Boro had been so ineffective. Coops looked close to tears, and had been brave to undertake such a telling interview at an emotional time. And it was good to see that the good hiding by Villa had hurt the players as much as the fans.

Villa boss John Gregory arrived in the press room and naturally voiced his satisfaction over his team's win. He even said that he was disappointed that Villa had not scored another couple of goals. He seemed to be looking down at his lap a lot, and I was told afterwards that he was reading some of his comments off a piece of paper.

Gregory did have words of support for Robson, which were clearly not rehearsed. He insisted that Robbo would pull the team through, given the opportunity.

There then followed a rather long wait while all we media men sat patiently in the press room and waited for Robson's arrival. The only point of discussion was the game. Everybody I spoke to agreed it had been a shocking performance. I was regularly asked if I thought Robbo would resign tonight. I said not.

I had been accompanied to the match by two Evening Gazette colleagues, Phil Tallentire and trainee Caroline Briggs, who had to wait with me until 11.10pm before Robson finally surfaced. The manager had kept the players locked in the dressing room for almost 90 minutes of grilling.

Robson was red faced when he walked in, but mentally strong. He answered every one from the barrage of questions, many of which were centred around his own future. As expected, he pledged to carry on the fight.

There was little road traffic to contest with on the way out of the Riverside. So the drive home was a quick one. But I needed a hot cup of tea to gather my senses, and it was 12.30am before I finally crawled into bed with nightmare thoughts of the match still swimming around my brain.

Tuesday, February 15

I WAS in big demand today, Occasionally from frustrated fans, but mainly by national radio stations, who were queueing up for my services. No doubt I was an easy interviewee to track down after last night's embarrassment at the Riverside. However I found it difficult to fit them all into my schedule, mainly because they were clamouring for interviews at the same time.

The subject matter was Boro's gradual demise, and also the much publicised Paul Gascoigne incident, when he broke his arm following his rash challenge on Aston Villa's George Boateng.

I tried to accommodate everybody, though it wasn't easy. These radio interviews can be useful publicity for the Evening Gazette, so that's why I am encouraged to undertake them. The most interesting one I did was for the Forces Network. It's the first time they've ever interviewed me. But it was just one of many during the day. I concluded the final radio interview at 7.40pm, when I spoke to Radio Five Live.

Fortunately the standard of questions was fair and reasonable. Nothing stupid. As usual, I tried to answer everything forthrightly. There's no point being wimpish or diplomatic about it.

I said that Gazza had been reckless, and stressed that Bryan Robson clearly believed that Boro would turn the corner when the next win came along. But it's hard for any losing team to start winning, especially when morale is low. I felt that the manager was hanging on by his fingertips, not so much from internal pressure, but against the power of the fans.

I had made just one major phonecall myself, to Boro physio Bob Ward, to check out the condition of Gazza. I received some excellent up-to-the-minute comments from Bob, who revealed that he was about to take Gazza to hospital for his operation to have a pin inserted in his broken arm.

Bob also told me that Gazza used his mobile phone at Middlesbrough General Hospital last night to ring Paul Merson on the Villa bus in order to speak to Boateng and apologise, while stressing all along that there was no intent.

I had three major stories to write up for the Evening Gazette. I blasted everybody involved with the club over last night's shocking performance. Surprisingly only a few fans phoned me during the day to vent their anger over the result. I suspected that the fans were all in a state of shock. It was a different atmosphere to the recent defeat by Derby, when everybody was fuming. I sensed that much of the anger had been replaced with a fear of the dreaded drop.

On the afternoon I received a very useful tip off, that Andy Campbell would be named in the England Under-21 squad tomorrow for next Tuesday's international against Argentina. It was an excellent piece of information, which would give me a perfect back page lead for tomorrow. And I was pleased for Andy. It would give him a great boost ahead of Saturday's game against Coventry.

Andy Turner from the Coventry paper rang me to swap a few statistics. He had watched the match on TV last night, along with the rest of the country, and couldn't believe that Boro had been so bad. I told him that Boro had lost all self belief and ability, partly in the hope that my comments might filter through to the Coventry players and they might become very slightly complacent.

Maybe I was clutching at straws in this respect. But I did believe that Boro could still beat anybody if they could get their noses in front.

Just before leaving the office, I was informed that Gazza had been charged by the FA for misconduct. It was unexpected, because if a ban was imposed by the FA as punishment, surely it was going to run concurrently with Gazza's term of injury. And he would be sidelined for a few weeks. Unfortunately the story arrived just too late to include in the final edition of the Evening Gazette.

Wednesday, February 16

BRYAN Robson talked positively today about turning the season around and getting the team back on the rails.

I knew that he sincerely believed he could do it, and that he felt he had all the necessary resources at his disposal, as long as he was not hit by another flood of injuries.

I admired his determination, but I still could not see any signs that the situation was about to change. Maybe all it would need was for Boro to get their noses in front against Coventry on Saturday. It was frightening to think what might happen if they went behind.

Robbo provided me with plenty of information and I had no problems filling the back page lead in the Gazette, especially once I had spoken to Andy Campbell to gather a few quotes about his under-21 call-up.

After arriving early for training, Andy had not yet had the chance to reach the Rockliffe Park restaurant for breakfast, where he would have been informed immediately by Robson about his call-up.

So Andy was very surprised when Alastair Brownlee, Gordon Cox and I broke the news. He was pleasantly delighted, as well he might be. Yet he stressed that Boro's Premier League safety was the most important thing on his mind at that time.

The rest of the day was a bit of a slog to burn my way through my outstanding work. But I got there on the end. There were enough quotes left over from my chat with Andy to write up my final advance feature for the Sports Gazette, which was a bonus.

Still no rest for the wicked. At tea-time I received a call from Talk Sport to undertake another interview. They were pushy beggars. I had done two interviews for them yesterday. It's in my own time of course, when they ring me away from the office. It must also be stressed that there are no fees paid by these radio stations. All interviews are voluntary. However, Talk Sport told me they were running a Boro special and so I buckled as usual and agreed to answer a few questions, sitting in my study with the phone in one hand and a Neapolitan Cornetto in the other.

Friday, February 18

GEORGE Hardwick's 80th birthday was officially celebrated at a lively function in the BT Cellnet Club at the Riverside tonight, and a good time was had by all.

George's special guest was Brian Clough, who helped to ensure that the proceedings went with a bang. Cloughie was clearly struggling badly with arthritic kneecaps which were showing the stresses and strains of scoring more than 200 Boro goals. But he got up to make a lovely off the cuff speech, which had us all laughing, and he was full of praise for George and his wife Jennifer.

With Clough now approaching his 65th birthday, he was still very mentally alert. In fact both Brian and George were in fine fettle.

After Cloughie's speech, John Wilson from Juniper Publishing got up to make a speech. It was always going to be a hard act to follow Cloughie, but it was made all the more difficult when John had to deal with a heckler - Cloughie himself! But John held his end up very well and was well received. He displayed one of the limited edition framed picture biographs of George which were snapped up during the evening.

In fact it was John who had initially suggested to the club that an 80th birthday celebration for George might make a great night, and the club had jumped at the idea.

I was joined on a table with my wife Brenda and several other people who I knew very well, including Frank Spraggon and his wife Linda, and Mrs Peggy Shepherdson. Loyal Boro stalwart Terry Jackson was there with his family, plus Evening Gazette bowls correspondent Tony Frosdick and his wife Judith.

It was a useful meeting with Tony, who revealed in conversation that his father in law, Tom Fleming, had won a gold medal for bowls at the 1966 Commonwealth Games. Tom had slipped the net in my list of potential entrants for the Teesside's Sporting Greats book, so I made arrangements to ring Tony over the next few weeks to get the full lowdown on Tom's achievements.

The evening, and the wine, flowed well. Graham Fordy, Boro's commercial manager, had done a great job of organising the night, which included operatic singers and a comedian. The singers were not my cup of tea, but it was something different.

I went home empty pocketed, but not empty handed. Brenda won a Boro replica shirt in the raffle which was autographed by all the former club stalwarts in the room, including Clough, Hardwick, Johnny Spuhler, Gordon Jones, Ray Yeoman, Billy Day, Derek McLean, Bryan Orritt and Alan Peacock. A nice collectors' item.

We resisted Ron Darby's kind invitation to go back to the Blue Bell for aperatifs, and left at 1am.

Earlier, I had driven up to Hurworth to see Bryan Robson. He was optimistic about tomorrow's crunch clash with Coventry City, despite having just been informed by physio Bob Ward that Phil Stamp had been added to the injury list.

I felt that Robbo was at the crossroads in this match. If Boro scored first they would probably win, and then hopefully turn the season around. If they went behind, I feared the worst. Somehow I felt that Bryan was naive to the fact that this could be the most important game of his managerial career.

Once downstairs, I waited in vain to interview Mark Schwarzer about his trip to Chile with Australia. He had arrived home late last night and had been given the opportunity to sleep-in. I waited patiently until 10.30am before being forced to walk to the car to send over today's story, in order to meet my deadline. I was half way through dictating the story when Schwarz drove up, clearly in a mighty rush. An interview was out of the question.

However, I picked up a good story after lunch. According to my information, Boro had concluded arrangements to take Alloa's 21-year-old striker Martin Cameron on trial next week. I made some phonecalls to pick up a few facts and figures, and wrote up the story for Saturday's back page lead.

Saturday, February 19

WHAT a weekend! A Boro win! I even celebrated by buying an Indian takeaway on the way home. Then I got up early on Sunday to read the newspapers. I'd almost forgotten exactly which papers I had delivered, because I hadn't opened them for weeks. Even Bryan Robson had said he was planning to celebrate the victory with a few drinks. Surely not!

But it was a fact. Boro 2, Coventry City 0. Boro had three much needed points in the bag and everything was all right again. For the time being, at least.

The lads had done really well. Fired up from the start, two goals up in 20 minutes through Gianluca Festa and Hamilton Ricard, and then coasting. Suddenly Boro were seven points away from the relegation zone. It was seventh heaven.

It was a total change-around from the sombre mood before the kick off. A few fans I spoke to had expected the worst. I noticed that the press contingent was heavy, particularly from the tabloids. They expected Robbo to walk, or be sacked, if Boro lost the game.

John Sadler was there from the Sun, while a couple of London-based journalists were in attendance, including Mike Walters from the Daily Mirror. The general feeling in conversation was that Coventry would encounter few problems.

So, what a difference 45 minutes made. It was praise all-around at half-time as 2-0 leaders Boro seemingly had the points in the bag. In his match commentary, Alastair Brownlee had declared that Ricard's piledriver had almost knocked the net all the way to North Ormesby. The mood change was wonderful.

Bryan Robson was first manager into the press conference after the game, though Gordon Strachan followed soon afterwards, and stood staring at the floor while Robbo spoke. It was very unusual to have both managers in the press room at the same time. I've known times in the past when this has happened, and the two managers have begun to disagree with each other, threatening to create an ugly incident. But Strachan was very polite and gave Robson his chance to say what he wanted to say.

Robbo put the win down to the influence of the returning players, plus the fact that his defenders had not made any mistakes. I felt that there had to be something else because Boro were fired up from the start for a change. The reason for this wonderful innovation did not emerge at the press conference.

Strachen blamed himself for the defeat, but would not go into details, for some reason. He did not look a happy man at all, and his replies were brief and straight to the point. I've noticed in the past that Strachan takes defeat very badly. But that's not a bad trait for a manager. I did not hang around for player interviews, deciding to wait until Monday. It was all smiles on the way out. I met a steward who had bet on Festa to score the first goal at odds of 40-1. Another fella who would be enjoying a good night.

Monday, February 21

I HAD a long chat with Viv Anderson today about the quality of coaching at the Boro. Naturally Viv and Gordon McQueen were well aware of the criticism which had been directed their way by some fans, and I felt that it was time for a reply.

I reminded Viv of the feelings expressed in many of the letters sent to the Evening Gazette, and he said that he was happy to agree to undertake the interview if I felt that it would help. I said that I thought it would.

My questions were hard-hitting, just as the fans would want them to be. I questioned the team's preparation, the apparent lack of planning, and the seeming inability to change a system when things were going wrong. Viv answered the questions forthrightly, and went into great detail about the detailed match preparation which went on every week. Personally I felt reassured at the end of the interview. My main worry, beforehand, had been that Boro seemed incapable of changing things around if they conceded an early goal. Viv insisted that the options were always there to put into place, but that often it was better to stick to the original game plan for as long as possible because that was what the players had worked towards all week. I could understand Viv's argument, especially as he made it clear that complacency in these situations was the last thing on the coaches' minds.

Maybe the most amazing part of the interview came when Viv revealed the full amount of travelling involved every week by himself, Gordon and also Bryan Robson. In fact Robbo was planning to watch an international in Holland on Wednesday, while Viv was flying to Hungary. All to look at players and playing systems.

Clearly the coaching staff could easily put in a lot more hours every week than most working people. But I also sensed that they were still in a very precarious job. All this hard work would be wasted if the signings made, and the ideas put into place, did not pay dividends.

Even so, Viv's quotes made for a nice piece and I decided to give over the whole of my Wednesday column for the interview.

Earlier I had chatted to Robbo along with Alastair Brownlee and

Gordon Cox for some fresh quotes following the victory against Coventry. It emerged that not only did Boro take part in a 90-minute lock in after the Aston Villa defeat, but they had to give up their day-off the following day for a four-hour grilling. Judging by the manner of the win against Coventry, the point of the discussions had hit home.

I wrote up Viv's interview on the afternoon, and also the Boro juniors column for the Sports Gazette, following my chat with Dave Parnaby on the morning. The youth team were now in the quarter-finals of the FA Youth Cup and everybody in the Academy set-up was buzzing. Just like the first team at the moment.

Tuesday, February 22

I FINALLY managed to track down Mark Schwarzer today to chat about his trip to Chile with Australia. So far I had not read a single line about the tournament, which had also involved Bulgaria and Slovakia. I did not even know any of the scorelines.

Mark revealed that he had been held up on the road by a car accident on Friday, which had prevented me undertaking an early interview. However, he was happy to chat but insisted on getting changed first.

I was also on the look-out for Robbie Mustoe, who was due to return to full training before the weekend following a back injury which had ruled him out for a month. A Mustoe interview would give me a suitable back page story for Wednesday.

Unfortunately Robbie walked down the staircase from the restaurant at Rockliffe Park, just as Schwarz emerged from the dressing rooms.

Gordon Cox also needed a Schwarz interview, and as he set up his mic, I squeezed in 20 seconds with Robbie first. Or rather Robbie squeezed in 20 seconds with me. Being well aware of my tight situation timewise, Robbie simply reeled off the details of his back injury, his personal feelings while he was injured, his gradual return to fitness and his planned comeback date, without me asking no questions in between. Wonderful. That's what ten years of being interviewed regularly by me does to a man. Robbie answered all my questions before I could get them out.

The interview with Mark needed to be much more detailed. The Boro keeper revealed that the Aussies has not won a game in Chile, but then had been unlucky not to remain unbeaten. They drew two and lost the other match to the host country on a last minute disputed penalty.

Schwarz described the 13 hour journey, which involved three tiring flights, the environment in Chile and the playing conditions. However he had obviously enjoyed the trip and especially appreciated the opportunity to win three more caps, and have a heart to heart chat with Aussie coach Frank Farina. Mark was particularly keen to see the Aussies bring their future international dates in line with those in Europe. The big story of the morning was the apparent exclusive revelations by the Press Association that Paul Gascoigne was wanted by an Australian club, Sydney Marconi Stallions.

It turned out that Mark had played for this club before leaving Oz.

"Could Marconi afford to sign Gazza?" I asked.

"They have an annual turnover of 100 million Australian dollars," he told me.

They could definitely afford to sign Gazza.

I had written up the story before leaving the Gazette so all I needed from Bryan Robson was a few comments. He revealed that there had as yet been no official approach from Marconi, but stressed yet again that Gazza was part of his immediate plans for Boro and was not going anywhere. The boss's quotes did not detract from Marconi's interest, but made it clear that Gazza was unlikely to end up Down Under.

Most of my evenings during the winter had been spent slogging away on my other book, Teesside's Sporting Greats, which I was writing along with John Wilson for Juniper Publishing. Basically I had been writing up biographies from Evening Gazette cuttings on most of the 95 sportsmen and women who had been selected so far for inclusion in the book. Some of the cuttings went back to the 1930s and were yellowed and crinkled. In fact they needed to be handled rather gently, because they had a habit of falling to pieces if you were not careful and created a job for the hoover. Not my scene at all. Now the cuttings were almost exhausted and I had reached the stage where I needed to begin interviewing as many of the 'Greats' as possible so that I could dot the 'i's' and cross the 't's' to complete their full stories.

After tea I undertook my first interview when I rang Nicola Lavery, who represented Great Britain in the cross country ski-ing at the Winter Olympics in 1984. I had tracked her down to her home in Kendal following an appeal in the Gazette for information. Nicola was happy to chat, and it was a significant step forward for me in convincing myself that the book could be completed in good time for its late-July deadline.

Wednesday, February 23

DAVE ALLAN, Boro's head of PR, rang me today to give me exclusive details of the six shirts which had been produced by the club's kit manufacturers Errea for the fans to select one of them as the new Boro away shirt for next season.

Dave revealed that one of the six was black, and another was orange. I didn't fancy the thought of either of them, but then I suppose from Errea's point of view it was all about giving the fans plenty of choice.

I wrote up the Robbie Mustoe quotes as the lead item in the back page lead today, but also gave details of the six shirts, which were to be revealed to the fans during Saturday's match against Leeds United.

Also, I rang Rockliffe Park to pick up details of the reserve team for Boro's match against Everton at Billingham Synthonia tonight. Carlos Marinelli was back after injury, which should be a crowd booster.

John Motson rang me at lunchtime. The man himself usually contacts me when he is due to commentate on a Boro game for Match of the Day. It meant that Boro-Leeds would be the top game on Saturday night.

Motty is always as pleasant as pie and keen to brush up on his knowledge of everything that is happening at the Boro. He usually displays a good basic knowledge of the Boro squad, though I was surprised that he knew very little about Marinelli. I filled him in with a few details. If Marinelli was on the bench on Saturday, then John would be the best prepared commentator around. I'm always keen to help him out. I think it's great that John is prepared to pick up the phone and undertake his own research, bearing in mind the BBC's huge number of researchers.

Friday, February 25

I WROTE up the story today about NTL'S interest in buying Boro shares, putting the accent on 'would be', 'could be' and 'it was reported', even though I knew the story was correct.

I had been tipped off about the possible marriage some time ago, though it was strictly off the record. However, the Daily Express had leaked the story on Thursday, and I was forced to follow it up.

When I phoned NTL press officer Debbie Calgie, she was all prepared. "Where were you yesterday?" she asked. "As soon as I saw the story in the Express I rang my head office for an official comment, so that I was ready for you ringing."

"I was on day off," I replied.

"That explains it then," she added.

I have known Debbie for many years, ever since she was a reporter with the Evening Gazette. Unfortunately she was unable to do me a favour by adding to the official comment which she had already been handed down by her bosses. Not surprisingly it was: "We do not comment on media speculation."

I phoned the Boro PR office as well, but they did not come back with a statement, so I knew it was another 'no comment'.

It was all I needed. Unfortunately 'no comment' is so easily translated into 'yes it's true, but we can't discuss it in public at this moment in time'. So I wrote up the story, as I knew it, for publication in tomorrow's Gazette.

Later in the afternoon, I received a photograph from Boro of the six potential away shirts which had been produced by Errea. I wasn't keen on any of them, and neither was anybody else who looked at the picture. I was particularly concerned that the white, black and red one might win, because it was a combination of the black and white stripes of Newcastle and the red and white stripes of Sunderland.

Earlier I had been up to Hurworth to see Bryan Robson. He spoke off the record about his trip to watch the Holland-Germany match in Amsterdam on Wednesday, where he was checking out two of the German players. Unfortunately Germany were well beaten, so Robbo probably learned very little.

I did not hang around at Hurworth because I had a lot of work to get through at the office. I slammed the accelerator pedal down to the floor to produce one of those record breaking dashes along the A66 which I really do not enjoy. But deadlines are deadlines.

During the day I also wrote up a preview for Cornelius Carr's next defence of his WBF middleweight crown. It was to be against South African Ruben Groenewald at the York Hall in Bethnal Green on March 10.

Cornelius, or John as I know him best, had phoned earlier in the week to chat about his preparations for the fight. He knew nothing about his opponent at this stage, but was training hard and was confident. I told him that I was planning to travel down to London to report on the contest, and he suggested that I should attend the post-fight get-together for a couple of drinks. Sounded like a good idea.

Saturday, February 26

GIANLUCA Festa earned himself a few unwanted headlines today, though it was not easy to have a great deal of sympathy.

I had popped into the Evening Gazette for a photo-shoot on my lucky tie, for inclusion in this book, prior to travelling to Boro's home game against Leeds. When I arrived at the office, I was informed that Festa had been widely quoted in two of the tabloids.

His comments were very cutting and critical of the club, particularly of Bryan Robson. The timing was dreadful, just hours before a big sell-out derby.

When I reached the stadium I made a few inquiries and discovered that

Festa's barbed comments had been made in an interview for a private web-site, and the two tabloids had lifted the quotes.

When I was informed that the club had given permission for Festa to be interviewed by this web-site, it was impossible to feel any sympathy. Apparently the interview was carried out by an Englishman who spoke Italian, so in this case it was highly unlikely that too much misquoting had gone on.

However, Gianluca denied making the comments and was supported by Robbo, who went on to attack the media.

In this modern era of multiple media technology, where anything which is said by anybody to a newspaper, radio, TV, or Internet reporter can be read by the rest of the media immediately, I can't understand why players are allowed to deliver these comments in unnecessary interviews and why the club insists afterwards that the players have done nothing wrong.

Media coverage of Premier League football has reached saturation point and nobody can say anything without it coming to the attention of every media network.

Not that the media is perfect, by any means. I don't like the way in which the media is allowed to speculate willy-nilly and get away with things when they are well wide of the mark, especially when they say things which damage the club and hurt individual players. But when the club shoots itself in the foot you can't blame the media.

Gianluca did deny making the comments in an interview after the game, and had also made a similar denial to Bryan Robson before the game kicked off. But he shouldn't have been in this position in the first place. It goes without saying, of course, that Boro have their own web-site anyway.

The Festa comments were all forgotten during the match, especially as Gianluca got stuck into the action. But his wretched day was made complete when he was sent off.

The Italian was dismissed three minutes from time for a second bookable offence. But the ten men hung on comfortably for a share of the spoils in a goalless draw. Despite the lack of goals, it was the best game I had seen at the Riverside since Boro were promoted two years ago.

Even so, there should have been two goals at least. Referee Uriah Rennie had a stinker, as he always seems to do at the Riverside, and supported his linesmen by chalking out a perfectly good goal apiece by each side.

Otherwise it was a great game to watch. I spoke to Gary Gill from Radio Cleveland as we waited for the press conference afterwards. Gilly was enthusing bucketfuls about the end to end football.

David O'Leary was first manager into the press room. He criticised the ref for Leeds' disallowed goal but, as ever, was full of praise for his young side, despite their missed chances. However, I did not like the patronising way he said: "I hope you great experts will agree", when referring to something which he had just said. But you have to admire the magnificent job he has done at Elland Road so far.

Bryan Robson, while supporting Festa, also criticised Mr Rennie, but stressed what a great game it had been for the fans.

While waiting for player quotes afterwards, I chatted to Clive Hetherington from the Northern Echo and Ian Murtagh from the Daily Star about some of the talented Boro kids who were on the production line. There was a feeling that Robson, too, could bring through some top talent before the end of next season, especially as some of the older heads could be reaching the end of the road at that time

There was no immediate chance to wind down when I got home. One of our sister newspapers, the Newcastle Journal, was short of sports reporters due to holidays, so I wrote up a couple of match follow up stories for them, ready to phone across tomorrow afternoon.

Monday, February 28

I TOOK delivery of the six Boro strips which had been produced by kit manufacturers Errea for the fans to select next season's away strip. Dave Allan, Boro's head of PR, dropped them off at the Evening Gazette. Then I dropped a bombshell on the rest of the lads on the sports desk. I told them they were to be photographed wearing the shirts, and would have to vote which one they preferred. Surprisingly there were no dissenters. The plan was to give me a quirky story for Paylor on Wednesday, while at the same time providing the Boro a bit of free publicity over their voting campaign.

However, I didn't bank on Gazette photographer Steve Elliott taking all six of us into the company car park for the photograph. It was freezing in the icy wind, especially when I stripped to the waist to change into my short sleeved shirt. I was wearing the blue and navy Errea shirt which clearly had very little chance of winning.

We knocked a ball about for a while to keep warm, though I've no idea where it came from. The photo shoot was a bit anarchic, but we got there in the end.

Afterwards I gave the lads special slips to vote 1, 2, 3 for the shirts they preferred and to comment on the one they had been wearing.

The black, red and white shirt was the overall winner in our voting system, though it wasn't my choice.

Earlier I had driven to Rockliffe Park amid regular squally showers to see Bryan Robson. As we were sitting in the restaurant beforehand, there was a dilemma for Gordon Cox because his mic was missing. He thought it must be in Alastair Brownlee's case, despite the fact that Ali and I repeatedly told him that it was lying in the large plantpot downstairs.

The dilemma reached a crisis when we received the call to enter Robbo's office and walked as far as his door. Coxy still would not believe that the mic was anywhere but in Ali's case. In the event Ali bravely delayed the press briefing by going back downstairs to retrieve the mic.

The mood in Robbo's office was ebullient, despite Bryan telling us that he had entertained the club's bank manager at his home on Saturday night. Maybe the news was good on that front as well.

Bryan was very upbeat about the game at Southampton on Saturday and was determined to leave no stops unturned to try to win the game, because it could bring virtual Premier League safety for the club. Robbo was not so positive about the home game against Arsenal the following weekend, because key defenders Gary Pallister and Gianluca Festa were due to be suspended.

"I think I'll ask the groundsman to brick up the goals," he said.

Back in the restaurant, I heard the word "Brazilians" used in conversation. My ears pricked up.

"We've got a couple of young lads from Brazil coming in on trial," Ron Bone admitted. "Their agent is paying for everything. We don't know if they are brilliant or useless. Leave it until later in the week."

Bearing in mind that the Brazilian striker who had arrived on trial earlier in the season was not rated good enough to play for the local Sunday League teams, it was probably good advice.

Tuesday, February 29

I RECEIVED a call last night to tell me that Bryan Robson had decided to change the players' day off to today. It was a bit of a blow because I had nothing in the bank, storywise. Potentially, there was a large hole in the middle of the back page of the Evening Gazette.

Fortunately Mike McGeary had reported on the Boro reserves' match last night as usual, at home to Liverpool, and this provided the source for a half decent story.

I rang reserve team coach David Geddis, who gave me some useful quotes about Dean Gordon, who had played in his third reserve game last night since returning from his cruciate knee ligament operation. I felt there was every chance that Deano would be back in the first team squad for Saturday's trip to Southampton.

The photo of the sports desk staff wearing the six Boro potential away shirts provided plenty of mirth and merriment in the office when it was handed around. However it was well worth it. I felt that the office interest in the picture would be reflected by the reader interest. My article on the shirts, plus picture and headlines, which was officially laid out in the sports page this afternoon ready for inclusion in tomorrow's paper, looked a good read.

Chapter Eight

MARCH

Wednesday, March 1

WHITE rabbits, white rabbits, white rabbits. I uttered the famous phrase as soon as I walked into Rockliffe Park this morning. Maybe it would help Boro to win a few games in March and rise up the table.

However it was me who needed a bit of luck today. I was short of fresh ideas for stories and was looking for a bit of inspiration. I had been tipped off that Boro were looking at three Hungarian players, but Bryan Robson soon dismissed that one.

"Hungarian football is in a dreadful state at the moment," he said. "I don't think they've got three decent players in the whole country."

I knew that Viv Anderson had flown out to watch the Hungary-Australia game recently and I had been led to believe at the time that he was concentrating on the Aussies. Robbo's comments about the Hungarians confirmed this fact.

I tried a few other avenues.

"Any signings at all in the offing?"

"No."

"Any new contracts being drawn up?"

"No."

"Any of the injured players on their way back?"

"No."

Robbo was not being obstructive. There was nothing happening.

I was still stuck for a story as I stared glumly at the reception area carpet at 10.10am. I needed to have my story phoned over to the Evening Gazette in 20 minutes. Then Brian Deane walked by. It was manna from heaven. I jumped up off my seat. He's a lovely lad, Brian, but not fond of interviews. However I was desperate. Two questions, and two answers, and I was made up. Brian stopped at the door to the changing rooms and gave me a couple of brief replies. A story at last! I already had plenty of information about Boro's quest for a place in the FA Youth Cup semi-finals in tonight's derby match against Newcastle United, so it was easy to fill the rest of my allotted space on the back page.

Graham Hiley from the Southampton evening paper phoned me later in the day to swap stats. "This is a cup final for us on Saturday, because we will go above you if we win," he said.

"It's a cup final for us as well," I replied. "If we win we will be virtually safe."

Looked like a good game was in the offing.

I wanted to know what it was like dealing with Saints' new boss Glenn Hoddle. "He doesn't give much away," came the reply. Hmmmm, I can imagine that. Rather Graham reporting on the Saints than me.

It was good to watch the Boro Under-18 side reach the semi-finals of the FA Youth Cup without having to keep reaching for my notebook every second. The lads beat Newcastle in front of almost 8,000 fans at the Riverside and my Evening Gazette colleague Phil Tallentire was officially reporting on the match. Just as well, considering that I was due my usual day off tomorrow.

The supporters seemed to thoroughly enjoy the match, many of them no doubt watching the young lads for the very first time. It's been hard working plugging the lads' matches and trying to drag the fans along, but the supporters have finally responded superbly. However it reminded me that only 192 fans had turned up for one of the early rounds of the Youth Cup last season, when the Riverside had seemed like a morgue.

Thursday, March 2

I DROVE through to Middlesbrough Municipal Golf Club tonight to give a talk to the North Riding Referees Society. Well, more of a question and answer session than a talk.

I find that questions and answers always make the night much livelier than just a boring monologue from me.

Generally it went well and I thoroughly enjoyed the night. In fact the grilling which I had anticipated, and which I have experienced at refs' gatherings in the past, surprisingly failed to materialise.

However I am probably not regarded as a 'ref basher' as such, so maybe that was taken into account by the meeting. I was asked what I knew about the rules of the game, as I expected, and why I hadn't bothered to take a referee's exam. But the tone of the questions were fairly mild and I was able to convince the members that It was my job to be a reporter and not a ref.

We touched on the subject of my least two favourites refs, Uriah Rennie and Paul Alcock, and I was quite open as to why I did not rate either of them.

With the refs' questions out of the way, the subject quickly switched to talk of the Boro, which was dear to the hearts of most of the people in the room. I've always felt that refs love their football as much as anybody. That's why they stay in the game in such a capacity. On Teesside, they also love the Boro. So what followed was an in-depth dissection of everything involving the Boro, and I think we all enjoyed it. We even came to the same conclusions.

Afterwards I was delighted to be presented with an special North Riding refs' paperweight by Premier League ref Jeff Winter to mark my visit. Afterwards I chatted over a couple of pints with Jeff, who I have known for several years, and with Graham Frankland, who is also from Middlesbrough and on the Football League list.

Friday, March 3

I ARRIVED at the Evening Gazette today to discover that Paul Gascoigne had been handed a three-match ban by the FA for the forearm incident involving Aston Villa's George Boateng, which had left Gazza with a broken arm.

The length of the ban was more than the FA had previously dished out for similar incidents which had been caught on video, but not spotted by the match referee at the time.

I must admit that I did expect a three-match ban for Gazza. One reason was because it was obvious that the FA would eventually change their own stance, so that punishment for 'video offences' would reflect the suspension period which would have been imposed had Gazza been sent off at the time. I also thought that the ban would be for three matches because it was Gazza. If you are going to make an example of somebody, then Gazza always seems to be easy prey for the football authorities.

What I did not expect was that the ban would not start until March 20, which was the time when Gazza was due to return to playing. It meant that the FA had effectively imposed a six-match ban, instead of three. My first reaction was that it was vindictive. When I had cooled down, I settled for the fact that it was simply unfair.

I can't ever remember the FA deliberately delaying a ban to wait for a player to recover from injury. After all, in Gazza's case the injury was punishment enough, especially after the stop-start season he had suffered. When I arrived at Rockliffe Park, assistant boss Viv Anderson had a similar reaction. He said that it looked as if Gazza had been made a scapegoat and he questioned the wisdom of the decision.

I was still at the training headquarters when Adrian Bevington from the

FA rang me. He knew that I would be looking for a comment, and had pre-emptied my call.

I really appreciated him ringing, especially as he did go to some lengths to give the FA's side of things. He stressed that Gazza was not being made a scapegoat, and that the same punishment which had been metered out to the Boro midfielder, would be given all to all future law-breakers who were caught out by video.

I respected Adrian's comments, while being unable to agree with the 18-day gap before the ban would start. I wondered what would have happened to Gazza if he had elbowed Boateng instead of using his forearm.

After chatting to Adrian, I suddenly realised that it was 10.25am. The dreaded deadline was almost upon me. I had to dash out to the car and quickly phone the story over to the Evening Gazette's copy department. It was a bit of a panic but I was just in time.

The rest of the day was quite leisurely. The Boro players were not due to arrive at Rockliffe Park until late morning, prior to their afternoon flight to Southampton, so I had no time to wait for interviews. I drove back to Middlesbrough and managed to clear my desktop by the end of the day. Which was nice.

Saturday, March 4

REPORTING on matches at The Dell is not for claustrophobics. I joined the assembled multitude as we crammed like sardines into the minuscule Southampton press box, which at best resembles squeezing into a strait jacket.

The long thin press box is so narrow that, once you have plonked your backside on one of the uncomfortable wooden stools, you can't even extend your A4 notebook out in full in front of you. So you have to jot down your notes sideways, while elbowing your nearest neighbour in the ribs at the same time. You also pray that nobody around you passes wind at any time during the game.

If Boro had tried to persevere with a press box like that, then they would have failed. The fire brigade officers on Teesside which have condemned it long ago.

However Southampton have no choice but to maintain their press box as an ongoing facility, while they await the building of their new ground. I accept that they can do nothing about it, though I won't look forward to sitting in it again next season, even if it will be for the very last time. Southampton can't do anything to improve the view either. I found myself sitting in front of a vertical 12-inches wide strip of wood which blocked my immediate view out of the press box. In addition, when I turned my head to look at the pitch, I could not see the left hand goal for an ornate stanchion which was supporting the main stand.

However Sports Gazette readers should feel assured that my match report was near perfect. I think!

It's the same for everybody in the press box, of course, even the Chinese reporter who was sitting a few seats away from me. He was phoning over his copy in his own language. To whom? I found it all rather unusual. There weren't any Asian players in either of the two squads.

Despite their accepted problems with the press box, it must be stressed that Southampton are one of the friendly clubs in the Premier League.

They look after you very, very well, from the minute you walk in the door, as I discovered. I realised that I had forgotten to send a fax during the week requesting my press pass for the match. There are some grounds where this could be a major problem. But I was in luck. The lady in reception was most helpful and quickly drew up a press pass for me.

Once inside the press room I bumped into the effervescent Rachel Whatley, formerly with Century Radio, and now working and living in Southampton. Rachel used to travel the length and breadth of the country with us, following the Boro, until her move south. However she was keen to see everybody again and the feelings were reciprocated. Rachel revealed that she was off to the United States next week for three weeks of reporting on tennis tournaments. Not bad if you can get it.

I also had a brief chat with former Boro midfielder David Armstrong, who has been living on the South Coast for several years now. He has put on a bit of weight, but looks well. He was working for a local radio station and I could hear his forthright comments in the press box during the match.

Then Gary Gill from Radio Cleveland arrived, having driven the 300-odd miles by himself and facing the return trip also on his own. Not a journey I would have fancied in similar circumstances. I arranged to contact Gary on Monday to discuss his plans to represent the Boro in the London Marathon.

Len Shepherd had driven me in some comfort to the South Coast and we were accompanied by Nigel Gibb and Nick Wood from the Northern Echo.

Before the match I was given permission to go down to pitchside for a photo shoot to get a few pictures for inclusion in this book. Fortunately a few of the Boro players stopped for shots as they were running out on to the pitch for the pre-match warm-up.

The match itself was not particularly exciting, though Boro avoided defeat on the tight pitch and drew 1-1, Hamilton Ricard scoring from the penalty spot.

After the game Bryan Robson came into the press room and did his bit, though I missed the opportunity to listen to what Saints boss Glenn Hoddle had to say. However, I did see Hoddle and his amiable No.2 John Gorman walking around the small stadium and conducting radio interviews.

I had asked the press stewards for an interview with Dean Gordon, who had made his Boro comeback in the game following six months on the sidelines following a cruciate knee ligament injury.

So I was ushered, along with Nick Wood and Gordon Cox, to an area near the Boro dressing room, from where Deano eventually appeared. He was bubbling as ever, and provided plenty of good quotes.

I also did an interview with Colin Cooper and chatted with Brian Deane, who was making his comeback after a rib injury. Brian was relatively satisfied with the afternoon's events, but felt that Boro should have won it.

Just as we were preparing to leave, I bumped into Stuart Ripley. It was good to see him again, though I have had the chance to chat to him several times over the years since he left the Boro. Stuart, who was injured and could not play in today's match, was looking out for his old teammate Gary Gill, so I directed him to the press box.

On the way out of The Dell, Nick and I stopped to admire the model of Southampton's new stadium. It looked remarkably similar to the Riverside, being a 32,000 all-seater and fully enclosed. It was due for completion at the end of next season.

I had secured the short straw and was driving home, and it was around 6.15pm when we got away. There was only one incident of note, when an ice-cream van without lights suddenly pulled out in front of me on to the A46 near Warwick. I managed to avoid a three vehicle pile-up with Mr Whippy and the car in front of me, though unfortunately my emergency stop awoke the lads who were asleep in the back. They were annoyed, as well they might be, because I did not stop to buy a couple of 99s.

Eventually we did stop, at Trowell, for a mushroom double Swiss meal in Burger King, and then finished off the rest of the journey on virtually empty roads. It was 11.45pm when I arrived home and quite a bit later when I crawled into bed.

Monday, March 6

I DROVE up to the site of the former Ayresome Park stadium with Evening Gazette photographer Steven Brough today for a photo-shoot. Boro were unveiling their new Holgate leisure wear and had selected the houses on the 'Ayresome Park Estate' as a back-drop for Curtis Fleming and Robbie Mustoe to be photographed modelling some of the new gear.

Residents in the houses must have wondered what on earth was going on as Curtis and Robbie occasionally stripped to the waist in the streets to change their shirts in front of a gathered horde of cameramen, photographers and assorted others.

I was not too interested in the leisure wear, but was keen to talk to Gary Gill from Radio Cleveland, who I knew was also attending the shoot.

Gary had accepted an invitation from the Boro some time ago to officially represent them in the London Marathon, and I wanted to talk to him about his training schedule, and exactly how he felt about the daunting prospect of running 26 miles non-stop.

However it was blowing a gale around the houses where the photo-shoot was taking place, so I arranged to ring Gary on his mobile later in the afternoon, once Steven had taken a picture of Gary in his running gear. If I had tried to conduct an interview in the street, I would not have been able to keep the pages of my notebook still in that wind.

When I phoned Gary, he told me that his only previous experiences of marathons was the chocolate bar now known as Snickers.

However it turned out that Gary was preparing properly for the London Marathon with a detailed training schedule, though he had not been happy to read in the Southampton matchday programme on Saturday that the Saints' official representative in the event was a regular marathon runner.

However Gilly had set himself a target of finishing in less than four hours and was ready to give it his best shot.

I also rang Ian Benoliel, who was one of the seven Boro fans who had appeared on Sky TV'S Soccer AM on Saturday morning. The other lads were Nigel Batchelor, Colin Howell, Kevin Leonard, Mark Gibson, Shane Myers and Mark Everton.

Ian's long trip to Southampton at the weekend, which included a diversion on the way to Sky's TV studios outside London, was now followed by a business trip to Scotland.

He was driving up and down the glens when I spoke to him on his mobile, so I kept losing his signal. However I continued ringing back and we managed to complete a half decent interview with a little perseverance.

Ian and the lads had thoroughly enjoyed their TV debut, and appreciated the chance to meet up with Gianluca Festa, who had also been a guest on the programme. Boro's Italian defender had been able to fit in the trip to London because he was sidelined through suspension.

I also spoke to Academy director Dave Parnaby on the phone to pick up the latest on the youth team scene. I needed to make the call because I had been unable to drive up to Hurworth this morning for various reasons. My Evening Gazette colleague Andrew Wilkinson had travelled to interview Bryan Robson instead, to pick up the day's back page lead.

Tuesday, March 7

I TOOK advantage of a chat with Steve Vickers at Rockliffe Park to grab a few useful quotes for tomorrow's Evening Gazette. I needed a story to cover for the fact that the players would be on day off.

Steve had returned to the Boro starting line-up at Southampton on Saturday, after finally recovering from a torn Achilles, and had played so well that I had no second thoughts about giving him the man of the match award.

Steve is one of those players who never gets fazed, whatever is happening around him, and he can always be relied on to give interviews even when things are going badly.

However on this occasion things were going well, and Steve was happy to stop and give his views on the latest developments. Naturally he was delighted to be back in action and, as Dean Gordon had done in Saturday's interview at The Dell, stressed that he had never felt that Boro were ever involved in a relegation battle.

The players were more positive about the overall situation than I was, but perhaps that was a good thing. You wouldn't have wanted it to be the other way around. However I was still not happy, just seven points above the bottom three, especially as most of the clubs below Boro were continuing to pick up points.

Gordon Cox and I had gone in to see Bryan Robson earlier, without the company of PR officer Louise Wanless, who was visiting the dentist.

Robbo went into some detail about the amount of scouting that he and coaches Viv Anderson and Gordon McQueen had carried out since Christmas. The Boro boss was particularly appreciative of the fact that there had been no mid-week games. The trio had never missed an opportunity to take in games all over Britain and the Continent, having spent a helluva lot of time both on the road and in the air.

I gathered that the list of potential summer targets which they had been compiling was already huge, as a result of all this advance work. But I wasn't able to prise out the names of any of the men on the list.

Robbo was also enthusing about Christian Ziege, who had emerged as such an important member of the squad during the season. The Boro boss was particularly delighted about the way in which the German was scoring a glut of goals in training.

Bryan said: "Christian scores goals for fun. Sometimes he powers them in. Sometimes he just strokes them home. He's such a quality player. In fact I'm thinking of playing him at centre-forward."

I knew that Robbo was talking tongue in cheek, but the more I thought about the idea on the drive back to the Evening Gazette, the more I liked it. At the very least, Ziege could be pushed into an attacking midfield role.

Before lunch I worked on finalising arrangements to travel to London on Friday to watch Cornelius Carr's next world title defence against the South African Ruben Groenewald at the York Hall, Bethnal Green.

No sooner had the arrangements been completed with the Evening Gazette's travel agents, than Cornelius phoned me out of the blue to announce that the fight was off. He had damaged his hand in training and had been told to rest it for six weeks.

Naturally Cornelius was gutted. All that training wasted, not to mention the loss of his purse. However it was good of him to ring and fill me in with the details. I would have to write up the story for tomorrow's Evening Gazette, bearing in mind that I had already missed one edition and was close to another. However my first job, upon putting the phone down, was to cancel my hotel and train tickets to London!

Constant interruptions during the afternoon meant that my Paylor on Wednesday column was rather late in being completed. When you are behind with your work, it's amazing how you get more phonecalls than usual. When the column was finally completed, I started work on writing up the whole of Saturday's Dean Gordon interview as a Pink feature. At the end of the day I left the office somewhat narrow eyed.

After tea and a much needed snooze, I phoned former world quadrathlon champion Brenda Holliday for an interview for the forthcoming Teesside's Sporting Greats book. As with all the people I have interviewed for the book, Brenda had a great story to tell. In winning the world title she had swum two miles in the sea off Brighton, walked 31 miles to Tunbridge Wells, cycled 100 miles around Brands Hatch and then run a marathon to Gravesend. And all in less than 20 hours. Wow!

Sounds like a good training programme for the Boro squad in July.

Wednesday, March 8

I COMPILED my weekly letters column in late morning, and decided to use one about Juninho as the lead letter. I had personally received only a couple of letters this week, which was true to form. When Boro are doing badly, we are flooded with letters. When they are on an unbeaten run, we don't receive many at all.

So I took this particular letter from the small pile which had been sent in for publication in the Sports Gazette. The letter writer was desperate for Boro to hang on to Juninho, and pressed his case at great length.

I did not agree with the thoughts expressed in the letter but I felt that it was well written, and was worthy of highlighting. I knew that there was still a wealth of support for Juninho on Teesside and that many fans supported the views in the letter. At the same time, I did not believe that the majority of fans believed that Juninho was the same player who had excited them three years ago and helped the club reach two Wembley finals.

Still a good player, yes, and he could a valuable asset in any team, provided the price was right. But Juninho had generally failed to deliver on his return to the Boro, despite his efforts. I felt that the £5.9m fee which had been agreed with Atletico Madrid could be better spent at the end of the season, unless Juninho could find another gear in the next two months. From street conversations, I was beginning to feel that most fans now felt the same way.

It would be a sad way for the Juninho and Boro love affair story to come to a close, but it's a fact that there is little sentiment in football.

Despite my problems in putting the letters column together, it was a very productive day because I had a bit of time on my hands. There was no need to go up to Hurworth, so I wrote up Steve Vickers' quotes from yesterday and then phoned David Geddis for a report on the reserves' game at Bradford City last night.

Boro had lost 2-1 to a late goal and, while David was disappointed with the result, he was full of praise for the overall effort and performance from his young side.

During the morning we had a visit at the Evening Gazette sports desk from a works experience girl named Robyn, who had arrived all the way from Louisiana in the United States. She was staying with relatives in Middlesbrough, and had been to see one of the Boro games during her stay, but couldn't remember the opposition or the score! However she was good company, and fortunately did not bore us all with tales of American football.

On the evening I drove through to the Castle and Anchor in Stockton to meet up with Alastair Brownlee, Gordon Cox and the rest of the lads for our regular night-out. There was only one subject as ever, and it was good to see that the general mood was a lot healthier than it had been on the previous occasion. The general consensus was that we would be watching Premier League football again at the Riverside next season.

Friday, March 10

I HAD another mad panic to make sure that the back page story was phoned over to the Evening Gazette on time for the first edition.

Curtis Fleming had agreed to give a pre-match interview at Rockliffe Park to Alastair Brownlee, Gordon Cox and myself, but stressed that he needed to change into his training gear first.

You can always bank on Curtis sticking to his word, but I was getting a little worried before he finally arrived at 10.25am to talk to us about the Arsenal game and Marc Overmars, Dennis Bergkamp and Co in particular.

Bryan Robson had already stressed that Curtis would be carrying out a man-marking job on Overmars, if the Dutchman was playing, and I needed some decent quotes from which to develop a lead story for tomorrow night's Sports Gazette.

Fortunately Curtis was in a positive frame of mind, as ever, and was genuinely looking forward to the game. So his quotes were worth waiting for.

Afterwards, I made the usual dash to the car to phone over today's story, which told of Keith O'Neill's trip to London to see a back specialist. Keith was hoping to get to the bottom of his niggling problem for once and for all.

Robbo had earlier given us his pre-match briefing from behind a mound of videos which were piled high on his desk. The video season had arrived. Agents everywhere were sending films of their clients around every club in Europe in the hope that some manager, somewhere, would see something that he liked.

I had already asked Robbo if he was interested in Norwegian striker Rune Lange, who had been strongly linked with the club.

"I'll tell you after I've looked at the video," he said, taking it from the top of one of the piles on his desk.

Robbo then proceeded to run through the names of all the other players featured on the videos on his desk. I hadn't heard of any of them, and I suspected that he hadn't either.

They had all arrived in the morning post. However Bryan did stress that he would try to look at as many of them as possible.

He said: "I would need around 60 hours a day to look at all the videos. I've gone through 15 already this week."

There was nothing which had taken Bryan's fancy this week, but then he had already compiled a potential list of summer targets from the personal trips that he and his coaches had made over the past few months.

While I was waiting for Curtis, Ron Bone came over for a chat with Alastair and stressed that one of the four Brazilian teenage trialists was looking good in training. Maybe there was another South American youngster heading towards the club.

Sunday, March 12

THERE were smiles all-around on Teesside as Boro finally ended the Arsenal hoodoo by beating the Gunners by 2-1 at the Riverside.

However not everybody was happy. A few of the London-based hacks who had travelled North were none too pleased to have given up their Sunday.

Arsene Wenger was none too pleased afterwards, either. The Arsenal boss had not seen his side win away from home since early December, and their chances of finishing in the top three Champions League positions in the Premiership were diminishing.

Wenger blamed his side's inability to take their chances, which was fair enough. This was the main reason why they lost the game. However Wenger summed up the way in which he was under pressure by criticising the officials for bad decisions. It was a little out of character.

Otherwise there were smiles in and out of the press room. The fans were treated to a great game on the hottest day so far this year, while the players played out of their skins, particularly in the second half.

Paul Ince and man of the match Hamilton Ricard scored the goals, though Dennis Bergkamp pulled one back and gave us all a nervous final 20 minutes.

Bryan Robson had been heard to say before the game: "I have got a feeling, this is the one."

The Boro boss could not have been more correct. As we waited for his arrival in the press room, the biggest smile of all belonged to PR officer Louise Wanless.

She said: "As soon as Bryan comes through the door I'll tell him to smile. If I had a party hat, I'd put it on him."

The point of Louise's comments was to reflect the fact that Robbo's TV mannerisms portrayed him as a dour, often dull individual.

It could not be further from the truth, especially when things were going well within the club. He has an excellent sense of humour and is usually very quick with his quips around the club. Maybe there was a good argument for Robbo improving his technique in front of the cameras.

Saturday, March 18

ONE of the biggest problems in driving to The Stadium of Light is finding somewhere reasonable to park within adequate hiking distance of the ground.

I drove towards the stadium from the west, but did not fancy any of the roads in front of dodgy looking locked-up premises, and headed for the city centre instead. I eventually found a secure car-park on the fringe of the shopping area which cost £4 for the afternoon, and then walked over the Wearmouth Bridge in the direction of the ground. It was then that I discovered a myriad of factory-dominated side streets. Not only would they have done nicely as a parking spot, but they would also have saved the Evening Gazette £4.

It was stifling driving up the A19 in the hot sunshine, and I made the mistake of leaving my jumper in the back of the car. It was not a good decision, because the blustery wind was very cold. It turned out to be rather uncomfortable sitting half naked in the shade in the press box, especially as I could see that half of the stadium was bathed in bright sunshine throughout the game.

As soon as I had arrived at the stadium I met up with the Boro PR team, who were walking around the ground.

I had spent the week painting and decorating the hall, stairs and landing at home, so I inquired whether I had missed anything.

"Nothing" was the answer. Maybe I had selected the right week to take off work, especially for the purposes of this diary.

The Sunderland press room is much bigger and better than Boro's, though there was a similarity in that there was no access to players afterwards. We did ask for Christian Ziege to attend for an interview, though he did not show, probably because he was having treatment for a dead leg suffered in a collision with Sunderland goalkeeper Thomas Sorensen as he was scoring his equalising goal in the 1-1 draw.

There was plenty of food available before the game, though all that was on offer at half-time was potato and leek soup and a roll, which was unusual. However it was gratefully accepted, because I was frozen to the bone.

Before the game it was good to have a chat with John Hendrie, who was doing some commentary work for Tyne Tees TV, before appearing on the Cafe Sport programme tomorrow afternoon. John seemed to have moved away from the coaching side of football following his managerial stint at Barnsley, and was now keeping reasonably busy on the media side of the game.

The press box at The Stadium of Light is situated on the lower tier of the main stand, and necessitates a difficult walk through the massed ranks of Sunderland supporters in the concourse in order to reach it. However the facilities are fine and the view is half decent.

At the end of the game, the travelling Boro fans were locked in for what seemed an unnecessarily long time. The fans could see us hacks grafting away in the press box once the rest of the stadium had cleared, and began chanting Bernie Slaven's name. The Living Legend gave them the customary wave.

However I could not see the point of locking in the fans for 20 minutes or so, especially as it would make them easier to be identified when they eventually walked out en masse. However I heard no reports afterwards of any aggro - certainly not like that which had followed Boro's 2-1 win at the stadium two years ago.

Bryan Robson was first into the press conference and spoke well. However, he dodged the last question when asked by the doyen of sports writers, Bob Cass, what he had thought about referee David Elleray, who had a poor game.

"I'm not getting involved with that," said Robbo. "I have had too many fines."

"Go on Bryan," shouted Ray Robertson from the back, which created a bit of mirth.

But the Boro boss was happy simply to praise his players.

Peter Reid's interview was punctuated throughout by an irritating ringing mobile phone which came from the other side of the partition which split the press room into two.

"That's got to be the worst phone ring I have ever heard,." said Reid, and it was impossible to disagree with him.

Still the phone continued ringing.

Eventually, Tyne Tees presenter Jeff Brown pointed out that it was Tim Rich's phone which was annoying everybody. But Tim, from the Newcastle Journal, remained unmoved as he sat taking notes on the front row and was oblivious to the fact that everybody else would have preferred to see him disappear and answer the damn phone.

I left the stadium at 6pm, and bumped into regular Boro fan Gary Thornburn outside, plus office staff Yvonne and Jane from the football club. The general feeling was that the draw was a good result, even though Boro should really have won it.

The drive back home was a doddle, once I had finally reached the car in the otherwise deserted car park, and a mushroom double Swiss and large fries from Burger King finished the day off nicely.

Monday, March 20

NEIL Maddison was sporting a shiny, navy blue foot today as a result of being caught by a mistimed tackle during Saturday's derby game at Sunderland.

The Boro midfielder displayed his 'trophy' as he limped through the reception area at Rockliffe Park, with one sock off and the other on. His foot was literally bruised from one end to the other.

He said: "It happened in the first ten minutes, but I just got on with the game. I didn't even dare take my boot off at half-time because I knew that it would swell up."

Neil had battled through the pain barrier and in the event had been one of Boro's top two performers in my book, second only to skipper Paul Ince.

His determination summed up the current mood in the camp. You could tell that every player was champing at the bit to play his part. None more so than Maddison, who had to wait a long time this season for a decent run in the side, but who had been one of the major reasons for the recent unbeaten run.

Gordon Cox and I took advantage of his arrival to interview Maddo about the Sunderland game, and about the team's future prospects. As ever, he spoke well and with real conviction.

There was only one interruption, from an angry Gary Pallister, who complained that it seemed that police speed cameras were always set up in Hurworth at a time when the Boro players were coming in for training.

He had a point. The patrol cars with their speed cameras were regularly in operation in two different parts of Hurworth, but never at what might be regarded as a sensible time when the children were going in to school. They were more likely to be found between nine and ten o'clock, when the roads were quiet.

I must admit that I always drove relatively slowly through Hurworth, because I enjoyed the atmosphere of the village so much. But I doubly checked my speed in the vicinity of the potential speed traps, because I simply could not afford to risk losing my licence and be expected to carry out doing my job.

Earlier, Bryan Robson's press briefing had started with a generally light discussion while we downed a welcome cup of tea.

Haircuts had started off the chat. David Beckham had displayed his new £300 close crop over the weekend, while Robbo was sporting the shortest cut I had seen since he arrived at the club.

"I've been to a different hairdresser," said Bryan.

You could tell. It was particularly short on the sides. He seemed happy with it, but only just.

He added: "When the razor came out I had to hold my hand up and point out that I was 43, and not 23."

The discussion subject then switched to Christian names, after it was stressed that Brooklyn Beckham had had a similar haircut to dad. We did run through a list of names which some people, not too far away from Robbo's room, might select for their own children. Too irreverent to mention here, unfortunately.

Once the tea was consumed, Robbo stressed that he had decided not to enter the transfer market before Thursday's deadline. I suspected that there was not much money in the coffers, in any case.

I knew that Robbo had already drawn up an extensive list of potential targets, but it made sense to delay any new signings until the summer, especially as the team was playing well at the moment.

Back at the Evening Gazette, I received the usual flood of phone calls which normally come in following a week's holiday. Unfortunately very few of them were offering stories. I also had to wade through a bit of correspondence, including criticism of my recent comments about Juninho.

It was disappointing. I believed that many fans were still blinkered about the Brazilian's current level of contribution. I knew that he was capable of playing a lot better but only he could unlock the door to improved performances. It was silly for fans to claim that Juninho would do better with better players around him. The truth was, if he was playing well, he would look great with lesser players around him.

At this rate it was a racing certainly that Juninho would be going back to Atletico Madrid in the summer, and I felt no satisfaction for thinking this way.

Tuesday, March 21

THE morning newspapers were full of stories today claiming that Brian Deane had suffered a hairline fracture of his leg in Saturday's derby game at Sunderland.

I had reported the fact yesterday that the big striker had gone for an X-ray, so I made the assumption that the latest stories were true. I arranged for a colour picture of Brian to be accommodated in the back page before travelling up to Rockliffe Park to pick up the story.

However Bryan Robson was a bit non-plussed by the newspaper reports.

"Brian is OK," he said. "He's sore, and doubtful for Saturday, but there's nothing broken."

Bearing in mind that the TV texts had copied the story from the papers, and that the radio stations were probably carrying the same negative line, I still had a decent exclusive story informing the fans that nothing was broken after all.

With Boro on a day off tomorrow, Bryan also provided me with another story for tomorrow's Evening Gazette. He revealed that Boro had signed one of the four Brazilian teenagers who had been training with the club.

Arturo Bernhardt, 17, had signed a two year contract and was currently sorting out his personal affairs in Brazil before returning to Teesside. The lad held an Italian passport, which meant that there was no work permit application needed. Arturo had been playing as an amateur back home, so there was no fee involved.

I also discovered that Boro were heading off to Africa for a brief three-day and two-match trip in Libya at the end of the season. Robbo invited me along and I was delighted to accept.

My attempts to discover a few more details about the Brazilian lad left me with no free time to play with, and I had another rushed job in sending over the Deane story for the back page of the Evening Gazette.

Once back at the office, I had to start from scratch on my Paylor on Wednesday column.

On Monday, Bernie Slaven had provided me with a few details about his trip to Rome to see Fabrizio Ravanelli, so that was a good start.

But I had a better story to lead off the column because a firm of sports auctioneers in the West Midlands had sent me a press release to say that a number of items of memorabilia previously owned by the famous Teesside referee Kevin Howley were being made available for sale next month. The auctioneers gave exact details of all the items involved, including a silver whistle presented to Kevin after he had become the youngest ref ever to take charge of an FA Cup Final at the age of 35 in 1960.

I can remember watching that match on TV, I think, though I can't remember Kevin. Wolves beat Blackburn by 3-0 and I can recall a player from Blackburn called Dave Whelan breaking a leg, and a little winger called Norman Deeley scoring at least one of the goals.

There were an alarming number of phonecalls again today so, by the time I had completed the column and a 90-minute Internet course in the Gazette's training headquarters, I was well behind on my regular work when I left the office at 5.30pm.

During the evening I phoned Moorsholm athlete Esther Cruice, who was preparing for her third consecutive Paralympics in Sydney later in the year. Esther, now living and working in Nottingham, had just flown back from a world cross country event in Portugal this morning but was most helpful and chatty. It was another story tied up for the Teesside Sporting Greats book.

Wednesday, March 22

THE Juninho situation was quickly developing into a saga. With Boro virtually safe from the threat of relegation now, the Brazilian's future had taken over as the major talking point among the supporters.

Today I edited three letters from angry fans for inclusion in my Paylor's Postbag. The general theme of all three letters was that the Evening Gazette was helping to soften the blow for Boro eventually not retaining the Brazilian. They claimed that we were writing our Juninho stories from the club's point of view.

The claims were complete and utter rubbish. It was better for the Gazette if Boro signed Juninho, because Juninho stories sold newspapers. We had a lot to lose if the Brazilian was sent back to Madrid in the summer.

It was also a fact that we didn't have a clue what the club was going to do, regarding Juninho's future. But it didn't take a genius to realise that Boro would baulk at the prospect of paying the previously agreed fee of £5.9m to sign Juninho. He clearly wasn't worth it on his current form. However, it was a very emotive issue. Those fans who wanted Juninho to stay had become very vitriolic. But they had a right to have their viewed aired, and that's why I was printing them.

I decided, too, that the Juninho subject needed a fresh airing in the Sports Gazette, where there was space for it to be debated properly.

So I contacted two members of our punters' panel, Michael Dixon and Philip Barker. The former was very supportive of Juninho judging by his previous comments in our regular Tuesday column, while the latter was clearly beginning to have doubts.

As I hoped, Michael told me that he would definitely pay £5.9m to sign Juninho, while Philip said that he would not.

These were exactly the replies that I needed to hear from both men if I was to project both sets of opinions on Juninho. I was able to develop the theme by asking further questions about Juninho and related subjects. The result was a very revealing "FOR" and "AGAINST" article, which I hoped would be of great service to the readers.

I wrote up the feature on the afternoon and included my own introductory piece, indicating the options which Juninho and the Boro faced in the summer.

Earlier I had written up my story about Boro's new Brazilian signing, the 17-year-old Arturo Bernhardt. It made the perfect lead item for the match report from Boro's FA Youth Cup semi-final first leg at Arsenal.

My colleague Philip Tallentire had travelled to Highbury to report on the match, which Boro lost 1-0. He filed his story before nine o'clock, before rushing off to Kings Cross to catch the train back to the North-east.

The evening was again spent working hard on the Teesside's Sporting Greats book. I phoned double Commonwealth gold medal cyclist Paul Curran and was astonished to discover that he had broken his back in an accident with a motorbike in 1996, which had effectively ended his competitive career.

When I first joined the Evening Gazette, many moons ago, I spoke to Paul several times when he was at the peak of his career. I had just assumed that he gradually faded from the cycling scene as the years caught up with him. So it was disappointing to hear that he could no longer comfortably sit on a racing bike.

At ten o'clock I switched my attentions to basketball and phoned Anne Gollogly, who won 103 caps for England. It was half past eleven by the time we finished chatting. But, once again, it was another fascinating story and one which had been largely untold in the Gazette. It was all good copy for the book.

Friday, March 24

I WAS surprised to discover that Bryan Robson had allowed Alun Armstrong to go to Huddersfield Town on loan, in a beat-the-transfer deadline deal which was completed very quickly yesterday afternoon. It was particularly disconcerting as Boro were not certain to have two fit front runners to face Sheffield Wednesday tomorrow. Andy Campbell was fine, but Hamilton Ricard was away with Colombia and Brian Deane was rated at 50-50 as he battled to shake off a leg injury. Bryan admitted that he was taking a risk by releasing Armstrong.

He said: "It's a slight gamble, but then Alun needs to get a regular game and this move should benefit everybody. If we get injuries then Alun will come back to us at the end of the month. However he is not getting in our side, and Andy Campbell is ahead of him now, so this is a great chance for Alun to get match fit."

While Armstrong had gone to Huddersfield, Steve Baker had joined

Darlington on loan, and Ben Roberts had extended his loan at Luton. Steve would enjoy the opportunity to get in some first team football and would shine at Third Division level. Ben was out of contract in the summer and likely to move on to pastures anew to find himself a No.1 role somewhere.

There were no incoming players before the deadline, as I had reported exclusively on Monday, though Robbo had signed Campbell and Robbie Stockdale on long term contracts. He had also been dealing with the contracts of quite a few of the younger players during the week.

Six had been offered new deals, namely Sean Kilgannon, Stuart Parnaby, Luke Wilkshire, Richard Kell, Mark Hudson and Anthony McStea, while five other youngsters had been released. Informing young lads that they were not quite good enough to make Premier League players was one of the more difficult sides of football management, but this was Robbo's sixth season as a gaffer and no doubt he was getting used to it.

Afterwards, Alastair Brownlee, Gordon Cox and I spoke to Mark Schwarzer, who talked glowingly about the team's intentions to try to finish the season in a higher position than last term, when they were ninth.

After lunch, I spoke to former Boro midfielder Paul Kerr, who was planning to leave his role with Allied Dunbar to take up a full-time job with the PFA. He would be based in the North but would travel around the clubs.

At the moment Paul was carrying out both jobs while he worked his notice with the insurance company, so we arranged to talk again at the end of next month with a view to me writing a story.

Saturday, March 25

BORO virtually assured themselves of Premier League safety with today's 1-0 win against Sheffield Wednesday - but not everybody was happy.

There were revelations that many angry words had been expressed in the dressing room after Boro had ground their way to three points against the relegation threatened Owls.

The main argument seemed to surround the penalty miss by Juninho, which cost Boro the chance of a comfortable 2-0 lead after only 16 minutes.

Andy Campbell had put Boro ahead five minutes earlier and was then brought down shortly afterwards by Owls goalkeeper Kevin Pressman.

Most fans would have expected Christian Ziege to take the spot kick, but Juninho stepped forward instead and his effort was well saved by Pressman.

What could have been an easy win then gradually subsided into a bit of a battle.

Bryan Robson made his situation clear at the press conference afterwards. He said: "I told the players weeks ago that Christian Ziege was the penalty taker when he was on the pitch."

When asked if Juninho would be taking any more penalties, he added: "I think Christian Ziege will do that from now on."

Otherwise Robson praised the hardworking performance and another clean sheet.

Sheffield Wednesday's acting boss Peter Shreeves also insisted his team had done reasonably well, though I thought they had not done quite as well as he did. Shreeves raised a few laughs with his comments, but I felt he needed something a bit more than humour to keep Wednesday in the top flight.

The Juninho saga was again the main talking point everywhere. The Brazilian did reasonably well and was always looking for the ball, though there was little end product.

One fan, Ronnie, approached me before the kick-off and warned me not to get dragged into the battle between the club and those fans who wanted to keep Juninho. Ronnie was probably right.

"Whenever you are asked a question, just refer to the fact that we beat Arsenal without Juninho," he said.

Maybe it was useful advice, because I had been led to believe that one or two fans actually believed that I was leading some kind of a campaign to get Juninho out. Ridiculous. I was just trying to stick to the facts and the reality of the situation. It was my job to tell the fans what was going on. Nothing would have pleased me more than to see Juninho playing out of his skin and helping the team to win games.

Juninho declined to comment after the game, as might have been expected. But Gary Pallister gave a long interview in which he offered some sympathy to the Brazilian.

A delighted Campbell, who signed a new four and a half years contract on Thursday, enthused about his triple whammy. He had signed a new contract, scored a match winning goal, and been informed afterwards that he had received a late call up for the England Under-21s' key European Championships qualifier against Yugoslavia.

"I'm absolutely speechless," he said, but he wasn't really.

I hung around in the windy concourse afterwards along with the Monday paper reporters as we waited for quotes. Doug Weatherall from the Daily Mail, Neil Custis from The Sun, Nick Spencer from the Daily Telegraph and Nick Wood from the Northern Echo were among those assembled, though Spencer had to leave at six o'clock to catch his train and missed the later quotes.

It was almost half past six before I had finally picked up all the relevant information and escaped from the stadium. I popped into the Gazette on the way home to collect my customary Sports Gazette. Should be a decent seller tonight, what with a home win and a lively double paged feature about Juninho.

Monday, March 27

I RECEIVED a welcome call out of the blue from Hull-based boxing trainer Steve Pollard to reveal that Peter Richardson was planning a comeback.

Richo, one of the best boxers produced in Middlesbrough in the past 50 years, had not fought for more than two years. I had assumed that he had hung up his gloves after suffering a bad shoulder injury in his last fight, which needed an operation to pin it.

However Pollard stressed that Peter was feeling fine now and was in full training again. The Teessider was going to manage himself this time around, though Pollard was operating as his trainer and adviser.

Discussions were already planned with a couple of big boxing organisations to try to conclude a four-fight deal which would culminate in Richardson fighting for the British welterweight title.

I hoped that it would come to fruition, because Richo had missed out on the chance of a British title fight in the first part of his pro career.

Pollard rang me just as I was scanning through my Boro match report in the Evening Gazette. It was the second match report I had written, and I was wondering whether it was better than the first one - though I would never know the answer.

The original match report had disappeared from the screen on my lap top yesterday morning just as I was sending it by e-mail to the Gazette. There was some kind of a blip in the system because the match report replaced itself with a test message which was supposed to have been sent last Tuesday.

Once I had finished head butting the wall of my study, I had no choice but to dust down my old typewriter and hammer at the keys to compile a second report. As I did so, I found myself full of envy for those people who have nothing to do on a Sunday but lie on the sofa and contemplate their navels.

For various reasons, I was unable to drive up to Hurworth today, so my colleague Andrew Wilkinson went instead. The press briefing was taken by Viv Anderson, who revealed that Boro would be sitting down with Juninho AND Paul Gascoigne at the end of the season to discuss their futures.

However I still got through plenty of work on the subject of the Boro, in addition to several other matters. I wrote up a piece for the Herald and Post and then knocked out a double page feature on Andy Campbell, using some of his quotes from the weekend.

Tuesday, March 28

THE official announcement of the Boro's share sale to NTL caught me rather by surprise, coming as it did at 1.25pm - just in time to miss the main edition of the Evening Gazette by a few micro-seconds.

The official news of the Boro-NTL partnership arrived by fax from the football club, and as might be expected, was rather vague.

No information about the amount of money involved or what it would be spent on; no specific details of why NTL particularly wanted to be a part of the club.

I phoned Boro's head of PR, Dave Allan, to find out why the timing had been perfect for every single one of the Gazette's media rivals. He apologised, but stressed that the whole thing had been controlled by NTL's headquarters. NTL's local PR Debbie Calgie had also had no input into the matter.

There was nothing I could do about it but follow up the story as best I could tomorrow. However I still wrote up the basic story tonight as our back page lead for our City Late edition, which is printed shortly before 4pm and includes the early racing results. However we print only a few thousand copies, and so I could not get the news across to as many Boro fans as I would have liked.

I was particularly annoyed because I had already amassed a great deal of information on the Boro-NTL deal, partly through hard work, and partly as the result of a fortunate phonecall out of the blue last week. What was annoying was that I had the chance to print the story earlier, but had not done so because the information had been divulged to me off the record. I could have leaked it today, or even yesterday, but I had decided to wait for the official go-ahead. Too late. Maybe there was a lesson to be learned from this incident. At least I had saved face by repeatedly telling the fans that the two bodies had been in negotiations for some time.

Earlier I had driven up to Hurworth to see Viv Anderson for the press briefing. Bryan Robson was still away, and I suspected that he was on the Continent and involved in detailed negotiations with more than one player.

Viv revealed that Boro wanted to bring in four new players during the summer, and the NTL cash would help in no small way. I think the club appreciated that they needed to do something which would MAKE the fans renew their season tickets. The fans needed to believe that the value for money side of following the club would improve dramatically next season. Even so, I had personally not met one individual fan who could say with his hand on his heart that he would definitely not renew, though I knew of a couple of families who were dropping at least one of their tickets. The total cost of three or four tickets was clearly a major problem for many families.

Back at the Evening Gazette, I hammered out my Paylor on Wednesday column with a lead item about a Boro fan in Pittsburg, Pennsylvania, who was offering his 'BORO FC' car registration plate as first prize in a competition being run on the Gazette's Boro web-site.

I had to phone Teesside's Premier League referee Jeff Winter at lunchtime to check on a technical point. I thought at the time that Jeff's mobile gave an unusual ringing tone after I had dialled his number. It turned out that he was in Copenhagen.

I needed a bit of advice from him concerning the situation during Boro's match against Sheffield Wednesday on Saturday when Kevin Pressman had handled a backpass from Peter Atherton, but match referee Andy D'Urso had taken no action.

Pressman had already been booked in the game and I needed to know whether he should have been booked again for handling the backpass, and therefore sent off.

Jeff stressed that the rules of the game did not state that goalkeepers should be cautioned for handling backpasses. It made a nice item for my Wednesday column, because several fans had contacted me to say that not only should Mr D'Urso have awarded Boro an indirect free kick six yards from goal, which was correct, but that he should also have ordered off the goalkeeper.

Towards the end of the afternoon I found time to write up an April Fool's spoof for Saturday's Sports Gazette. It was the brainchild of my colleague Andrew Wilkinson, and involved the Riverside Stadium being moved 400 metres across the railway line and closer to the A66. This was necessary because of Global Warming, which was increasing water levels in the River Tees during high tides and causing potential problems with the stadium's foundations.

We even devised a factfile of the huge machine which would move the whole stadium, in its entirety, at an inch a day.

It was a bit of fun writing it; I had to hope that the people who read it were blessed with the same sense of humour!

After tea, I drove back into Middlesbrough for a charity Race Night, which had been organised at the Dorman Long social club in Oxford Road. I had sponsored one of the horses in the eight races.

Alastair Brownlee had hoped to make it as well, but he had been to see his big bosses in the South during the day and didn't make it back to the North-east in time.

However there were a lot of familiar faces present, including one of Gordon Cox's best pals, Ian Durrant, who is a horse racing expert who divides his football interest between Boro and Scottish side Hearts.

What followed was one of the most amazing things I have ever witnessed. As the film of the third race was about to start, Ian suddenly chirped up: "Oh no, I know the race."

It just looked like any race, at any meeting, especially as the film was hazy and difficult to make out as the horses stood at the start. Yet Ian knew immediately that the race had been held at Ascot in the early 1990s. As soon as the race was under way, he pointed out that horse No.4 was the winner.

I was pretty pleased about this, as I had invested £1 on horse No.4, but everybody around me was not so delighted. They had backed other horses. So, too, had Ian.

It turned out that Ian was perfectly correct with his incredible powers of identification. He even gave us the real names of the horses and the jockeys as the race unfolded, and No.4 romped home.

I've seen people on TV who have memorised the running order of a shuffled pack of cards. But I don't think I've seen anything as remarkable as Ian's feat. Those of you who have been to one of these race nights will know exactly what I mean.

Wednesday, March 29

I PHONED Boro chief executive Keith Lamb today for a few more details on Boro's partnership deal with NTL.

There wasn't a lot more that he could tell me about the deal, though we did chat generally about the club and its plans for the future.

Keith is always good for an occasional chat. He tells it like it is and always had a realistic approach - and often a new slant - to not only the Boro's future plans, but also the state of the game in general.

He did stress that the planned 7,000 seat extension to the East Stand would not be going ahead this summer despite the influx of NTL cash. However he added that the club was still committed to constructing the extra tier should England win the battle to stage the 2006 World Cup. Boro were determined to keep their place on the list of World Cup stadia. I also phoned Adrian Bevington in Barcelona to try to find out whether Andy Campbell would be making his England Under-21 debut in the rescheduled European Championship qualifier against Yugoslavia tonight.

Teessider Adrian is one of the leading PR men at the Football Association and always travels with the Under-21s. He was enjoying his first brief break in a very hectic trip since arriving in Spain, but was happy to chat. However, Adrian stressed that he had received no advance info on the England line-up, which would not be announced until an hour before the kick off.

As it turned out, not only did Andy play, but he scored the first goal in England's 3-0 victory. I picked up the news on Teletext during the evening. It was great for Andy and would give his confidence another massive boost, especially as the players around him in the Under-21 side included the likes of £11m Liverpool new boy Emile Heskey and other established Premier League stars like Frank Lampard and Rio Ferdinand.

Thursday, March 30

I SPOKE with Graham Fordy today about the team's end of season trip to Libya, and suddenly it didn't seem so attractive.

Bryan Robson had offered me the opportunity to fly out with the team and I had jumped at the chance. In return for the official invite, I had expected that I would be asked to relay information back to the club as well as to the Evening Gazette and our sister newspapers in Newcastle.

Unfortunately my plans to report back on a daily basis with the stories of the tour were put on ice, when Graham asked how I intended to relay my copy from Libya.

"I know that mobile phones don't always work," I said.

"There is no satellite link at all," said Graham.

"But surely there must be phones in the hotel."

"There are, but you could stay in Libya for the whole three days and fail to get an outside line."

Graham knew what he was talking about. He had visited Libya twice already. I was still keen to go, though wondered how the Gazette would react when I informed them that they might not receive a word of copy until I arrived back at the office.

At the same time I wondered how anybody, anywhere would ever be able to read a match report unless I went out there.

Friday, March 31

ALAN Moore was the forgotten man of the Boro this season. Having fought a long battle to recover from two major calf operations, he had gone under the knife again to have a knee problem corrected.

To say that it had not been a happy time at all for the Irish international was something of a major understatement. However Bryan Robson was at last hopeful that Alan's injury problems were finally behind him. The Boro boss was looking for Alan to get back into top gear by the start of the new season and challenge for a first team place. Clearly the ball was firmly in Alan's court to grasp the nettle and start knocking on the door again. At the same time it would be good to see him prove a few of the fans wrong and show that he could perform at the highest level when fully fit. Robson clearly believed that Alan had the ability to get back to where he was a few years ago.

With Boro's next game at Spurs still three days away, I was reluctant to interview Bryan about the match at this early stage. So I broached the subject of the overall injury situation regarding Moore, Phil Stamp and Keith O'Neill.

Stampy was another who had been so unlucky. He had started the season in the team and was flying in the opening games of the campaign. Then he began to suffer one setback after another and never had the chance to consolidate himself.

The lad deserved much better luck, though Robbo revealed that there was no magic wand to stop Phil from picking up occasional injuries and everybody just had to keep their fingers crossed.

Keith's situation was a little more complex because he was battling to recover from two or three inter-linked worrying problems in his back. He was making progress, which was a good sign, but only slowly.

The Irishman was another who could be listed as injury prone, said Robbo, but mainly as a result of Keith's whole-hearted and committed displays in which he never shirked the responsibility of getting involved in physical contact.

The trio seemed to be Robson's only current injury worries, until Gordon Cox, Alastair Brownlee and I chatted to Gianluca Festa with a view to netting an advance feature for Monday's match at Spurs. It went well and included just one brief break while Gianluca traded friendly insults in Italian with Christian Ziege.

Festa's English continues to improve and he is well capable of answering any question thrown his way. The results made for a useful feature interview. However, when he threw in the fact that he was doubtful for the Spurs game with a hamstring injury, it suddenly became a useful news interview as well.

Coxy and Ali also interviewed Neil Maddison, who was returning to full training today after recovering from a foot injury. However I had spoken to Neil only last week and so I sat out of the proceedings.

Once that I had phoned in my fresh story on Festa to the Evening Gazette, I drove back to the office to get on with the job of compiling a concise list of all the football and rugby match reports which would be appearing in tomorrow night's Sports Gazette. This was needed by chief sports sub-editor Martin Neal, so that he could design in advance the Pink paper's pages.

After lunch I wrote up the Moore story for tomorrow's back page and then hammered out a fresh story on Boro's potential summer signing spree for the main story in the Pink.

Robson had said already that he was looking for four new faces at the end of the season. But today he made it absolutely clear that he wanted to buy really big, and was looking for official backing from the club. I was sure he would get it.

This was no sop to try to appease those frustrated season ticket holders who were thinking of not renewing for next season. It was simply a determined bid to try to ensure that the club took a major step forward.

Chapter Nine

APRIL

Monday, April 3

GETTING to White Hart Lane can be something of an ordeal, whether you try to do it by road, rail, air, sea or river.

In past seasons, I've always made the trek to North London by road because all of my previous visits have been for three o'clock kick offs. But today Boro were at Tottenham for a live televised match, which kicked off at 8pm. From my point of view, it necessitated an overnight stay in London.

Today's White Hart Lane ordeal involved getting soaked to the skin several times and having most of the breath crushed from my body.

Before leaving Teesside, I wrote up today's back page story for the Evening Gazette from quotes which I had saved from Friday's press briefing. I selected some quotes from Bryan Robson calling for Boro to go out and win their first away match since October. It turned out to be an excellent choice of story on my part.

My walk from the Evening Gazette to Middlesbrough railway station had to be made in continuous rain. I was just grateful that I had packed a hat.

Upon arriving at Darlington station, I had around five minutes to wait before my mainline connection arrived to ferry me to King's Cross. Just enough time to buy a brunchburger and a cup of tea.

The train was actually early. Well, there's a first time for everything. I jumped on, found my seat and proceeded to enjoy the burger. When I reached for the tea, I discovered that the woman who had served me had failed to fix the plastic top correctly on the cup. The contents had gradually oozed out and soaked through the seat next to me. There was a huge wet patch on the seat. I could only hope that nobody arrived to sit next to me during the journey, because I was sitting in the wrong seat and the one with the wet patch was mine. I endured a few nervous moments whenever the train stopped at other stations on the way, but fortunately, I escaped the threat of a damp backside.

There was an orchestra on the train, or so it seemed. The whole journey was punctuated by non-stop ringing tones from mobile phones. If I had recorded them all, I could have composed a symphony. Maybe I was jealous, because my mobile never rang once, and I missed the opportunity to try to talk louder than anybody else when I answered it.

After arriving at Kings Cross, I was soaked again walking the mile and a bit to the Bloomsbury Park Hotel. I normally enjoy a quick kip at the hotel before heading off to the match, but this time it was impossible. Singing workmen were constantly hammering away in renovating the corridor outside my hotel room door.

I decided to make an early start for White Hart Lane, which was just as well. I was soaked walking back to Kings Cross and then caught the Victoria Line to Seven Sisters. Then I switched from the tube to the railway station at Seven Sisters.

When I walked on to the rail platform I could not believe my eyes. The station was absolutely packed, both with commuters and Spurs fans. And the scenes which followed were absolutely remarkable, and certainly illegal.

The first train arrived within minutes. As it slowed down, I could see that there were people already standing on it because all the seats were taken. The attempts of several thousand people to try to board this train were absolutely frightening. They pushed, jostled and fought to get on. Incredibly, most of them made it, crammed up inside the train just like they would have been on the football terraces in the golden days. It was obvious that nobody could move a muscle. I was certain that more passengers would suffocate than actually reach their destination.

I didn't make it aboard myself, but quickly realised that I would have to bite, scratch and punch my way on to the next train if I was to make sure that I would actually reach the stadium to report on the match. I made it on to the train, but only just. There must have been 40 of us crammed in the 'boarding and alighting' area. I could not move any part of my body. I don't know how the doors managed to close, nor how the small woman underneath the mop of black hair in front of me managed to breathe.

Fortunately White Hart Lane was only a few minutes' journey away, and I don't think anybody died. Not in my carriage, leastways.

The rain had eased slightly when I arrived, so I bought a tray of chips for my tea and ate them in the street. Mike Walters from the Daily Mirror turned up and stopped for a chat, and then Bernie Slaven did likewise. Mike had driven through London to reach the ground, while Bernie had motored through sleet and snow from Teesside. It had not been easy for any of us.

Inside I met up with Nick Wood from the Northern Echo and Tim Rich from the Journal, and also had a long enjoyable conversation with Chris Harte from the London Sports Reporting Agency. Chris, who was my inspiration for writing this book, has written three similar sporting diaries among many other publications. He told me that he was currently working on a book about his sporting memories from his long career in journalism.

The rain was picking up again as kick off approached, which was a pity because the Spurs press box is virtually at pitch side and does not offer protection from the weather. As a result I spent the 90 minutes trying to keep the incoming droplets off my A4 notepad, although it was impossible to cope whenever a huge blob of water cascaded from the roof of the stand.

As I was waiting for the kick off, Christian Ziege agreed to a request to have his photo taken with a young lad at pitchside. The steward taking the picture clearly had problems operating the camera and Christian stood there for several minutes. It seemed an age before the flash finally went off.

The match was superb, Boro winning 3-2 with one of their best performances of the season. Hamilton Ricard scored twice, while the other came from a Stephen Carr own goal. Boro were hanging on at the final whistle and I was relieved to hear it for a few reasons, mainly because I was very cold and wet.

Afterwards, Bryan Robson came into the press room and enthused about the win, but I missed George Graham's apparent sour grapes attack on the referee because I wanted to hang about on the staircase in the hope of picking up an interview or two.

A German journalist, who had asked me if I could set up an interview with Ziege, followed me.

I was in luck. Robbie Mustoe stopped for a long chat which would make an ideal Sports Gazette feature, and then skipper Paul Ince talked positively about the team and the overall situation at the club. This was my back page lead for tomorrow.

It was the German journalist's birthday, too, because Ziege and Spurs' German midfielder Steffen Freund came walking up the staircase together. So my friend was able to carry out a double interview in his own language.

I had arranged to make my way back to Kings Cross with Nick and Tim. I managed to write up my match report for tomorrow and most of the Ince interview while I was waiting for them to file their stories to their own newspapers.

We left White Hart Lane at 11.15pm and decided not to risk walking to White Hart Lane railway station at this time of night, especially as we were carrying briefcases. So we set off to walk the two and a bit miles along the well-lit main road to Seven Sisters tube station in the pouring rain.

We were about half a mile short of our destination, when a bus arrived which was clearly heading towards the station. So we hopped aboard. Nick revealed it was his first journey on a bus for many years. Shame! Amazingly there was a friendly Boro fan on board, who seemed to know more about Boro's forthcoming trip to Libya than I did!

The trip back to Kings Cross was eventless and I left my two pals at the Shaw Plaza Hotel, which looked very impressive on the outside and was a damn sight more plush than the hotel I was staying in. Maybe the Gazette can find it in their hearts to stump up the cash for me to stay in the Shaw Plaza next time.

I had another three quarters of a mile to walk to my hotel, but thankfully the rain was not soaking through my clothes.

I downed a quick cuppa while I finished off writing tomorrow's back page lead, and I crawled beneath the sheets at 12.30am with the rain blasting against my window and the window panes rattling annoyingly in the wind.

Tuesday, April 4

IT was raining cats and dogs as I walked back to Kings Cross from the Bloomsbury Park Hotel. Nothing new there then. However it was a bit of a battle avoiding all the commuters' brollies. All these people, in such a hurry. The streets had been deserted when I walked back to the hotel in the early hours.

I had been awoken at the hotel by my 7am alarm call. The window was still rattling. I showered and then ate an excellent English breakfast before telephoning my stories to the Evening Gazette following last night's victory against Spurs.

As soon as I boarded the 9am train, I bumped into regular and long-time Boro fan Gary Stevenson, who never misses a match. So he provided a welcome bit of friendly chat for the return journey. Neither of us was sure whether we had the correct tickets for this early train, and I was mentally prepared for a bit of argy-bargy with the conductor. Fortunately both tickets seemed to be in order when they were checked.

Upon our arrival at Darlington, we caught an immediate connection to Middlesbrough and I was back in the office for 12.20pm. I quickly hammered out my weekly piece for the Herald and Post and then started on my Paylor on Wednesday column.

I phoned Rob Nichols at Fly Me To The Moon because the fanzine was set to produce its 250th edition for Monday's big game against Manchester United. Rob provided me with a few useful anecdotes for my story. However he revealed that he was disappointed that the United match had been moved from Saturday to Monday for TV viewing, because the fanzine suffered from reduced sales for night games. It was a pity considering that this was a special edition.

I had been asked to switch my day off from Thursday to tomorrow. It meant that I had to write up tomorrow's Evening Gazette back page story today because Bryan Robson and the players were all on day off tomorrow. Fortunately I had plenty of Robbo quotes left from Monday night and managed to put a story together.

All in all, I was pretty knackered when I left the office at a quarter to five. But not as knackered as my dog Holly. She had given birth to three pups last night while Boro were scoring three goals at Spurs. Maybe I would have to call one of the pups Hamilton.

Thursday, April 6

CHRISTIAN Ziege was Liverpool-bound, according to the morning papers. I didn't believe a word of it, and doubted the suggestion that the story had originally surfaced in the German media.

Bryan Robson had the same reservations and was absolutely fuming that such stories had been written in the first place. He believed they had been manufactured by people who did not have the club's best interests at heart. The problem, of course, is that stories such as these can have a potential unsettling effect.

Robbo would not comment officially in detail on the reports, merely pointing out that Liverpool could not afford Ziege, and in any case the player was not for sale.

Not wanting to give any particular prominence to this story, I concentrated on one or two different lines.

Bryan talked in general about the current unbeaten run and the poor form which was shown by the team between Christmas and mid-February.

He insisted that the bad run early in the year was largely due to the injuries which the team had suffered during this period and that was the reason why the squad in general had struggled to cope. He stressed that it would have made a huge difference if the squad had possessed another four top quality players.

I had already reported the fact that Robbo wanted to bring in four new players for next season. The manager's inference today was that these new signings would give extra depth to the squad and provide the consistency which had been missing this season.

Afterwards, I had a brief chat with Gary Pallister before getting a flier away from the training ground. The big centre-back was still having problems with his back and I suspected he would not be fit to face his old pals from Manchester United on Monday.

His back had flared up on a couple of occasions during the season and it seemed that this was a problem which was not easily going to go away, except with rest. It had clearly left Pally thoroughly frustrated.

Friday, April 7

I WAS surprised to see Henry Winter from the Daily Telegraph walk into the Boro's training headquarters at Rockliffe Park at nine o'clock this morning.

It turned out that Henry had attended the Newcastle United FA Cup semi-final press conference at Durham County Cricket Club yesterday and had stopped over in the North-east to undertake a pre-arranged interview with Paul Ince.

Henry was keen to discover what was behind Boro's dramatic improvement in form over the last two months and I was happy to fill him in with the details. Not only is Henry a good sports writer, but he doesn't slag people off for the sake of it. So I knew he would give the club a fair crack of the whip in his write up.

No sooner had Incey arrived and joined Henry in the press room, than Bob Cass from the Mail on Sunday turned up. He had arranged to have a chat with Gary Pallister, and the pair disappeared up to the first floor restaurant.

Once in Bryan Robson's office, the Boro boss gave me a decent exclusive by revealing that Paul Gascoigne had suffered a fresh problem with his left arm, which he broke in February, and had spent two days in hospital on a drip.

Gazza had apparently picked up some kind of an infection, which needed immediate treatment. It was clearly a blow for the midfielder, who had received two kinds of luck this season - none and bad. However the scare was now over and I saw Gazza come in for training. Unfortunately the illness had set him back a week and he was not included in the 18-man squad which Robbo handed me for Monday's game against Manchester United.

Downstairs again, Alastair Brownlee, Gordon Cox and I interviewed both Brian Deane and Curtis Fleming to gather a couple of advance pieces previewing the game.

Both players talked well and, while it was clear they expected a very tough game against United, it was evident that confidence was high and neither player was unduly concerned about the threat from the big stars in the United line up.

Monday, April 10

SIR Alex Ferguson looked totally exhausted, knackered, depressed and fed up when he appeared in the press room at the Riverside Stadium. Yet his Manchester United side had just won 4-3 against Boro in one helluva game.

I had watched him interviewed on Sky TV only a few moments earlier, where he seemed to be quite chirpy. But when the United boss entered the pressroom he looked tired, morose and unhappy.

He proceeded to give us a long monologue about his view of the game, which was both informative and realistic. But when he had finished, the questions started from the floor, and Sir Alex became agitated and snappy.

Even the amiable John Murray from Radio Five Live, who asked a totally acceptable question about United's underpar first half performance, was given short shrift.

But Sir Alex stayed the course, to his credit, and did not leave the room until he was invited to do so by the press steward.

Bryan Robson had good reason to feel more disappointed because his team had lost the match, but was much more cheerful. He was pleased with his side's overall performance, but not too happy with that of referee Paul Durkin, who had disallowed a goal from Hamilton Ricard which clearly affected the result. The ref had also booked Christian Ziege for no obvious reason.

Ziege had got himself in a tangle with United skipper Roy Keane, whose aggressive approach had led to him being replaced by Sir Alex for his own good. The Boro fans had felt Keane should have been sent off instead, and I've never known such a vociferous and angry reaction from the home supporters when Keane left the pitch in the final ten minutes.

The match had been a classic, Boro having dominated the first half. They led at the interval on merit with a goal from Andy Campbell.

The watching press, who included big guns like Martin Samuels from the Daily Express and Lee Clayton from the Daily Star, had been impressed with Boro's first half display.

But as we tucked into onion bhajis, spicy meat pies and chocolate covered caramel shortcake at half time, I agreed with Ian Murtagh from the Daily Star that I would still happily settle for a point.

Our fears were soon realised. Boro trailed 3-1 after 75 minutes, through goals from Ryan Giggs, Andy Cole and Paul Scholes. But, in a great finish, Paul Ince and Juninho scored either side of a hotly disputed but perfectly legal goal from Quentin Fortune, and United just edged home. I was keen for a player interview afterwards, but there weren't many players around. In the event Hamilton Ricard agreed to stop for a couple of minutes, for which I was very grateful.

He answered all my questions in his best English, with a smile on his face, and I gathered a few useful quotes. It's impossible to have a full in-depth chat with the Colombian, unless you speak fluent Spanish, but his English is coming along very well and he understands everything you say.

Afterwards I drove home and filled in my match facts sheet over a cup of tea before climbing into bed after midnight. Surprisingly, despite a match of such magnitude, I did not feel that much adrenaline was running through my veins, and had few problems dropping off to sleep.

Tuesday, April 11

ONE or two fans telephoned today to express their disgust at the number of Manchester United fans who had appeared in the West Stand at last night's game. The United fans were easy to recognise because they stood up and celebrated United's four goals.

The Boro fans who phoned me didn't know how the United fans had got there. Neither did I, especially as they seemed to be sitting in seats normally occupied by Boro season ticket holders.

I could only assume that some Boro fans had passed on their tickets to United fans, and then stayed at home to watch the game on TV. That was a risky business because the tickets were non transferable, and fans breaking the rules could have their tickets withdrawn without financial recompense.

I discussed the implications of the story with the news desk, who were keen to write up an article for tonight's Evening Gazette. They did so, and it eventually appeared on the front page. The story contained a warning from the club against any fans who were found guilty of giving away their seats.

I was busy writing up my match report, in addition to hammering out the back page lead afterwards. I then moved quickly on to my Herald and Post article, before switching to my Paylor on Wednesday column. Last night's Robson interview and his criticism of referee Paul Durkin formed the basis of the back page lead, while the Hamilton Ricard chat provided me with a useful piece for my column.

Towards the end of the afternoon, I was keen to pick up a feature for the weekend's Sports Gazette. I rang Andy Campbell and Mark Summerbell, but nobody was at home.

I was beginning to think that my luck was out, when suddenly it was in. A large feature dropped out of the blue on the PA sports wire service which had been written by Damian Spellman, who is PA's man in the North-east.

The feature contained lots of fresh quotes from Paul Ince, which were clearly made following last night's match. It was manna from heaven. I scraped away all the surrounding copy, kept the quotes and then manipulated them into a story of my own. Bingo! Not my usual style, but it certainly was enough to take the pressure off me later in the week.

On the evening I phoned Carole Knight-Moore, the former international table tennis player, for a piece for the Teesside's Sporting Greats book. It was several years since I had spoken to Carole, so it was pleasant to chat about her career again. We talked for an hour and a quarter.

Carole was a forthright person during her playing days who did not always have a perfect relationship with the international selectors, but there was not much she failed to achieve in the sport and she was a great ambassador for Middlesbrough.

She stopped playing in the mid-80s, even though she could probably have gone on for longer. However now she is giving a lot back to table tennis both in coaching and promoting the sport, which is great to see.

Wednesday, April 12

IT WAS marvellous to see more than 14,000 fans brave the elements to watch Boro's Under-18 side play Arsenal in the semi-final second leg of The Times FA Youth Cup at the Riverside.

It was a full package job. Very cold, blowing a gale, and raining cats and dogs. Not the kind of night on which you would normally expect to see so many people leave their firesides to watch the team's teenage players in action.

But turn up they did, wearing their waterproof clothes and thermals, and as a result the roads around the stadium were virtually gridlocked for the best part of three quarters of an hour.

I was one of many who missed the kick off because of the heavy traffic. I thought I had plenty of time when I left the house, but I hit dense traffic on the A66 near the St Hilda's turn off, and came to an almost dead stop. Eventually, in sheer frustration, I drove off, down the slip road for the Odeon and up Marton Road, before turning left into the top end of Borough Road.

However all that I achieved was to hit the slow moving traffic coming through North Ormesby. The number of cars and swear-words uttered from my lips was higher than ever. What I would have given for a bit of proper traffic management by the police.

I did consider turning around and going home again, and I'm sure that many fed-up fans did exactly that.

However I had been invited to the Evening Gazette's private box at the Riverside and did not want to miss the opportunity of a decent night out. The box had been given over to the Gazette sports desk for the night, and it was an opportunity for the lads to enjoy a rare night out socially.

It was two minutes after kick off before my wife and I finally walked into the box, at the same time as assistant editor (sport) Allan Boughey, who had been stuck in the same traffic. Having eaten no tea, I was desperate to start tucking into the fare which was on offer.

The lasagne and chips went down very well, as did the free drinks during the course of the evening. The only disappointment was that the Boro lads did not do themselves justice. Trailing 1-0 from the first leg, they levelled the aggregate scores very quickly when Gerard Robinson scored a superb goal. However an error by Aussie keeper Brad Jones, who otherwise handled the ball well in the difficult conditions, led to the Arsenal equaliser and the visitors were always the stronger side afterwards. The wet and bedraggled crowd were given little to cheer throughout the 90 minutes, and Boro went out by 2-1 on aggregate.

The poor football was counter balanced by the antics of an over officious steward who kept us amused for some time. He kept popping up in front of the box, insisting that no alcoholic drinks should be on display. The steward insisted that he was carrying out the requirements of the Law, as he clearly had been told to do by his superiors. However I would have understood his concern if there had been any fans in the West Stand. But the stand was totally empty. Therefore the law could not possibly apply in this case because there were no fans to see the alcoholic bottles on display in the private box. Only if any of those fans in the East Stand had brought binoculars with them was there any risk of the alcohol being spotted by supporters.

However the steward would not give up his personal campaign, even when he spotted some of the sports desk lads merely drinking orange juice. He told them to stand at the back of the box, from where they could quite clearly not see the game. At least we could see the funny side and had a laugh about it.

With a day off looming tomorrow, I was not reporting on the match. This pleasure had befallen our Boro youth team man Phil Tallentire, so

I took advantage of the situation by remaining inside the box and watched the game through the window. Phil, wearing several warm layers of clothing and no doubt sucking some Victory Vs, had to brave the conditions outside.

I was amazed to see that virtually all the seating in the West Stand lower area was saturated by the continuous rain. And many seats were bombarded by constant dripping from the overhanging stand above. I had not realised that all the Boro fans suffered in this way when it rained. It reminded me of my trip to Spurs last week when I had received the same treatment.

Earlier in the day I had driven up to Rockliffe Park to see Viv Anderson for the daily briefing. Afterwards I carried out a quick interview with Gianluca Festa for a piece for the Sports Gazette, before racing back to the Gazette to write up my back page lead.

Friday, April 14

I HAD been tipped off last night that Boro legend Wilf Mannion did not have very long to live. It was still a shock to me when the news came through at 10.25am that the Golden Boy had passed away in the early hours of the morning.

I was dictating today's back page lead over to the copy typists at the Evening Gazette when the news broke.

There were only 30 minutes left before the first edition of the paper was 'put to bed', but it created one of those amazing beat-the-deadline situations at which journalists always seem to excel.

As I was relaying my preview of tomorrow's game against Coventry City to our copy department, a team of Gazette journalists was already springing into action to phone around and interview Wilf's family, friends and playing contemporaries. They quickly put together a front page lead story to replace the original story which had been planned for our Friday edition.

I had already written and stored Wilf's biography a couple of months ago. This was retrieved from my personal directory at the Gazette and immediately slotted into the Gazette on a newly designed page inside the paper.

When Wilf's death was announced, I had already left the Boro's training headquarters and had reached Neasham when the copy typist rang me. As soon as I had relayed today's back page story, I drove back to Rockliffe for a reaction interview.

Boro had just started training and so Bryan Robson and the players were otherwise engaged. But news travels fast and Alastair Brownlee and Gordon Cox had already gathered a few quotes from Robbo. Coxy replayed a tape of the quotes for me, and I had phoned them into the Gazette within minutes.

No doubt the Gazette readers would not have realised that the well presented story about Wilf's death which appeared in the newspaper that night had been hastily put together with the minimum amount of fuss and without delaying the print time.

While the writing of the stories about Wilf was rather clinical, there was still a lot of sadness over his passing away.

I had got to know him personally, having interviewed him on several occasions over the years. Wilf was a very friendly and likeable guy, who still loved his football and had been a regular attender at the Riverside Stadium before he became ill.

I knew that he had no axe to grind against the current regime at the Boro and was thrilled to be invited to attend games. However he always harboured a little bit of bad feeling over the way he had been treated by the club shortly after the war.

At that time, Wilf was a truly great world class player and should have had the opportunity to earn a bit of extra cash in his life to reflect his special talents. But Boro had always held him back and refused to pay him any more than the maximum wage, while other top players at the other clubs were receiving special perks.

Mannion did move to Lancashire in 1948 to take over a shop and wanted to sign for Oldham Athletic. But Boro always blocked the move and Wilf eventually had to return home and carry on as before. He still continued to give the club magnificent service, but always felt a bitter taste over the way in which he was treated. He did eventually receive a testimonial from Boro along with George Hardwick in the 1980s, but never had the chance to achieve the level of financial security which many top sports stars enjoy in modern times.

I had not seen Wilf for almost a year before his death and I knew that he had been very poorly. So I realised that his time was near. However I have no doubts that Wilf is still out there somewhere, practising his close control with the new lighter ball, and discovering that he could do more tricks and leave even more players in his wake than he ever achieved while on this earth.

In a poignant way, Alastair Brownlee will always remember the day of Wilf's death because the Boro TV and Century Radio man was celebrating his 41st birthday today.

Just in case anybody didn't know about Ali's momentous occasion, Gordon Cox played the "Happy Birthday" tune loudly on his mobile phone whenever we bumped into anybody within the corridors of Rockliffe Park.

It was great to see PR officer Louise Wanless back at the club after being poorly recently and she joined us at the press briefing with Bryan Robson. Louise's outgoing personality and helpful nature is a vital feature of my daily trips up to Hurworth.

Robbo talked about tomorrow's game with great confidence and also reflected on the continuing stories linking alleged transfer targets with the club. It was clear that Robbo was not keen to comment on regular press speculation all summer.

However he did tip me off that the two trialists who were at the club, the Ghanaian Emmanuel Armah and the Austrian Richard Stroymayer, had not come up to scratch and would not be staying.

Afterwards, Ali, Coxy and I interviewed Andy Campbell about his breakthrough to the first team. It gave me a nice back page story for tomorrow. Andy's new found confidence on the field was reflected by his positive mood off it, and I was delighted to see him reach this latest rung of the ladder in his football career.

Back at the Gazette, all the talk was about Wilf. We held a meeting to plan the next stage of the newspaper's tributes, and as a result several members of staff were handed various follow-up jobs .

I was asked to write two pieces about Wilf for the Sports Gazette, one of which needed to be around 100 centimetres in length in order to make a two-page special feature. It's normally difficult to write any story to such a length and it seemed a bit of a mammoth request at first. However, once I had started, I found it easy to discuss Wilf's life and playing career and threw in a few anecdotes here and there.

The second story was fortunately much shorter in length and contained some fresh reaction stories which I was able to piece together, including one from Boro chief executive Keith Lamb.

All in all, it was a hectic day but a rewarding one in professional terms. I knew that the Mannion family would be pleased with not only our high profile approach, but also the reverence and respect in which we were treating the story of Wilf's death.

It had been a busy week altogether, and after tea I was back on the road again with my boxing hat on to travel to the Borough Hall at Hartlepool for the North-east Counties Finals of the ABA Championships.

The subject of my visit was the highly rated middleweight Stephen Swales from the Phil Thomas School of Boxing in Middlesbrough.

I arrived shortly after 8pm, but it was closer to 10.30pm when Swales eventually took to the ring against Shaun McDonald from Hull St Paul's

ABC. It was a good contest and well worth the wait. McDonald came to win, but Swales was always the better boxer and won every round of an excellent scrap.

The atmosphere was made perfect by Swales' travelling band of fans, who screamed their support all the way through the contest.

Afterwards I interviewed Stephen and also his amiable coach Ron Cave, who I have known for many years. Ron, who has coached many boxers to national titles, was hopeful that his man could go all the way to the final and maintain the excellent success rate which Teesside has in the ABA competition.

It was a good night all round, especially as there were so many people to chat to. I discussed everything from football to politics with another good friend, John Dryden from the Wellington ABC in Middlesbrough, and also spoke briefly with another mate and coach Denis Power, who is now a well respected boxing referee.

There was a good crowd at the show and I spotted top Cleveland County darts player Ray Hutchinson from Hartlepool, and his brother Kevin, and we had a chin wag. Ray revealed he was in his 18th season as a county player.

Presswise there was a low turn out, though I had two sports editors to keep me company on the press bench - Roy Kelly from the Hartlepool Mail and Neil Watson from the Sunderland Echo, both of whom were reporting on the fortunes of boxers from their own circulation areas.

By the time I had finished my interviews, strolled to my car on the road above Hartlepool Fish Sands and driven home, it was approaching midnight. I quickly rattled off my report over a cup of tea and was in bed shortly after the bewitching hour.

Saturday, April 15

JUST when you start to look forward to throwing away those winter woollies, the cold and rain returns with a vengeance.

The torrid 90 minutes of Boro's disappointing defeat at Coventry City was certainly the coldest match I have endured so far this season.

My feet had gone numb long before the end of the game and I found it difficult to talk coherently once I had returned to the relative warmth of the press room after the match.

Ironically there had been no warning of the Arctic conditions when I left home in bright sunshine on the early morning. However I have learned from bitter experience never to be under-prepared, and I was still wearing all my layers and carrying a pullover for good measure.

Len Shepherd's son Andrew joined Nigel Gibb, Nick Wood from the

Northern Echo and I in the car, so we had a full load of five for the trip to the Midlands. The weather grew worse the further south we travelled and by the time we had reached Coventry, it was raining constantly.

We managed to find a parking place in Highfield Road of all places, though it necessitated a long walk around to the other side of the ground in the pouring rain.

Highfield Road is one of those stadia which has not yet been redeveloped, and so the press facilities tend to be a bit basic, though perfectly adequate. We were delighted to see that hot coffee and tea were available in the press room when we arrived shortly after 1pm, plus two huge plates of assorted biscuits. I ate so many of the biscuits, most of which were dunked in my tea, that I was unable to find any extra space to consume my regular pre-match Snickers bar. I worried at the time that this might lead to an under-par Boro performance and I was proved right. Sorry lads, it was my fault. I ate too many biscuits.

I delayed taking my seat in the stand for as long as possible because of the cold and damp. As soon as I did find a seat, I was warmed by the sounds of Jimi Hendrix on the Tannoy. Nick remarked that this was probably the first time that a Hendrix record had been played at a football ground since his death in 1970, and it was impossible to argue, mainly because I was too cold to talk anyway.

The match did not start until six minutes past three in order to remember the anniversary of the appalling Hillsborough disaster, which occurred 11 years ago to this day.

Boro's players were also wearing black arm bands following the death of Wilf Mannion yesterday. Some of Coventry's players were also wearing arm bands, though others were not. I could not work out what that was all about.

Boro were never really at the races in the game and lost 2-1, their goal coming from the penalty spot from Christian Ziege, who was the only Boro player to make an real impact in the game.

I did manage to escape the cold at half time, though it was a difficult task. All the fans sitting in the corner of the main stand at Highfield Road were expected to leave through one single and narrow exit, which proved nigh on impossible when everybody wanted to go out at the same time. To make matters worse, people began trying to return to their seats, back up the exit, before I had even reached it.

It took eight minutes to get from the press box to the concourse and even then I had to pass a couple 'snogging' on the exit steps on my way out. I am sure there is not a lot that Coventry to do to improve the situation, but I've not seen the likes of it at any other ground this season. After the game Gordon Strachan entered the press room and was his usual flippant self, but there were no signs of Bryan Robson or Viv Anderson.

Eventually I went looking for vital quotes and managed to catch Paul Ince on the staircase, along with Gary Gill from Radio Cleveland. It was good of Incey to stop, especially as he had scored the first own goal of his career in the match.

Ince described everything as 'shambolic', from the game to the officials, and that just about summed it all up perfectly.

Then I managed to get hold of Viv Anderson just as he was leaving the ground. Viv agreed to answer a few questions, and I suspected from his replies that neither of the Boro coaches had attended the press conference because they feared they would have faced fines for expressing their forthright views about the officials, especially concerning Coventry's second goal. Boro were adamant that the goal should have been rubbed out for offside.

The drive home was a doddle, with very little traffic on the roads, and I was in the house before ten o'clock. The drive up the A19 was weird, due to a thin red shaft of light which stretched high into the sky ahead of us. Various explanations were offered as we approached it, and the most acceptable of them was that the aliens had landed.

However when we finally saw the cause of the light, it came from a huge flare of gas which was being burned off, probably at the works at Wilton. Once we could see the actual flare, the shaft of light disappeared. Why such a phenomenon was created in the first place, I will never know. Answers on a postcard please.

Monday, April 17

BRYAN Robson tipped me off today that Boro were hot on the trail of French midfielder Christian Karembeu, who was now with Real Madrid.

I was impressed. There was not much that Karembeu had not achieved in the game, having won the World Cup two years ago. He was also a right-sided player, which was something Boro had been lacking. No doubt the prospect of watching Karembeu would excite most Boro fans.

It was a useful tip off from Robbo. However I could only keep my fingers crossed that the story did not surface anywhere else until negotiations between Boro and Real Madrid had reached a conclusion.

Robbo revealed that the deal could all be done and dusted in about a week's time. Clearly the Boro boss had been working very hard behind the scenes.

"Once the deal is done," Robbo told me, "We won't be able to announce it officially. But I'll give you the nod and you can start to speculate about our interest in him."

When I am sitting on these kind of stories, I don't even tell my wife - and she is a Boro season ticket holder. That's not intended as a slight on my wife, because it's probable she wouldn't tell anybody. But when I am told something in confidence by the club, I keep it in my confidence.

However, I was not the only person who knew about Boro's chase for Karembeu, and I feared for the security of this particular story.

Otherwise there was not a great deal of news. Robbo denied an interest in Newcastle striker Duncan Ferguson and Lee Clark of Fulham, as had been claimed in the Sunday papers.

He did reveal that he had had very strong words with the referee and linesman following Saturday's game at Coventry, when Robbie Keane's winning goal had been allowed despite a strong suspicion of offside.

Robbo suspected that he might be carpeted for what he said to the two officials, so it was something to check on later in the week.

In reception, I managed to grab a few quick words with Alun Armstrong, who had picked up a bout of sciatica during his month's loan at Huddersfield Town. However he was due to start training and would be returning to the Terriers for a second month, which could culminate in a First Division play-off final appearance at Wembley. It gave me a useful story to 'nose off' today's back page lead.

While I was waiting and hoping that something else might turn up, Neil Maddison walked by and revealed that he was the 'King of the Karaoke'.

In order to test out this claim, Gordon Cox from the Boro website produced his microphone, and Neil gave us his version of Neil Diamond's Forever in Blue Jeans at full pelt. I must say that Maddo's version was better than the original, though I will make no further comment.

Back at the Evening Gazette, I received a call from David McVeigh from The Times, who was after a bit of chatty information about the Boro. I gave him a rundown on the Alun Armstrong situation, and he was made up.

I'm writing more boxing stories these days, so I was pleased that Tony Whitby from Middlesbrough ABC rang me to give me the lowdown on Savdhul Zaman, who was boxing in the Junior ABA Championship semi-finals at the York Road, Bethnal Green, on Saturday. Savdhul is one of a family of four highly promising boxers from Middlesbrough. I saw his elder brother Abdul box at Hartlepool on Friday.

Later in the afternoon I phoned Gary Gill for details of his performance in yesterday's London Marathon. Gilly was clearly a tired man. He was even talking slowly. He admitted that every muscle in his body was agony, and that his legs had buckled when he tried to get out of bed this morning. But then he revealed that he had actually enjoyed it.

Gary did rather well, too, finishing 6,500th out of 41,500, and came home in a very respectable time of 3hr 46min. What's more, he raised around £3,000, to be split between Willie Maddren's MND Fund and South Cleveland Holistic Cancer Care appeal.

Gilly was also the first former Boro player to finish, coming in ahead of Paul Kerr, Mark Proctor and Bernie Slaven.

Tuesday, April 18

I INFORMED Bryan Robson today that the results of a PFA based survey had been announced which revealed that the average player over 20 years of age in the Premier League earned £8,000 a week.

"Don't print that," he insisted. "Or I'll have a queue of players knocking on my door in the morning."

It was too late. The story was already being printed, and I asked Robbo for his comments.

In truth, he was happy to talk, and even claimed that players' wages would continue to rise before they eventually levelled out once pay-per-view television was fully established around the world.

Robbo had no complaints about the level of players' salaries, even though his own wages in his playing days did not match the equivalent potential earnings today.

But he did point out that he took a back seat when contracts were discussed with prospective new signings, because he did not want to be seen to be doing anything which might create a wedge between manager and player.

Robson also talked about Paul Gascoigne and the midfielder's long battle for full fitness. The Boro boss denied yet again that there had been an approach for Gazza from the American Soccer League, but added that he would be looking at all possibilities during the summer. He was determined to find some method of keeping Gazza match fit following the disastrous injury-hit year the player had just endured.

Afterwards, I interrupted Mark Summerbell while he was tucking into his breakfast of beans on toast and requested an interview. He was happy to oblige, once he had washed his breakfast down with a hot drink.

Gordon Cox and I chatted to Mark in the reception at Rockliffe Park. For a player who can be so aggressive and fearless on the pitch, Mark is a quiet laid-back lad off it, but very friendly. He was not a good talker when I first interviewed him a couple of years ago. However, like all experienced players, Mark has become interview-wise and provided plenty of thoughtful quotes.

The Durham lad had played in all of Boro's previous 13 games. It was his best ever run in the side and he had done very well, though he stressed that it was a continuous battle for the younger players to stay in the team.

The rest of the day was a bit of a battle for me. Once I had reassembled the office car which Coxy had dismantled in the car park, I raced back to the Evening Gazette. I wrote up my Paylor on Wednesday column before lunch, though I did not have time to take a break, and then got through the best part of two Sports Gazette features on the afternoon.

Wednesday, April 19

ADRIAN Bevington from the FA rang me in the early evening to reveal that Boro were to be charged for their players' antagonistic behaviour towards the match officials after the fourth Manchester United goal had been awarded nine days ago.

This was the goal where Quentin Fortune looked to all the world at least five yards offside when he netted. TV evidence later showed that the goal was in fact a good one, and the assistant referee had made an excellent decision to insist that it should stand.

However the Boro crowd were incensed at the time, and so too were the Boro players. They surrounded referee Paul Durkin and complained vociferously, in the hope he would overturn his decision.

Boro's actions were nowhere near as bad as the angry scenes which had occurred at Old Trafford in January when Andy D'Urso had been threatened in a very nasty fashion by the United players after awarding a perfectly good penalty in Boro's favour. But it did have some similarities.

Adrian had rung me to explain the reasons behind the FA's decision to charge Boro, even though they had failed to take any action against United for their more serious incident in the first meeting between the two clubs.

Adrian explained that it was the Old Trafford incident which had led the FA to introduce a policy of carpeting all clubs for similar actions in the future. It was to be their policy to charge clubs on every occasion, and they aimed to be consistent. He stressed that this was not one case for the rich and another for the poor, because United would be charged should they ever repeat the episode.

I understood and appreciated Adrian's reasons for ringing and also his arguments. Personally I felt that it was a mistake to carpet Boro because it did imply to outsiders that, while Boro had been charged, European Champions United had escaped scot free. I felt it would make the FA look like hypocrites, rather than achieve what they were setting out to do.

However I told Adrian that the FA would get a fair report in the Evening Gazette even though it wasn't up to me to write the story tomorrow, because I was on day off.

I had already spoken to Adrian earlier in the day when he confirmed that the FA were considering a report from referee Neale Barry over certain remarks made by Bryan Robson to the match officials after the defeat at Coventry on Saturday. This story had given me an exclusive back page lead tonight.

Thursday, April 20

FUNERALS are normally dreary, dowdy affairs. But there was a sense of fulfilment and togetherness as Wilf Mannion was laid to rest.

A sense of fulfilment for the wonderful experiences which Wilf had enjoyed as a player both with the Boro and with England, and also the way in which he was always venerated and treated with great esteem by the people of Teesside throughout the whole of his life.

And a sense of togetherness for the way in which the people of the conurbation turned out in their thousands to witness Wilf's funeral cortege and pay their respects to one of South Bank's finest sons.

In that respect I felt a sense of celebration; for a rewarding life which had brought such much pleasure to so many. Rest in peace, Wilf.

At the same time I was saddened to hear of the death of Ken Dodds, who was another Teessider who lived and breathed football.

Ken, who lived in Parliament Road, was an avid collector of football memorabilia long before the hobby became fashionable.

I visited him on a few occasions at his home and saw part of his huge collection of shirts, caps and photographs. Ken was well known to many top players before and after the Second World War, not only those at the Boro, but also from other big clubs.

One of his prize possessions was an Arsenal shirt which the legendary Cliff Bastin had worn in the FA Cup Final in the Thirties.

If Wilf is currently plying his unique footballing skills on some far off football pitch, then Ken is standing applauding him from the touchline.

After tea, I phoned Marrie Wieczorek for an interview for the forthcoming book, Teesside's Sporting Greats.

Marrie, who works as a coach at the Middlesbrough Football

Community Centre, has been a top quality player in her own right for more than 20 years, having played three times for England in 1980.

I have known Marrie for much of this period and so our conversation carried on for much of the evening, and covered several sporting topics other than her own career.

In fact, by ringing her, I took away her opportunity to watch either Arsenal or Leeds in UEFA Cup semi-final action, both of which were live on Sky TV tonight. However it was an enjoyable chat, and I gathered plenty of useful information for Marrie's story in the book.

Friday, April 21

IT was a particularly Good Friday for Keith O'Neill, who revealed that his back had never felt better at any time during the past ten months.

Keith returned to Rockliffe Park today following a week at the German clinic run by the world-renowned specialist Dr Hans Moller-Wohlfahrt, who had investigated O'Neill's ongoing problems with his back.

Keith described Dr Moller-Wohlfahrt as the best doctor in the world. He was clearly very confident that his problem had finally been solved and that he could get his career back on the rails.

Alastair Brownlee, Gordon Cox and I interviewed Keith after he had emerged from his car at the Boro's training headquarters. He was full of smiles and it was great to see.

The interview went very well until Alastair asked Keith if he thought there were too many foreign players in the game. I winced a little bit, but Republic of Ireland international O'Neill replied with great diplomacy. However it looked as though Keith's season was virtually over and now his target was to get himself fully fit for pre-season.

Other than the arrival of O'Neill, it was all quiet on the western front at Rockliffe Park because the players were not due to train until early afternoon, before setting off for tomorrow's game at Chelsea.

Earlier, we had interviewed Viv Anderson about the game at Stamford Bridge. He made it clear that another under-par performance would not be acceptable.

Saturday, April 22

THERE'S something about Stamford Bridge which I don't very much like. I've nothing against Chelsea, but there's something about their stadium which is unnatural and sends the wrong kind of tingle down your back.

All the better then, to see Boro score their first goal at the ground for

21 years and come away with a share of the spoils from a 1-1 draw.

Maybe I should have realised that Boro would not lose this one when I spotted a car with the numberplate PIG BA on the way down the M1. It was a good luck omen if ever I had seen one.

Gordon Cox from the Boro website was back with us today, and in fact drove all the way to London and back again. Rather him than me. However it was good to travel with the Talking Tache again, even if there were five of us crammed into the car.

We spent much of the journey on the way down immersed in a general knowledge quiz, hosted by quizmeister Nigel Gibb. Nigel always runs our quizzes with a firm hand, and reserves the right to make up his own rules. He docks points for foul and abusive language, specially that which is aimed at the question master. So the final scores don't always reflect a person's general knowledge, more his ability to keep his mouth shut when the answers given in Nigel's book are clearly contrary to fact.

The heavy rain which had waved us goodbye at 8am on Teesside gradually dissipated as we travelled further south. There were no problems on the roads and we climbed out of the car close to Stamford Bridge at 12.15pm to be greeted by warm sunshine.

I arrived in the press room before one o'clock and met up with Clive Hetherington from the Northern Echo, who had travelled down by train. He had missed Boro's win at Spurs because of illness, and I hadn't seen him at a Boro away game for some time. So it was a great opportunity to catch up on old news. Clive Tyldesley from Independent TV was also there, writing a piece for the Daily Telegraph on this occasion, and he was keen to find out the latest Boro news.

The press facilities are fine at Chelsea, though gaining access to players is difficult. There is a spacious press room beneath the main stand, leading up to a press box at pitch level. The Boro fans were alongside us in the main stand, and in great heart. I spotted two of my good pals, Lennie Downs and Gary Thornburn, who I suspect had also travelled down the M1 on the morning.

The afternoon was a potential recipe for disaster when I discovered that I was regularly losing the signal on my mobile phone. In fact I doubted whether I would manage to be lucky enough to send over the whole of my match report to the copy room at the Sports Gazette in time for publication. However, despite many frustrating problems during the first three quarters of the game, I managed to hold on to the signal in the closing stages and had finished phoning in the report by the time the final whistle went.

Boro were battered in the opening ten minutes and went behind to a goal from Gustavo Poyet, though Hamilton Ricard equalised before the interval. Boro did well in the second half and were full value for their point.

Bryan Robson talked positively in the press room afterwards and, so too, did Gianluca Vialli, even though the Chelsea manager must have been gutted at losing two potential Champions League qualifying points.

I have always admired Vialli for the way in which he handles press conferences. Even though he regularly receives several testing, and sometimes stupid questions, he never loses his cool, laid back persona, and always answers every question diplomatically without ever showing any signs of aggression or frustration.

After the conference, one of the southern based national newspaper reporters was selected as our representative to go into the players' tunnel and pick up interviews. He came back with quotes from Paul Ince and Gianluca Festa, among others, which gave me vital words in my notebook.

Coxy and I left Stamford Bridge at 6.30pm and exchanged abuse with Alastair Brownlee, Gary Gill, Bernie Slaven and Boro TV producer Simon Hanning, who were driving out of the stadium at the same time. Just how Ali manages to 'con' his way into receiving VIP car parking passes at some of the Premier League grounds I will never know. On the walk back to our car, we met up Nigel, and Lennie and Andrew Shepherd at the nearly Fulham CIU Club.

We broke with tradition and held a second quiz on the journey to the services at Leicester Forest East and our much needed KFC zingerburger meal. This quiz was even more amusing than the first, thanks to the alcoholic intake enjoyed of some of the participants.

Ali phoned us later to say he was driving past Sheffield and wanted to know if any major bands had come from that city. The answer, of course was Human League and Def Leppard. After duly receiving the answers, Ali then informed us that he was driving through the mountains. My brain was scrambled by that comment, but I managed to pull myself together before we arrived back in Yarm. I was back home for 11.20pm, which was not bad going.

Tuesday, April 25

I HOPED for news of Christian Karembeu today, but Bryan Robson stressed that the progress which had been made over the past eight days was minimal because the player's agent was ill in bed.

It was a disappointment to me, because I was desperate to reveal the story in the Evening Gazette. However Robbo insisted that the story was not yet strong enough for me to print it. He was worried that another big club would get wind of Boro's interest and try to muscle in.

Robbo was still very confident of getting his man, though he added that he had not yet agreed a fee with Real Madrid. I realised at this point that the actual signing, if it was to take place, was at least two or three weeks down the line.

However Bryan made it clear that a deal to sign Australian midfielder Paul Okon from Italian club Fiorentina was nearing completion.

I had been slipping Okon's name into the Evening Gazette on a regular basis, to alert the fans that this signing was likely to happen. Even so, I knew that Okon was not a big name, and would not lead to a rush of season ticket sales. Nor would it excite other pressmen and lead to huge headlines in the tabloids.

However, Robbo was adamant that Okon would be a useful signing, who would strengthen the team. The Aussie was also available on a free transfer, which was a major bonus.

I had been tipped off that Okon had already visited Rockliffe Park and was said to be very impressed with the facilities. Apparently he also watched Boro's recent game against Manchester United.

Time was a bit tight today, but I asked Bryan a few quick questions about next week's derby game with Newcastle before running through the rain to the car to phone today's story to the Evening Gazette.

Then I drove back through the dense spray on the A66. I can't understand why we drivers don't all slow down by ten miles an hour in such conditions. But we don't. Maybe we just like splashing through the puddles. As soon as I returned to the office, I wrote up my Paylor on Wednesday column, skipping lunch in the process. The afternoon was utilised to hammer out Robbo's Newcastle quotes in a feature for the Sports Gazette.

Wednesday, April 26

COLIN Cooper revealed that he was due to play the 500th league game of his career at West Ham United on Saturday - followed by his 600th league and cup appearance against Newcastle United next Tuesday.

The news was a bit of a bonus for me, especially as I had approached Colin only for a routine interview. The information sparked a few more questions and ensured that I was able to put together a nice feature for the weekend.

Coops is enjoying a purple patch with Boro and no doubt there are a lot more appearances to come, because he looks after himself and loves the game. In two stints with the Boro he has proved to be a great servant to the club.

I had driven up to Rockliffe Park through the pouring rain mainly with the intention of picking up a player interview for the Sports Gazette, so it couldn't have worked out better.

I had already written up today's back page story because Bryan Robson announced yesterday that he was flying out to Paris today. I used the revelation as the basis of today's piece, because Robbo was almost certainly looking at potential summer targets in the France v Slovenia international match.

I knew that Robbo had previously flown to France on scouting expeditions on several occasions this season, so I threw in a few of the names who had been linked with the club. Robbo was on the look-out for a 25 goals-a-season striker, and I concentrated on naming French forwards, including the likes of Sylvain Wiltord.

Another reason for driving to Hurworth was to gather the first interviews for a series of posters which the newspaper was planning to give away with the Sports Gazette during the summer.

The interviews were all about the Boro players' personal choice on a few trivial and mundane matters and involved a series of short, sharp questions such as did they prefer McDonald's or Burger King, or EastEnders or Coronation Street?

I devised the questions in the car on the way up to Hurworth, disregarding potential questions such as Soap or Shower Gel, Blair or Hague, and Blonde or Brunette. Receptionist Catherine Keers helped me to finalise the list.

I approached Paul Ince first. He was quick with his answers, but baulked over Celtic or Rangers for some time before finally answering 'either', rather diplomatically. Then Mark Schwarzer had a go. I discovered that both Incey and Mark were Weetabix men who had a soft spot for Jennifer Lopez!

Friday, April 28

ROBBIE Mustoe announced that he was hoping that Celtic might be the new opponents for his testimonial match, though he added that there was still a lot of work to get through on the subject.

He had originally hoped to be playing against Rangers, but this one was knocked on the head some time ago. Celtic had been the next best bet, though Robbie was also looking at the possibility of attracting overseas opposition.

I suspected that the game would now take place early next season.

I spoke to Robbie along with Alastair Brownlee, and we looked ahead to the matches against West Ham tomorrow and Newcastle on Tuesday. Robbie revealed that he was still awaiting his first goal of the season, having never yet failed to score in any campaign since he established himself in the league.

As Boro had neither scored at West Ham in the Nineties nor won a derby game this season, I was torn between which match I would prefer to see Mustoe finally break his duck. Eventually I settled for both of them.

Earlier I had arrived at Rockliffe Park to discover that I had missed a 'first' at the training ground while I was enjoying my day off yesterday. Bryan Robson had been giving his early morning press briefing when the gentle refrains of 'Match Of The Day' entered the air. Robbo was being interviewed by Gordon Cox at the time, so PR officer Diane O'Connell made a desperate bid to find the accursed mobile phone and switch it off.

However Diane could find no phone. And still the music persisted. After more intensive research, she discovered that the offensive noise was coming from Coxy's legs. At first it was thought the mobile phone was strapped to his leg. But no. He was, it turned out, wearing musical socks. Yes, musical socks. I've witnessed some horrendous juvenile habits in my time, but this one beats the lot.

Today, it transpired that Coxy was wearing a different pair of socks, which did not perform any particular tricks. So the briefing went off without interruption.

My theory that Boro would struggle to keep the Christian Karembeu story secret was proved correct. The story of Boro's interest in Karembeu had been broken in one of the tabloids, and Robson was not a happy man.

He pointed out that very few people had known about his approach for the player. I sensed there was a suggestion that the story might have been leaked from the assembled gathering within his room.

That was certainly not the case from where I was sitting. I hadn't told a soul. However I did have enough information to indicate that the story had been passed on by someone from within the club, albeit innocently, but it wasn't up to me to point the finger.

The frustrating thing was that Robson would now be less likely to give us vital tip-offs in the future, and I didn't need that situation.

Back at the Evening Gazette, I received a tip-off that Graeme Souness had watched Boro reserves in their match against Manchester United on Wednesday. Apparently the Blackburn Rovers boss had been concentrating on Boro, rather than United.

I spoke to a reporter in Lancashire who said that Souness was looking out for two full-backs and a striker for next season. Boro's full-backs on Wednesday were Robbie Stockdale and Craig Harrison, while Gerard Robinson and Tom Jones played up front.

I would not have been surprised if Souness had been running the rule over Neil Maddison, who was with him at The Dell a few years ago. Maddison would do a good job for Blackburn, just as he does for the Boro. However I wouldn't like to see such a committed and wholehearted player like Maddo leave the club.

Saturday, April 29

ANOTHER wonderful day out in London for everybody concerned as Boro won 1-0 at West Ham United. It was a glorious day weatherwise to boot.

We left the drizzle of Teesside behind us at 8am and picked up Nick Wood from the Northern Echo at Wetherby.

I had checked the weather forecast before leaving and was expecting up to 18 degrees of heat in London. So I left my coat and jumper at home.

But Nick was wearing a huge overcoat when we picked him up.

"People at work say I look like Dr Who in this coat," he said, as he climbed alongside me in the back of the car.

He proceeded to wear the coat all the way to London, despite the emergence of the sun, which was blasting in through the windows.

I had made the mistake of having one drink too many on a night-out last night, and did not feel at all too well for a while. I could not even finish my breakfast at McDonald's on the way. Shame!

However I felt fine long before we parked up near Upton Park. It was wonderful to step out into the hot sunshine. I had taken my camera, so Dr Who took a photo of me outside the ground.

Inside, I was quizzed by London based journalist Tony Flood on every detail of the latest Boro statistics. The only thing he didn't ask for was the inside leg measurements of the players.

The West Ham press room is OK, but not one of the best. Upon entering you have to walk through two back to back doors, which is very confusing. But the hospitality was fine, with two huge trays of biscuits accompanying hot tea and coffee.

The press box at Upton Park is a bit tight, but perfectly adequate, and the view from the front of the top tier is excellent.

Former Hammer Paul Ince was loudly booed by the home fans every time he touched the ball, but he had a great game, and so did the team as a whole. Boro's winning goal came from the penalty spot from Brian

Deane, after Andy Campbell had been brought down by goalkeeper Ian Feuer.

When the penalty was awarded the Boro players went into a huddle to decide who was going to take it, because neither Hamilton Ricard nor Christian Ziege was on the pitch. Juninho was playing, but he stood well away from the discussions, having missed two in a row. Eventually Deane accepted the responsibility and stepped forward. He stuck the ball away well.

After the match, Bryan Robson was first into the press room. He was asked the obvious questions. Was it a penalty, what did he think of Paul Ince's barracking and was Juninho staying at Boro?

All were answered diplomatically, and Robbo also stressed that he felt that Steve Vickers' display at the back was the best game he had ever played for him.

Harry Redknapp followed Robbo into the room and spoke very honestly. He had no complaints about the penalty and simply rued his side's missed chances.

But, like most Cockneys, he could certainly talk. He went on and on. I wanted to talk to at least one Boro player, so I decided to try to leave while the interview was still in progress. To do so, I had to force my way with some difficulty past a burly steward who initially had no intentions of allowing me to leave the room.

"I thought you were going to punch him," Dr Who said afterwards.

Certainly I had been thinking of head butting him in the stomach.

However I made it downstairs to discover that most of the Boro players were already on the coach. I managed to grab last man Colin Cooper, who had celebrated his 500th league appearance with three points.

Gary Gill from Radio Cleveland was with me at the time, but his tape cassette recorder decided to go on strike. So I asked Coops a few quick questions by myself while the rest of the frustrated players, who were keen to get away, were banging desperately on the inside back window of the coach.

West Ham employ a similar interview system as Boro and Chelsea, where one member of the press is allowed down to the dressing room area to collect quotes. The pressman who was selected was John Cross from the Daily Mirror. He returned, having spoken to Juninho, and gathered some decent stuff. So Dr Who and I listened to the tape to transcribe the quotes.

It was a quarter to seven before we finally got away from West Ham but it was a glorious night, and a fitting way to end a great day out.

Nigel Gibb had brought his quiz book and so we had a question and answer session in the car which lasted until the arrival of darkness made it impossible for him to ask any further questions. Dr Who, making his debut in one of our quizzes, quickly became agitated by the imbalance in the degree of difficulty of the questions and also the rigidity of the rules. I had warned him in advance but to no avail.

He did provide the best answer of the night, which was so good that I can't even remember it. However Lennie Shepherd was a runaway winner of the event despite having had a couple of pints while he had waited for us to carry out our interviews at Upton Park. Maybe there is a message there somewhere.

I drove home and we stopped at Blyth on the A1 for a burger. I was back in the house at 11.40pm, just as Match of the Day was finishing.

Chapter Ten

MAY

Monday, May 1

ANOTHER Bank Holiday, another 7am start. I had compiled my Boro match report and match facts as usual yesterday, but I had to write up the back page lead for the Evening Gazette before setting off for Rockliffe Park.

I put together a story based around Juninho's quotes from Saturday, and tried to ensure that it was well balanced.

I still did not believe that the little Brazilian would become a Boro player in the summer, because the fee was too high. I had a duty to pass on this belief to the fans, because it was based on titbits of information which I had picked up during the course of my daily visits to Hurworth. I have to try to tell the readers what is going on, even if the truth hurts. However I also made sure that I did not give the impression that the story was a personal opinion, bearing in mind the strong feelings held by some of the supporters, especially those who wrote me abusive letters.

When I arrived at Hurworth, I was blasted by a heatwave when I emerged from the car. It was only nine o'clock in the morning.

When Bryan Robson arrived, he suggested that the press briefing should take place in the sunshine, which was an excellent idea. The Boro boss talked enthusiastically about tomorrow's match against Newcastle United.

I had expected that Christian Ziege would again be ruled out of the game, but Robbo revealed that he expected the German to play.

"I've spoke to Christian," said Robbo, "And he tells me that he will be OK. But I'd rather it was kept quiet and so just say that he is in the squad but he is doubtful."

I didn't want to go that far because it was not quite true. But I certainly didn't want to write anything in the Gazette which made it easier for Newcastle on the night, so I had to find some middle ground for the readers which did not totally eliminate Ziege from their thoughts when they set off for the Riverside.

Afterwards Alastair Brownlee, Gordon Cox and I chatted to Phil

Stamp, who had made a welcome return to the Boro starting line-up at West Ham. It was his first start since Boxing Day after picking up a frustrating hamstring problem.

Once the microphones had been withdrawn, I asked Stampy a few general questions about his battle for full fitness. The results would make a nice story for Paylor on Wednesday.

Ali, Coxy and I also spoke to Curtis Fleming, who provided some excellent quotes about the need for Boro to put the emphasis more on winning games than on simply trying to entertain.

I could not agree more. In any case, when the team was playing winning football, then it would entertain the fans anyway.

I knew that Curtis had thoroughly enjoyed playing his part in the battling win at West Ham, while I had thoroughly enjoyed it myself from the stands. It was just the kind of game at which Curtis excelled. As far as the Hammers fans were concerned, Boro might not have looked a particularly entertaining side. But I was proud of the team on Saturday, despite the fact that they created few chances. It made me wonder what kind of entertainment some fans were expecting to see. I, for one, had been
thoroughly entertained by Boro's performance at Upton Park.

It was discovered during the Curtis interview that Ali was wearing socks which wore the word 'GOAL' emblazoned across them. Fortunately they didn't play a musical tune, but they were particularly dreadful. However, Ali revealed that the socks were being worn to celebrate the fact that he had scored his first five a side goal for four years last night. It could have been worse, I suppose. He could have had the word 'GOAL' tattooed on his neck.

Having burned my nose in the hot sun, I retreated to the unnatural heat of the Evening Gazette office. I wrote up a piece about Boro for the Herald and Post, before breaking the back of my Paylor on Wednesday column.

The usual sandwich shops were closed at lunchtime. However, having walked to Burger King through the sparse groups of zombie-like people tramping aimlessly around the otherwise empty streets of the town centre, I was just grateful that I was able to work every Bank Holiday.

Tuesday, May 2

I HAD been looking forward to seeing Bobby Robson for the first time this season, and hearing his comments.

But the Newcastle United boss failed to show for the post match press conference after Boro were held 2-2 at home by the Magpies tonight.

Bobby passed on a message via the press stewards to say that he didn't want to attend the press conference because he was worried about what he might say. I was a bit surprised. Nobody is forced to say what they don't want to say at press conferences. A simple 'no comment' is enough to evade the dodgy questions.

However Bobby was apparently incensed by some of the decisions made by referee Mike Riley and did not want to risk saying something which might end up with him having to answer an FA disrepute charge.

Mr Riley had certainly had a bad game. He had given Boro most of the 50-50 decisions in the style of the old-fashioned 'homers'. But I don't think the ref made any particular decisions which affected the result.

Bryan Robson did show up, and managed to avoid the burning question. It was "Do you accept that you got your tactics totally wrong at the start of the match?"

Boro had kicked off with a strange 4-3-3 formation, with at least three men playing out of position, and the whole team had a nightmare. The Magpies led 2-1 after 20 torrid minutes but it could so easily have been 4-1.

Finally the word was passed on to the pitch for Boro to revert to a sweeper system. Once this had been done, they began to play. However they were chasing the game for a long period and were grateful for Gianluca Festa's diving header which produced the equaliser amid much relief 11 minutes from time.

Juninho had earlier put Boro ahead in the fifth minute and went on to produce a man of the match display. I was pleased for him, because I knew he had been frustrated during his spell on the bench. His performance tonight was warmly appreciated by the fans.

The Brazilian had made a strong point in his last two outings. Suddenly I sensed there was renewed pressure on the Boro management to look again at the Juninho situation.

Many fans still wanted to keep him, and on this form it was clear that he could represent good value if a new deal could be struck with Atletico Madrid. Clearly Boro would not fork out £5.9m for Juninho and then add a similar sum in wages on top, so the original deal was still unlikely to be acceptable. Maybe a new deal could be struck.

However, if Robson intended to sever the club's links with Juninho at the end of the season, I felt that he had done himself no favours by playing the Brazilian in the past two games.

Many fans who had begun to accept that Juninho would be leaving Teesside, would surely now be believing that Boro should be busting a gut to keep him after all. And they had a strong argument.

If Juninho did go back to Spain for good, Bryan would have created a lot of grief for himself and the club which he could have avoided.

The result apart, it had been a good night out. I met up with my old pal Alan Oliver, who reports on the fortunes of the Magpies for the Gazette's sister paper, the Newcastle Chronicle.

Alan revealed that he was off to Barbados for two weeks' holiday when the season ended. I must be going wrong somewhere.

However I was delighted to see that Alan was getting on well with Bobby Robson. Bobby's arrival at St James's Park had brought to an end a long succession of managers on Tyneside who had made it very difficult for Alan to do his job. He certainly deserved a bit of luck for a change.

The Boro press box had been packed with all the major journalists from the North-east, except those who concentrated purely on Sunderland.

There were one or two outsiders, like Alam Khan from the Yorkshire Evening Post, who is always good for a chinwag. In fact I was delighted that Alam was there. While I was waiting in vain for Bobby Robson to appear, Alam had slipped down to the Boro dressing room area and interviewed goal hero Festa. He willingly handed me a couple of useful quotes for tomorrow's Gazette back page before he headed off back to Leeds.

Wednesday, May 3

DAVE Flett from the Luton newspaper phoned to say that it looked as though Ben Roberts, who was on loan at Kenilworth Road, would not be joining the Hatters full-time in the summer.

I had known that Ben was unlikely to accept the offer of a new deal with Boro if he could find himself an attractive move elsewhere, especially one with first team prospects. I could understand his decision, because Ben had a great deal to offer and was good enough to play regular league football at a high standard.

However, Dave revealed that Ben had apparently received an offer from another Premier League club, to go as a No.2. It was an interesting new development and I would need to have a chat with Ben as soon as I could get hold of him.

I wrote up all the stories today from last night's derby draw against Newcastle United, and the Evening Gazette's back page headline was 'Sign Me Up'. It was a story about Juninho's fine man of the match performance and his battle for a permanent move back to Teesside. It kept the story bubbling nicely in the melting pot, just as I suspected it would throughout most of the summer.

Friday, May 5

I CHATTED to Steve Gibson this morning about the ups and downs of Boro's current season and also the future of the club.

The Boro chairman was as disappointed as anybody that the team had not made any progress in terms of league positions, but was clearly excited about next season.

He stressed that the financial situation of the club had never been better, especially following the huge cash injection from cable giants NTL. However he warned that the club faced a major double challenge next season. As the wage bill continued to spiral, they had to balance the books and at the same time continue to make progress on the pitch. It wasn't going to be easy.

Steve revealed that the club's new signings would add several million pounds to the club's wage bill. He inferred that there would be an increase in season ticket prices. I knew that many fans would not be happy to fork out more cash, though I could appreciate the club's situation. They had to remain competitive both from the football and commercial points of view, if they wanted to keep pace with the big clubs. If Boro did not continue to expand, then they would risk going backwards.

I had phoned Steve to pick up a piece for the Evening Gazette's end of season supplement, which was called Come on Boro.

Earlier on the morning I had interviewed Bryan Robson for the same reason. We also talked about the Watford game tomorrow, and Robbo revealed that teenagers Carlos Marinelli and Luke Wilkshire were in the squad. However I knew that Robbo was desperate to win the game and equal last season's tally of 51 points, so I suspected neither of them would start the game.

Afterwards, Alastair Brownlee, Gordon Cox and I interviewed Mark Schwarzer, which sorted out tomorrow's Gazette back page lead.

On the afternoon I fitted in a trip to Radio Cleveland to record Red Balls On Fire. Jeff Brown from Tyne Tees was the other studio guest. Jeff has been a good friend of mine going back many years and so we immediately established a good rapport for the programme, which was recorded live.

In fact the Boro debate went so well that Clem and Fischer altered their programme schedule as we went along in order to accommodate all the chat.

It turned out to be a 15-hour day for me because I had arranged two evening interviews for the Teesside Sporting Greats book. I phoned Guisborough-born canoeist Ian Raspin at his home in Nottingham, and then Sedgefield-born netball player Kendra Slawinski at Luton.

I can't complain about this extra work because I love doing these interviews with Teesside's top achievers and putting their whole biographical stories together. The more people I talk to for the book, the more I realise that it was a great idea to write it. However, I was rather tired when I replaced the telephone receiver for the final time at 10.10pm.

Saturday, May 6

NOT a happy day at the Riverside. Boro were woeful in their weak attempts to beat relegated Watford and were fortunate to escape with a 1-1 draw.

After the match, Bryan Robson was handed a microphone on the pitch to thank the fans for their support over the season, and was greeted by loud booing.

A lap of honour was also planned for the manager and players at the end of the match and this turned out to be a PR disaster. The stadium was only one third full as the entourage walked around, waving, and the biggest cheer they received came from the 1,200 Watford supporters in the south-west corner.

I suspected that harsh words were said in the dressing room after the game, because it was dreadful fare in the second half. No doubt Robbo had cooled down by the time he reached the press room.

He did, however, blast his forwards, and quite rightly so. They had been very poor. The game raised new questions about Juninho's future, though Robson again stressed that the decision over the Brazilian would be made in the summer.

Watford boss Graham Taylor had preceded Robson into the press conference and was smiling throughout. He said that Watford had re-emerged as a yo-yo club and that was tremendous for them, because it meant they were among the top 30 clubs in the country.

I agreed with every word he said, though it was impossible not to link Watford's situation to that of the Boro. Robson had achieved Premier League mid-table respectability for the club and that represented a massive step forward from the yo-yoness of my time in reporting on the club's fortunes.

Yet many Boro fans were clearly not satisfied with such progress and felt Boro should be better than they were. In fact I honestly believed there were some Boro fans who didn't care which division we are in as long as we were top of the league, and therefore would happily see Boro become a yo-yo club again.

It had created the foundations for an interesting summer, especially when it came to filling in season ticket renewal forms.

Earlier in the day I had a busy morning at the Evening Gazette. After helping to fill the sports pages in the Saturday daily edition, I wrote up the Steve Gibson and Bryan Robson interviews for Come On Boro.

Then I drove up to Portrack to see Shab from MSV, who had generously agreed to sponsor this humble book.

I've known Shab for several years and he has been a strong follower of the club for a lot longer. Despite running a successful business which does much of its trade on a Saturday, he still manages to get to many away games with his son Waqa.

Shab is well known at the Boro, and is now a personal friend of most of the staff and players. In fact, when you see the huge pictures of the Boro players hanging in his purpose built store at Portrack, you wonder whether there is a bigger Boro fan anywhere. And I'm not saying this simply because he is sponsoring the book!

Monday, May 8

LINCOLN is a nice place to be on a sunny summer's night. You can see the cathedral dominating the skyline from the main stand at Sincil Bank. It looks even more impressive after dark when it is fully lit up.

Boro were pretty impressive as well, even if they were playing only in a friendly match against Third Division Lincoln City.

The occasion was the testimonial match of Lincoln defender Grant Brown, who was born in Sunderland.

My experience of friendly matches is that they are often mind-numbing and contrived affairs. I've seen some testimonials where I have struggled to stay awake.

But this match was different. There was an atmosphere from the start, both sides wanted a piece of the action, and Boro went on to win an end-to-end thriller by 4-3. I don't think I am stretching things by saying it was the best testimonial I have ever seen.

There could easily have been twice as many goals. Most of those which did go in were top quality, especially two extra special strikes from Juninho which contributed towards him scoring a hat trick in 11 minutes. I could not help wishing he had been putting away such quality goals in the Premier Division.

The game was level at 3-3 at half-time, and Carlos Marinelli grabbed Boro's second half winner. Bryan Robson pitched in the kids in the second half and they all did well, totally controlling the game as Lincoln tired.

I was the only North-east journalist to attend the match, though Boro TV had a crew there. However, at one time I thought I would not get there at all, mainly because I had no transport. There were no available cars in the Evening Gazette fleet. I did not fancy going on the train because it would necessitate an overnight stop, and I needed to be back at work early on Tuesday morning.

In the event, the Gazette organised a hire car for me. It was a smart looking Peugeot 206, with only 1600 miles on the clock. Very nice indeed.

I arrived in Lincoln in good time, but took ages to find Sincil Bank. I drove to the east of Lincoln when I needed to drive south. When I did find the stadium, I could not work out how to get to it. I drove around the back of it twice over. In the event I parked at the end of a narrow side street and walked over a bridge straddling a fast running canal, in order to reach the stadium.

Outside I met up with regular Boro away fans Glyn Davies and Julie Henry. They were both a bit depressed about the way in which the season had developed and did not look to the future with much optimism.

I respected their views but it was depressing me that I was meeting up with so many Boro fans who held the same opinions. Personally I was looking forward with relish to the prospect of Boro playing a third consecutive season in the Premier League for the first time since I began reporting on the fortunes of the club. I was not sure what people wanted, or expected, because this was the most successful period that the club had ever had in my time and I did not want to lose it.

I remembered the Sincil Bank ground well from my last visit in 1992 when Lennie Lawrence's team lost 5-1. The press box was right at the back of the main stand and the local press were friendly. However I made the mistake of taking my seat too early, and the Tannoy was loud, tinny and irksome. It was difficult to make out what was being said, though I did pick out the fact that the ninth prize in Grant's testimonial draw was an autographed Bristol Rovers pennant. I could not imagine what the tenth prize would be.

After the game I managed to gain access to the dressing room area and had a useful chat with Gary Pallister, who had been making his comeback after injury. He was keen to ensure that he did not receive any glowing headlines in the Gazette tomorrow, because he was playing his way back only gradually.

Afterwards I followed the team up to the directors' lounge, where we all crowded into a tight little room and I sat alongside Robbo to pose a few relevant questions.

The club's facilities were basic, but fine, and the reception which the Boro received was excellent. In fact the players were mobbed for autographs by hundreds of waiting fans when they finally left the ground.

It was twenty past ten when I crossed the canal to return to the car, and twenty minutes to one when I finally dived into bed. But I had thoroughly enjoyed the night.

Tuesday, May 9

ANOTHER late night, this time at the Riverside Stadium, where the BT Cellnet Awards evening was staged.

It was a grand affair as usual, with an original meal, and plenty of free-flowing wine for anybody who wanted it. I couldn't over imbibe, because I was driving. But it was frustrating to discover that the white wine on the tables was one of the best, Sancerre, which would have eased its way down my throat very well.

I had given a lift to Roy Kelly, the sports editor of the Hartlepool Mail, eventually anyway. It had taken me an age to find his house. In the event I had to ring my wife on my mobile to ask her to ring him and find out exactly where he lived.

Roy was on my table, and I was seated in between Alastair Brownlee and Clive Hetherington from the Northern Echo, so there was plenty of good crack. Boro players Alun Armstrong and Mark Schwarzer were also in our midst. Alun was still trying to recover from his disappointment at the end of his loan spell at Huddersfield, who had failed to reach the First Division play-offs after losing 3-0 at Fulham on Saturday.

Christian Ziege won Boro's player of the year award, which was selected by the fans during the season. My personal choice was Paul Ince, though I knew that Ziege had also had a very good season and was very popular with the fans.

Unfortunately there was a bit of an administrative cock-up because Ziege had been allowed to return to Germany for treatment on his sore groin. However he did send a prepared statement, which was read out by BBC TV's Ray Stubbs, who was the evening's host. In fact Ray read the statement so quickly, that I could not manage to take it all down in my trusty shorthand note. So I had to go hunting for the said typewritten statement at the end of the evening. Fortunately I managed to secure it.

Paul Gascoigne was invited on to the stage to present a long service award to Robbie Mustoe, Andy Campbell took the young player award, while the ever smiling Hamilton Ricard uttered the word 'good' 47 times in receiving the goal of the season award. Well, probably anyway.

There was a nice touch when chairman Steve Gibson took to the stage to present an Unsung Hero award to Jane Woods, the Boro's ticket office manager, for her hard work in one of the club's busiest departments. The evening ended on a high with the arrival of the comedian on stage.

I never manage to pick up these guys' names, but he was by far the best I have ever heard at the awards night. Few people escaped the wrath of his tongue, especially chief executive Keith Lamb, but it was all taken in good taste. I think!

There was plenty of time for chat afterwards, and I left on the stroke of midnight, just as my car turned back from a Rolls Royce into a VW Golf.

Earlier in the day I had been in demand by Boro TV. They dispatched a camera crew to the Evening Gazette to interview and film me in various parts of the newspaper buildings. Alastair Brownlee asked me my views on different aspects of Boro's season, in different aspects of the Gazette.

It was a bit of fun, even though none of the individual question and answer sessions took less than three takes. The longest took six. We had to walk and talk while the filming was taking place, while carefully avoiding outstretched pieces of machinery and cables which could have sent us on to our noses. Simon Hanning, the producer, regularly insisted that we had walked either too quickly or too slowly - and told us to go back to our starting positions and repeat the questions and answers again.

During the course of the exercise my answers to the same questions changed considerably. In fact I probably ended up giving answers on my last takes which reflected completely different opinions to the first takes. But we got there in the end.

In the afternoon I spoke to Steve Gibson concerning a recent report by accountants Deloitte and Touche, which revealed how far the Boro had come during Bryan Robson's five years in charge. Steve was really upbeat about the report, because he felt that it told the whole story of Boro's dramatic progress from minor to major.

Wednesday, May 10

MY mail had turned vitriolic again. If ever a team had needed to play well and win a game, it was Boro against Watford last weekend. But it didn't happen, and potentially it had paved the way for a summer of discontent.

As I put together my penultimate Paylor's Postbag, I sifted through a couple of very naughty letters. Once in particular launched an incredible personal attack on me, as if it was all my fault.

To make matters worse, judging by the fax information on the top of the letter, the letter writer was a police officer. The letter was completely defamatory. If the Evening Gazette had allowed me to print it, which they wouldn't, then I would have been able to successfully sue this guy for a lot of money for his attack on my integrity.

I'm sure that the letter writer was a normal guy, leading a normal life for most of the week. But when you receive letters like this, it makes you wonder whether some of the people who go to watch the Boro would be better off gardening on a Saturday afternoon.

Friday, May 12

BORO today offered me a place on the club's end of season trip to Libya - and I had to turn it down.

The club had been allotted 24 places on the flight, to accommodate the full party, which included players and coaches. From the start, I was on the stand-by list. I had been keeping my fingers crossed for three or four weeks that there might be a place for me. I had even been carrying my passport around in my jacket, in case the passport number was needed for the club's documentation.

But I finally realised on Tuesday that I would not be going to Libya. I attended the awards dinner at the Riverside and discovered that the players and coaches had been inoculated two weeks ago for three serious diseases, including hepatitis B and typhoid.

I would happily have had the injections at the same time as the players, just in case there was a place for me. But I was not told anything about it at the time. I know it was nothing personal because the club were happy for me to go to Libya. It was merely an oversight.

However, I felt it was unfair that the players should be inoculated, but the press should not. So I rejected the invitation which was offered me today.

The Evening Gazette supported me in my decision even though, initially, they had wanted me to go. I know that many people come and go from Libya without having the inoculations first, but on the extremely rare chance that something happened to me, I wouldn't have had a leg to stand on insurancewise.

There was another problem, in any case, when I discovered the total cost of the trip. This was my fault. I should have enquired earlier. But I don't think the Gazette would have been happy to pay the bill.

As it was, I was disappointed to miss out on the trip mainly for personal reasons, having lost the opportunity to set foot on the African Continent for the first time.

Even so, I knew I would have encountered major problems in Libya. Boro's commercial manager Graham Fordy had warned me that there was no satellite link for mobile phones. My BT Cellnet-sponsored mobile phone would have been little use to me. Apparently it was also very difficult to obtain an outside telephone line in the hotels, unless you were prepared to wait until 1.30 in the morning. So I might have encountered major problems in filing copy.

Libya apart, it was a productive day. Before going in to see Bryan Robson at the Rockliffe Park training headquarters, I had a chat with midfielder Mark Summerbell. He was a little bit down following his dislocated shoulder, which was still held in a sling. The injury had otherwise brought a premature end to what had been an excellent second half of the season for Mark. However at least he would have plenty of time to get himself fully fit by the time that pre-season came around.

Robbo revealed that Hamilton Ricard had travelled to see a specialist in London to have a suspected hernia checked out. An operation was likely. It was the fashionable injury at the club at the moment.

We also discussed the Libyan trip, and Robbo wanted to know why Gordon Cox wasn't going.

"I've got 14 charges pending for offences against camels," came the reply.

Afterwards Alastair Brownlee and I chatted to Andy Campbell in the warm sunshine outside the training headquarters. Andy had just been called up for the England Under-21 squad for the European Championships in Slovakia at the end of the month. It had been a really great second half of the season for him, too.

Then Coxy and I waited to chat to Paul Ince for the skipper to provide us with his views on the season as a whole. Paul talked positively, and quickly, as ever, but I think I got most of it down in my notebook. It gave me a good story for the Gazette's Come On Boro supplement. On the afternoon I wrote up the Campbell story for tomorrow's back page, and also hammered out a lead story for the Sports Gazette on Christian Karembeu. Boro were very confident of being able to complete a deal to sign the French international once his club Real Madrid had played in the European Champions Cup Final on May 24.

On the way home from work, I popped into MSV in Portrack Lane to see Shab and sort out the finer details of his sponsorship of this book. We chatted for a while about the ins and outs of the Boro, and the comings and goings during the summer.

Shab is a good friend and a big fan of Juninho, and hoped the club would be signing on the Brazilian permanently next season. He felt, deep down, that it might not happen. I felt so, too. But I suspected that there would be many twists and turns in the three months ahead.

Sunday, May 14

THE press steward at Everton insisted before the game that Paul Gascoigne was in the Boro starting line-up at Goodison Park this afternoon. I knew that Gazza was going to Libya this week, but he hadn't even been listed in Bryan Robson's squad on Friday for the Premier League match on Merseyside.

"Are you certain Gazza is playing?" I asked.

"Well it says so here," he replied.

"But you haven't got Gianluca Festa in your list. Have you got the numbers five and eight mixed up?"

The steward decided to go away and check it. When he returned, I discovered that I was correct. The numbers were mixed up. If Gazza had been selected, it would have made a good story for the media. But he was not in the team for the final match.

If Gazza had played, then he would have sweated buckets. It was a red hot afternoon. Everton even added to the heat with a spectacular fireworks display on the pitch before the kick off.

The fireworks were great. The billowing clouds of smoke which followed were not. Within seconds, it was no longer possible to see the far side of the stadium. People around me were coughing and spluttering. Spoil sports! This new glitzy approach was now par for the course in the Premier League.

Len Shepherd, Nigel Gibb, Helen Shepherd and I had arrived at Goodison Park far too early. These away games are getting closer, season by season. We were able to park up close to the ground, taking advantage of parking restrictions in the nearby streets which did not apply on a Sunday. We soaked up the sun for a while before entering the stadium.

You have to climb three long flights of stairs at Goodison Park to reach the press room, but there is a lift for those who don't like exercise.

Everton's press room is very small by modern standards and the facilities are minimal, but they are also adequate. The room has a row of windows which look out over the myriad of streets which surround the stadium.

I made myself a hot cup of tea and sat with Bernie Slaven from Boro TV. He was compiling a list of names for the next crop of Bernie's About interviews and asked if I could contribute any new names to the list.

I couldn't. But I just happened to mention Lennie Lawrence in connection with Ben Roberts' loan spell at Luton.

"Lennie Lawrence, he'll do. Thanks Eric," said Bernie.

We watched Bolton's 2-2 draw with Ipswich on TV in the First Division play-off semi-finals while we were waiting for the Boro game to start at the ludicrously late time of four o'clock. Marcus Stewart scored his second goal of the game to equalise for Ipswich.

"Marcus Stewart would have been a good signing for Boro," said Bernie.

He was probably right. It was a great finish.

The press box lies at the end of a narrow corridor which leads directly from the press room. The box is tight, but the match was low profile today and there was plenty of room. I sat in between Ken Daley and Neil Bramwell from The Independent.

"Did you know that Boro have their worst away record against all the big clubs on this ground?" asked Ken.

Ken is a regular purveyor of anorak facts, most of which are depressing. Suddenly I didn't feel too confident. I had even forsaken my new lucky black briefcase in favour of my old brown one, just in case I was mugged.

In the event I need not have worried. Boro were brilliant. Brian Deane gave them an early lead with a header, and then Juninho settled it in the closing minutes with one of the goals of the season. Boro made it look easy.

Boro's travelling fans were magnificent. They were reminiscent of Watford's fans last week. They never stopped singing and tormenting the home crowd. If only the fans at the Riverside could generate the same kind of atmosphere.

At the end of the game, the Boro players went across to salute the fans and throw their shirts into the crowd. The fans were chanting "Sign On Juninho". It was impossible to disagree with them after that goal.

After the match Bryan Robson entered the press room and revealed that he intended to fly out to Atletico Madrid to discuss the Juninho situation, shortly after returning from this week's trip to Libya. This story already had more twists and turns than the road to Hurworth. I sensed that Boro might try to sign the Brazilian on a permanent deal after all.

Everton boss Walter Smith followed Robbo into the press room soon afterwards. Walter is not a guy who smiles easily, and this was no occasion to attempt one. He is clearly a hard man, but he had done a brilliant job at Everton with limited resources, even though his team was outplayed today. There was not much the local hacks could say to him. His press conference was over very quickly.

I managed to wangle an exclusive press pass to visit the Everton dressing room area, where I joined up with Alastair Brownlee, who had arranged to interview Juninho.

The Brazilian was undertaking a TV interview when I arrived, but then linked up with Alastair and me. He talked passionately, as he had done on several occasions in the past few weeks, and there were no doubts he wanted to stay with Boro.

Once again, Juninho insisted: "I don't have nothing to prove."

It was good old Teesside slang, and I understood his drift perfectly. I was beginning to feel he would have the chance to improve his local dialect in the near future.

Before leaving the stadium, I had a brief chat with Boro chief executive Keith Lamb. However, he and Bryan Robson were then dragged away in conversation with new Everton supremo Bill Kenwright.

Once outside Goodison, I discovered that my travelling colleagues had fooled me. They were not in the social club were I had arranged to meet them. In searching for them, I stumbled across a children's birthday party on the first floor of the club. Everybody turned to me and smiled when they saw me. I'm sure they thought I was the kids' comedian.

Fortunately I managed to track down my colleagues via my mobile phone. They had fancied another pub instead. So we met at the car. It was 6.25pm when we left Liverpool. I drove back, and we followed Bryan Robson in his BMW for several miles after leaving the stadium. However he lost us as soon as we hit the M62.

It was a glorious night. In fact it was the first time in my life that I had ever seen the sun shining on Saddleworth Moor. What a way to end the season!

Monday, May 15

I HAD just finished writing up fresh revelations about Juninho for the Evening Gazette's back page lead when I received a tip off that Bryan Robson was popping into the training headquarters for 11am, and would give a quick press briefing before leaving for Libya.

I raced out to the car and drove up to Hurworth, arriving at the same time as Gordon Cox from the Boro website.

He beat me into the car park and so I had to execute a clever little manoeuvre to make sure that he did not edge me out of my favourite car parking spot.

Alastair Brownlee arrived soon afterwards, while Robbo turned up with Gordon McQueen, deep in discussion.

The briefing was over rather quickly because Robbo was in a hurry, but I managed to stockpile a few bits and pieces for use later in the week. Juninho was the main topic of conversation, and Robbo confirmed that he would be trying to sign the Brazilian. It was the first time the Boro boss had admitted this fact since Juninho returned to the club.

However the underlying inference from Robbo's comments was still as clear as it had ever been. Boro would not pay £5.9m for Juninho's signature. I suspected that a lot of negotiating lay ahead, both with Atletico Madrid and with Juninho himself.

I had been tipped off that Juninho had flown back to Brazil today for an operation to have a plate removed from his leg. Robbo confirmed that it was true. The Boro boss also gave me details of another pre-season friendly. Boro were due to play in Jim Leighton's testimonial at Aberdeen on July 25.

No sooner had Robbo left to take part in an outdoor interview for Boro TV, than the biggest bee that I had ever seen flew into the room.

Coxy, was jumping around at first, but then decided to catch it. He did very well in throwing a player's training bib over the bee, in mid flight, in order to drop it to the carpet. Then he covered it with another six bibs.

The idea was to lift up all the bibs and thus release the bee outside. However when Coxy tried to pick up the bibs, the bee began to buzz rather ferociously.

At this point Coxy dropped the bibs and raced across the room at 90mph, but the bee was even quicker. It was a lot more frightened than he was. Emerging from the bibs, it fled on a direct flight path across the room and out of the open door, as if it knew the door was there all the time.

"So that's how you get bees out of rooms," I said.

Outside I had a brief chat with Boro PR trio Louise, Diane and Liz before heading back to Black Rock. It was so hot in the car that I felt sick by the time I arrived back at the office.

However this was no time for wimps. I had to write up several stories within a short space of time, so lunch was out of the question.

One of the stories was the Paul Ince interview from last week, which was to complete my list of jobs for the Come On Boro supplement. The powers that be were shouting for the story before I had completed it. But I got there, just.

One of the points made by Paul was that it had been a reasonably good season, but he had expected better.

I agreed that it had been all right. I could not see Boro as a top six side, and therefore I felt they had done OK. The major disappointment for me was the dire defeat in the FA Cup at Wrexham, followed by the Frank Worthington Cup quarter-final exit at Tranmere when Boro really did enough to win it on the night. If Boro had beaten Tranmere, they might have gone all the way to Wembley again, and then the season would have been acclaimed by everybody as a good one.

However, the dodgy spell in the middle of the season had cost Boro dear. In fact if they had won three Premier League games during that losing spell, then they would have finished sixth.

So maybe they are not too far away from being a top six side after all, if Bryan Robson buys well during the summer.

POSTSCRIPT

I WAS going to write a postscript to this book, looking back over the season and ahead to the future.

Then this letter arrived on my desk. I was surprised to read its contents, because I had blindly assumed that most fans had been carried away with the far-fetched promises made by the club and believed we should be winning the championship every season.

It's so easy for people to be sidetracked from reality. We forget that Boro have never won anything. Maybe they never will. I often tell myself that mid-table Premier League security is as good as it can possibly get. On other occasions I believe that it can get a lot worse.

If Boro can hold on to their Premier League spot and hold sway among the top dozen clubs in the country for several years, then maybe one day they can win a cup competition. But it won't happen every season. After all, it's never happened before.

In the short term I'm still nervous. Worried that the negativeness held by many fans could yet bring the club down. I'd rather see some of the really unhappy fans stop coming to the Riverside, save the huge financial outlay that it costs them to watch top level football these days, and have a bloody good holiday instead.

But you can't point the finger at the fans. In many respects the club are to blame, for raising supporters' expectations far above what it is reasonably possible to achieve in the short term. If there is any blame attached to the fans, it is believing that the club is something which it is not.

If we can all get our feet back on the ground, and Boro cut back on their wild promises, then maybe we can all move forward together. I sincerely hope so.

Anyway, back to this letter. It arrived, out of the blue, from Boro season ticket holder Kevin Bouttell. I have never met him, nor have I ever read one of his letters before.

But I feel that what he has to say makes a perfect postscript to this book, having been written with sincerity, honesty and downright commonsense. So here it is......
.

"Cast your minds back a few short years. It's 1994 and the last home game of a miserable campaign. There's only about 8,000 inside creaking, aged Ayresome, and you've quite happily queued for your half-time pie (lukewarm) and Bovril (scalding hot).

"Watching the clock on the North Stand is the only half-time entertainment. It doesn't move, frozen in time like the ageing stone terraces and creaking stands. We lose 3-2 to Crystal Palace and trudge home, reflecting on a poor campaign in which we finished ninth in Division One.

"Today's Premiership audience are a bit more sophisticated, yet a lot more cynical. A lukewarm pie and Bovril at half-time is not going to satisfy. They demand the best food, facilities, comfort and a TV within a few metres from them in the concourse to entertain them at half-time.

"And why not? After all, in the money mad world of Sky TV deals and Premiership millions, why shouldn't the fans enjoy a slice of it? But with it they also demand success, entertainment every week - and the best players.

"A few short years ago Boro's audience would have given anything for a few seasons established as a top division club. But this is Y2K, and this season the critics among the Red Book holders have been shouting loud.

"Suddenly we are expecting, nay demanding, a top six finish coupled with a decent cup run, while playing free flowing entertaining football. A bit like 96-97 but without the heartache of relegation please.

"Some would say that lured by the carrot of a spanking new stadium, signing big named players and listening to the promises emanating from Gibson and the club each season would automatically give them the right to this. But listen carefully to Gibson and he has never promised instant cures.

"This season has been blighted by that interminable post Christmas run (again) and a few games (yes, quite a lot actually) where the footy served up wouldn't exactly get a five-star review in the Egon Ronay Guide to Spectacular Footy.

"But hang on. This is Middlesbrough we're talking about, and we're still a small club no matter which way you look at it.

"Three Wembley cup finals and a succession of superstars seem to have given some fans delusions of grandeur. As a club we're still growing and only the very elite can demand top six finishes and be disappointed if they don't achieve it.

"Even Chelsea can't win a place in next season's Champions League. Blackburn had their glory year (just one) for sure, but where are they now? Do we really have the potential to be a bigger club than, say, Manchester City, with the fan base that they can call upon? And where have they been for the past few years?

"No, we're making steady, but this time (unlike 96-97) solid progress.

How many years did it take the current Manchester United era to become the force they are?

"Not for a minute will anyone inside the Riverside think we can emulate them, but given time and the backing of the town's fans, we can damn well try.

"Solid progress. That has to be the key. We now have the best training facilities in Europe to attract the top players to the cold North-east, and for all his mistakes over the years, a manager in Robson whose name can still attract players to a club that most of the world's biggest names have never heard of.

"Let's be patient, at least for a little while longer. It's expensive, believe me I know. And let's hope Boro do something about reviewing prices, for families at least, in the close season. But don't hold your breath.

"But come on, you know what it takes to support this club and I still share the same dream as you. Let's return refreshed next season and put the atmosphere back into the Riverside and watch the next chapter unfold. Believe me the best is yet to come.

"After all, what else would you do on a Saturday afternoon....or Sunday...or Monday night?"

Up the Boro